Ireland

England

Norman
Invasion
1066

France

Portugal

Spain

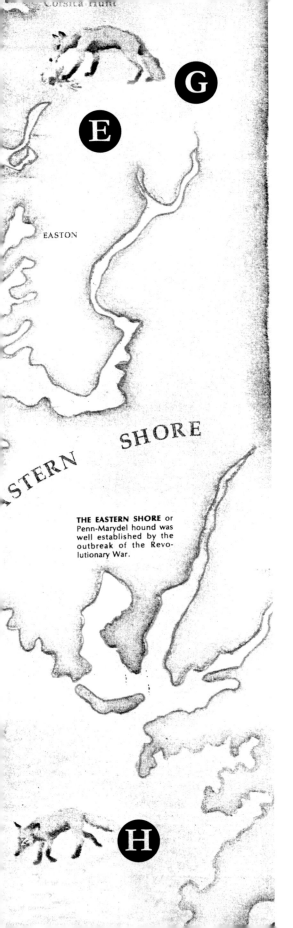

EASTON

THE EASTERN SHORE or Penn-Marydel hound was well established by the outbreak of the Revolutionary War.

STERN SHORE

A. WASHINGTON HOUNDS INVADE THE CAPITOL, 1832. During the administration of President Andrew Jackson, a Washington Hunt drag passed beneath the windows of the Capitol while Congress was in session. Hearing the baying of the hounds, the Honorable Harry Cage of Mississippi rushed out of the hallowed chamber and leaped upon a stranger's horse in order to catch up with the disappearing field.

B. ROBERT BROOKE, first known Master of Foxhounds in America. Brooke's descendants have continued to breed hounds to the present day. Records which span 300 years show that such famous strains of American Foxhounds as the Trigg and Walker can be traced to the Brooke hound. One hound, Brooke's Barney, was cited as one of the finest ever to have run in Maryland. To him are traced the majority of the present-day Brooke hounds.

C. JOHN STUART SKINNER, America's pioneer fox-hunting editor. In 1829, he founded *The American Turf Register and Sporting Magazine* in Baltimore.

D. CHIEF JUSTICE ROGER BROOKE TANEY, 1777-1864, hunted foxes as a youth at Battle Creek, the family plantation in Calvert County.

E. THE CORSICA NECK FOX accounted for many a Delmarva chicken at the turn of the century.

F. ROBERT BROOKE arriving with his foxhounds from Whitchurch in Hampshire, England.

G. PINE TREE FOX HUNTING CLUB. In 1898, this Queen Annes County club held a celebration to commemorate "the two hundred and forty-eighth anniversary of the introduction in America of foxhunting . . ."

H. ENGLISH FOX. Eight eighteenth century Talbot County planters asked that the schooner Monoccasy bring, on its return voyage from Liverpool, eight brace of foxes. The arrival of the foxes in Chestertown was celebrated at a gala ball. During the hard winter of 1779-80 offspring of these foxes crossed the fozen bay to populate the Piedmont country on the Western Shore.

A portion of this map has been reproduced from a map compiled and drawn by Robert Eldredge published by the Maryland Horse Breeders Association.

OUR PENN-MARYDEL HOUND

A HISTORICAL ANTHOLOGY

A sketch of an Eastern Shore Foxhound by Paul Brown

BY H. L. TODD ADDIS, MFH

OUR PENN-MARYDEL HOUNDS
A HISTORICAL ANTHOLOGY

Copyright © 2012

by

H. L. Todd Addis, MFH

Library of Congress Number: 2012913895

International Standard Book Number: 978-1-60126-329-2

Printed 2012 at
Masthof Press
219 Mill Road
Morgantown, PA 19543-9516

PAUL BROWN

Some months after James Scharnberg and I decided on a Paul Brown sketch for our cover, I came across a photograph of a lovely Eastern Shore bitch Forbid being shown by Ms. Patsy du-Pont's huntsman, Kevin Whyte. This Fair Hill Maryland Penn-Marydel gyp won the best of show at the 2004 Eastern Shore Fox Hunters October Hound Show.

Since artist Paul Brown died in 1958, I am sure that he did not use Forbid as his subject. The hound displayed on the cover and near identical conformation of Ms. du-Pont's hound is in no way meant to represent the chosen standard that Penn-Marydel should represent; however, I am sure they both should get honorable mentions.

Paul Desmond Brown (1893-1958) was a prolific illustrator and artist of equestrian sports and country life. Brown was born in Mapleton, Minnesota, and as a young child he began drawing horses and equestrian sports.

Paul Brown's drawing of an Eastern Shore hound displayed in Alexander MacKay-Smith's book, American Fox Hound 1747-1967.

Although he never owned a horse, he was an avid fan of horse sports and frequented hunt race meetings, polo matches, racetracks and horse shows. He studied everything about horses and became an expert at portraying them.

He is especially known for his gift of accurately depicting horses in motion. During his career, he wrote and illustrated 32 books and illustrated another 100 by various authors. In addition to books, his works appeared in numerous periodicals including *Collier's, Cosmopolitan, Liberty, Elks, The American Legion, Country Life, Spur, Polo, The Sportsman* and many others.

As a commercial artist, he is recognized for the hundreds of drawings used by Brooks Brothers of New York in their advertising and promotional materials. He died in 1958 in Garden City, New York.

TABLE OF CONTENTS

DEDICATION

This book, *Our Penn-Marydel Hound: A Historical Anthology*, is dedicated to the memories that my father and mother created for their family.

The term "No child shall be left behind" was in the forefront of child rearing and having his three sons and one daughter vigorously engaged in the sport of fox chasing.

The thrill and challenge of raising and hunting ones own pack of hounds penetrated my soul to the greatest extent. It could not happen without the full participation and enthusiastic encouragement of my wife Hampton (Happy).

Like the foals, my son and two daughters all retained their mother's temperament!

Until we meet again.

H. L. Todd Addis.

Clarkson Addis VMD

Ann Heinrich Addis

PREFACE

A book any true hound person, but especially lovers of the Penn-Marydel (PM) must have.

Dr. Addis has put together a history of the Penn-Marydel that is accurate, interesting and takes you right up to the present. The book is full of articles and information on not only the PM hound, but the people who have contributed to this, what I call, the PM hound awakening. Dr. Addis' contribution to this breed and to the people who hunt them is immeasurable and not just due to this excellent book. A renowned breeder and huntsman of PM hounds for 52 years, his drafts to other hunts and his hounds bred into other packs are substantial and impressive. As the Masters of Foxhounds Association (MFHA) "Keeper of the Stud Book", I can attest to that. His tenacity and outspoken persona coupled with honesty, knowledge and research make this a great read.

The PM Hound has become one of the most popular breeds of foxhounds in recent years. In what seemed like a very short time, MFHA member hunts started drafting PMs and breeding PM packs. Several hunts made complete turnovers going from English or Crossbred hounds to pure PM packs overnight.

Penn-Marydel packs have always been around, but mostly on the East Coast, as the name implies, in Pennsylvania and Maryland. Responsible for the registration of all MFHA packs, I've been very much aware of their increasing popularity. In what seems like just a few years, an explosion has occurred. From California, throughout Middle America, in the North, South and East, more and more MFHA packs were breeding to or drafting PMs into their breeding. It too became painfully obvious to me that PM breeders, hunters and lovers were always the keenest, most outspoken defenders of their breed. English, American and Crossbred hound breeders and hunters may love their hounds just as much, but don't come close to the enthusiasm seen in the PM society who believe passionately that PM hounds are the best. I asked myself why is this sudden popularity?

In order to find out, I started hunting with every PM pack I could find, member or nonmember of the MFHA. I had read and heard all the stereo typing; on one hand - PM were slow, babbled, dwelled, and extremely shy with conformation like a cross word puzzle; on the other - they had great voice, very biddable, a nose that could carry a line when other hounds didn't have a clue, and you could hunt them successfully in areas many hounds would bust out of. Hunting with the PM packs was the only way for me to form an opinion based on what I saw and experienced. I found out that all the good was true and that the negative depended on who and where they were hunted. Even the conformation, while there are glaring differences (for good reasons, they were bred to hunt in a specific area) can to a trained eye be as good looking as any other hound.

In 2008 kicking, shoving and shouting, the PM hunters influence and PM popularity convinced the MFHA Board of Directors to enter the PM into the MFHA Stud Book as a separate breed. Prior to that, PMs were simply listed as American hounds. Adding them was no easy task, but a task well deserved and appears to be working.

To my knowledge, Dr. Addis's book is the first book ever written about the Penn-Marydel and the people who made this breed popular. I believe it will be a classic that will survive the test of time.

Lt. Col. Dennis J. Foster (US Army, ret)
Executive Director, Keeper of the Stud Book
Masters of Foxhounds Association
Author of "Whipper-in"

FOREWORD

At long last, Dr. Todd Addis has written the definitive treatise on the Penn-Marydel Foxhound. It is a book long overdue and eagerly awaited, and one that belongs on every dedicated foxhunter's bookshelf or bedside table. Much of the content appeared in articles penned by the author for the newsletter, "Friends of the Penn-Marydel," and now it is available to those foxhunting enthusiasts who missed reading that delightful periodical.

Dr. Addis delves deeply into the diverse ancestry of the Penn-Marydel, whose origins are found in the early French breeds, the St. Huberts, Talberts, and, most influentially, the Gaston and Saintongeois. Indeed, all branches of the American Foxhound's family tree are deeply rooted in Gallic soil. Exhaustive research into the writings of Sir John Buchannon-Jardine, T. Ivester Lloyd, Joseph B. Thomas, and the often-controversial Sir Newton Rycroft, as well as Alexander Mackay-Smith and J. Blan van Urk, has given form and substance to what heretofore has been largely oral history.

Reading the stories of famous Huntsmen of Penn-Marydel packs of the past century is the most fascinating and entertaining experience a lover of venery can experience short of hunting with these extraordinary men. Their skill, patience, ingenuity, and dedication are amazing, and their contributions to modern foxhunting are invaluable. Such men as George Brice, Orville Roberts, and Albert Crosson, who are enshrined in the Huntsman's Room at the Museum of Hounds and Hunting North America, housed at Morven Park in Leesburg, Virginia, as well as Guy Mercer, Bart Mueller, John White, Arthur Brown, and Ben Funk, who are knocking on the door, set a standard of excellence to guide generations to come.

Our Penn-Marydel Hound is not only excellent in and of itself, it is a valuable addendum to the MFH's vastly flawed Centennial tome, which fails to mention the Penn-Marydel Hound and, basically, ignores its positive contributions to every pack into which its blood has been infused. And that includes most of the packs lauded therein. My own Keswick pack of mainly Bywaters American hounds owes much of its continued success to an outcross to Murtagh's "Boxer," bred by Joseph T. Murtagh, MFH, who had just accepted the joint-mastership at Rose Tree. That blood runs strongly in the pedigrees at Keswick today. Many of the modern packs whose breeding programs have gone awry desperately need an infusion of Penn-Marydel to balance the scale. May this book provide the inspiration!

Our Penn-Marydel Hound is a history and an anthology, filled with insight and humor, nostalgia and opinions, and . . . it's a DAMN GOOD READ!

Thanks, Doc, and Good Hunting!

–Jake (John J. Carle, II, ex-MFH)

INTRODUCTION

"The 'good' of other times let others state, I count it lucky I was born so late."
—Lord Ribbensdale

Over the past several years, a number of people have asked me if there is a book about the Penn-Marydel hounds that they could buy. My stock answer has been, "I am not aware of any that you could purchase." Their response has been, "Why don't you write one?"

Foolishly, I have given into these suggestions and am tackling this project with scant qualifications as a researcher and writer.

The readers of this book must firmly fix in their minds that the Penn-Marydel Foxhound has been developed and described for hundreds of years.

From my early interest and reading about the Penn-Marydel Association, Inc. and the naming of its Eastern Shore type of hound, I found Alexander MacKay-Smith's book *American Fox Hounds 1747-1967* to be most interesting. In this book he refers to the Pennsylvania packs as the Penn-Marydel packs back to 1914. Therefore, I must assume the Penn-Marydel Association did not coin the name Penn-Marydel hound but merely decided on a type and incorporated the name in 1934. To further clarify the PMD name MacKay-Smith writes, "Except for the war years, the Bryn Mawr Hound Show has been held annually since 1914. For the first dozen years stallion hounds from the Penn-Marydel packs were largely victorious."

Five books resting on my library shelves have given me the courage to proceed. The first three books were written by English authors. My favorite was T. Ivester Lloyd's *Hounds*. I quote Lloyd when he makes a complimentary statement about Sir John Buchanan-Jardine's book, *Hounds of the World*. "If you do not have the *Hounds of the World*, you surely are missing the best venery book ever published in the English language."

Having already mentioned the "King" of authors, Alexander MacKay-Smith, I wish to quote an astonishing statment by another Ameican author, Joseph B. Thomas. Mr. Thomas writes in his *Hounds and Hunting Through the Ages*, "Gace de la Barque estimates that in his time, which was early in the fourteenth century, there were in France twenty thousand gentlemen who kept scenting hounds in more or less large numbers."

If the reader of this book wishes to know just who was the breeder of our ancestors of our Penn-Marydel hounds I must rely on Sir John Buchanan-Jardine and T. Ivester Lloyd to narrow the possibilities.

Before I move on to chapter one in the first section of this book, further discussion of our hound loving Frenchmen is necessary.

Sir Walter Gilbey in his *Hounds in Old Days*, 1913 verifies earlier writing by stating:

> The Norman conquerors of England brought their hounds with them when they took possesion of this country and there is evidence to show that the breed known as St. Huberts (white or black) or Talbots were the foundation stock of the breed afterwards known as southern hounds. (History students: Remember the date 1066, William the Conqueror, the Norman Invasion.) The *Livre de Chase* translated between 1387 and 1390 by Edward second Duke of York, descirbes in length the best sort of "running hounds" which were used for the stag, proceeds to tell us that there are many kinds, some small and some large. The small were called kenets (currs) which would run or tree all kinds of game. Those which "serve for all game, men call harriers."

The importance attached to breeding a hound most suitable to the terrain and game to be pursued goes back over a thousand years. The stag, during the hunting season, which extended from the first day of winter (22nd December) to the feast of St. John (June 24th), was of higher value than any domestic beast. The stag consisted of twelve legal pieces—haunches, antlers, tongue, breast, etc., each of which was valued at 60 pence, making a total value of three pounds.

Taking some important descriptions of Sir John's French Gascon hound: "They hunt the hare fairly well, and the wolf splendidly; they hunt it by nature, and, as the wolf rarely ruses much, they excel at hunting it, their only fault being that they are too slow to ever kill. Many hounds of this breed have the paces and action of the wolf. (Could we not substitute the coyote animal in place of the wolf?)

"To sum up, throwing their tongues freely, in rather too low a tone, moreover too slow, these hounds have a superb appearance, very good noses, and great love of hunting. They are very hard by nature, but lack energy and activity. They have good constitution and for that reason are the finest that I have ever seen were those of the Baron de Ruble at the Paris Hound Show of 1863, and of which the breed had been kept in his family since the reign of Henry IV (1574-1589).

"Two Frenchmen with the titles of Baron interbred their packs for years and exchanged their puppies, M. de Ruble keeping only the black and white ones.

"The two barons introduced the blood of the Saintonge hounds (Saintongeois) (pronounced: santa now waz) origin not known, but thought to be a much improved Gascon hound. These Gascon-Sainteongeois are now the only pure French 'Chien d'Ordre' type of hound still existing quite without English foxhound blood; they have by far the finest music of any hound I have ever come across," so says Sir John Buchanan-Jardine. He goes on to write, "The Gascon hound ceased to exist but should be of great interest to English students of hound history, because I think there can be little doubt that the old blue-mottled strain of Southern hounds owed a good deal to Gascon blood.

"It will be remembered (so says Sir Jardine) that Gascony was for many years, roughly from 1150 to 1450, under the English crown, so that it seems probably that it was at that time that the ancestors of our old Southern hounds would be imported. Possibly the name Southern hound may have originated from the breed coming from Gascony, as they were by no means confined to the south of England; in fact, the last remnants of them today are to be found in Lancashire.

"In any case, about 1919 I made an attempt to breed up a pack of Southern hounds. I started by getting a blue-mottled bitch from the Holcombe Harriers and was lucky enough to obtain most of the Hailsham Harriers."

Sir John Buchanan-Jardine says the Gascon hound ceased to exist—well maybe my Govanor, a Penn-Marydel may be the only one to survive!

At this time a few thoughts and hound breeding experiences will be highlighted from Sir Newton Rycroft. These were published in the articles published in *The Hound Magazine* and republished in a book titled *Rycroft on Hounds, Hunting and Country*, 2001 authored by James Scharnberg, under a section titled "Blue Hound's":

The Holcombe Harriers in Kennels c. 1906. Photos are from Rycroft on Hounds, Hunting and Country.

"I can only declare a personal interest when I say that blue colour interests me because it signifies descent from a breed which in its pure form is now virtually extinct in Britain, though not in France. This the old Southern Hound, which I think was much the commonest hound used for hare-hunting in the seventeenth century and earlier. The great Beckford, I think, hit the nail on the head when he said of them 'Too dull, too heavy and too slow.' They were hounds in fact with tremendous voices and were also extremely low-scenting."

Among foxhounds the importance of this color is more easily recognizable, because it was the coat colour of one of the most famous of all foxhounds of this century, Cartharthorn Nimrod[24]. He was blue mottled and so was his great-grandam, Col. Russell Johnstone's Restive; and Restive's great-grandam in her tail female was an old blue mottled Devenshire harrier of Old Southern blood.

To continue in Thomas' book, page 51, "The English bloodhound is, from its appearance, unquestionably the descendant of the black and tan hounds of St. Hubert, as already mentioned; but the earliest distinctly English breed was the Talbot, the name originating from the ancient family of that name. This breed had many characteristics of the bloodhound in appearance and style of hunting; but its colors—white, black and tan, red and fawn—according to French, indicate that its origin was derived from the crossing of the white breed of St. Hubert, the black and tan St. Hubert, and the fawn hounds of Brittany. These ancient colorations, and in some measure the voice, still reproduce themselves with utmost precision in the Old American hounds. Numerous writings and many pictures fix very definitely the characteristics of Talbots and their more or less direct descendants, the Southern hounds, which breed is undeniably described by Shakespeare:

My hounds are bred out of the spartan kind so flew'd, so sanded, and their heads are hung with ears that sweep away the morning dew, crook-kneed'd, and dew-lap'd, like Thessalian bulls; slow pursuit, but match'd in mouth like bells, each under each.–Midsummer Night's Dream

(William Shakespeare, it is well known, was prosecuted for deer-stealing, by Sir Thomas Lucy. No doubt the Talbot hound was used by the deer-stealers.)

"In the seventeenth century, the slow Southern hounds began to lose popularity in favor of the fleet Northern hounds. These Northern hounds, not to be confused with the Western Harriers, hounds originated, according to various authorities, by a cross between the Talbot and Scotch deer hounds. Salnove, Setincourt and d'Yauville agree that it was this sort of hound that was so extensively imported into France. Stonehenge and Richardson state that from such hounds, again crossed with grey-hounds and large terriers, the modern English foxhound originated. Some experts have even suggested some mastiff blood was part of the mix. Savary, in his Latin poem describes them as, "slender, active, like strong greyhounds, carved of flank, long of muzzle, pointed of ear, cat footed, all nerves and very fast." "The Terrier has left its mark in short ears, a voice sparingly used and lacking the bell-like tone of the ancient hounds."

Chester County Day at Warwick County Park, 2005. Who says the Gascon Hound no longer exist? Michelob[92] the large blue tick dog hound at my left hand carries every gene of the old Gascon French Hound to give him the exact con-formation that is so well described by Conte le Couteulx de Canteleux in his Manuel de Venerie. *He had no faults in his first four seasons. His staying power in our hills with many rocks necessitated his return to my son's Bright Leaf Maryland pack, where by the gentler terrain extended his hunting for two more seasons.*

Reproduced from the pages of T. Ivestor Lloyd's book *Hounds*, 53-64.

The Old English Harrier

(Old Southern Hound Type)

BIG stone-built kennels as part of old farm buildings are a survival of the days when two or three neighbouring farmers often combined to keep a pack of hounds.

Another way was for each to keep a few couples at his own farm and to assemble the pack on hunting days. Fed chiefly on the "casualties" of the district, hounds luck was in inverse ratio to that of the farmers and inclined to be "streaky." This was levelled out a little by hanging, and, in those days, people were not particular how long flesh hung in the gallows.

Before sun-up the first part of the pack would be let out, kennelman's voice and the joyful cry

of hounds sounding for miles through the still morning air. Hoofs click on the cobbles of the yard and soften to a "plod, plod" as the farmer, his hounds about him, jogs past the new stacks which are waiting to be thatched, where the ruts made by harvesting carts are still fresh. Down a deep lane where the undisturbed air strikes warm as midday and the honeysuckle has but lately died on the stone-faced banks.

Its roofs glowing from a sun's ray, which has not yet reached the walls, another solid-looking farm-house stands and is greeted with a mighty bellow and a crack of the heavy-thonged whip. A farmhand opens the gate, more hounds dash out, and, stopping within a few inches of the new arrivals, proceed to walk round them, sterns erect and hackles up, in the manner hounds greet each other when they are acquainted but not *too* familiar.

Another red-faced, jolly old farmer greets the first, and the weather, harvest and prospects of sport are talked of as they take hounds on to the next farm, where more will be waiting. At length the pack is assembled, as also is as good a collection of yeomen as ever advocated beef and beer as cures for all ills. No less healthy and hearty is the parson who is with them. All are astride the broad backs of good strong roadsters that are capable of carrying the "Missis" on a pillion when required.

They spread over a field where the sun is turning the stubble to rich gold and hounds' noses go down. Soon old Blueboy's note is heard but does not carry conviction. A few yards on, he pauses and feathers, and, all doubts allayed, puts up his heavy-jowled old head and throws his tongue sonorously and with certainty. Bellman looks up, considers for a minute and then goes to the place. He puts down his nose and in due course proclaims the line and is joined by other hounds, each making sure of the line for himself. ("Unbelieving old beggars!" we can hear the modern huntsman mutter.)

The line of a travelling hare provides what was considered the best part of a hunt. Lop-eared, heavy-jowled old Towler, Jasper, Blueboy, Bellman and the rest of them slowly and with great pains unravel the line, several hours old, through all its meanderings where the hare has played or fed.

Puss, sitting in her forme, pricks her ears as the blue-mottles and black-and-tans draw near, claps closer for a moment and then, filled with the idea that they are hunting her line, slips off like a streak in the mist.

Now rings out the chorus—and more store was set by the note than by the forelegs. Old Trumpeter might have a front like a calf, but his was a lovely bass, and who cared if Cowslip's back was as long as a wet week when she had that rare singing note which ran up and down the scales? (I once had a blue-mottle Beagle bitch who had it. Her name was Merry and she used to throw up her head and—*trill* is the only word that fits.)

In those days the duties of kennelman and whipper-in were often carried out as spare-time jobs by an odd man or youth about the farm. A baggy-pocketed rascal who usually whipped-in on shank's pony and kept his eye on one or two of the hounds that might be a bit quick on a rabbit. These he would pretend to rate, letting them pounce and catch before doing anything to really stop them.

Second-horsemen with sandwich cases were things then undreamed of, but the followers had no intention of going hungry long enough to impair their enjoyment of the sport. Having despatched the first hare and rewarded hounds with the "innards" only, an adjournment would be made to the nearest farm-house or inn where hounds could be shut in a barn and horses baited. In the kitchen, the men would set about a tremendous breakfast helped down with gallons of ale. Blood pressure was a thing they never talked about, although they sometimes had to use leeches.

Another leisurely start followed and, there being no hurry, markets and prices would be discussed, or the ram one had bought at the fair the week before. They would count the coveys they saw and all the while the grand opera chorus towled and swung and circled like a swarm of bees.

Other packs were kept by squires or parsons

who had often had strains in their families for generations. Being better mounted, these bred a lighter, quicker hound. The restricted travel and transport facilities of those days did not allow bitches to be sent to dogs of different packs and limited the exchange of ideas and opinions. One thing over which they did often go to great trouble and expense was to keep the "harmony" of a pack just right. It is hard to imagine a modern master of hounds offering "a couple of basses for one tenor!" There was no Peterborough and so the hounds of a district must have evolved from those brought to that country by the Normans. This idea is born out by the fact that both the Old Southern type and the lighter Western Harrier have their prototypes in France.

In the villages of Lancashire and Yorkshire most of the cottagers had a hound or perhaps a couple, as important members of the families. When the horn sounded in the middle of the village at a very cold early hour, from doors and windows and over low walls would come the hounds, wild with delight at the prospect of sport. One old hound knew the hunting days and was always standing on the wall waiting for the horn.

Huntsman and followers, all afoot, would take the pack on to the moorland with its great outcrops of rock still vague in the morning light and wreaths of mist drifting over the heather.

On putting up a hare, one of these North

Country sportsmen was heard to remark to Puss, "Hey thee, lad, get oop an' join in t'spoort."

When followers came up to hounds at a check the huntsman often had a trying time, with each man cheering and otherwise trying to help his own particular hound. There were also difficulties should he decide to draft a certain hound, and only the "raw 'uns" would give satisfaction to some of the aggrieved owners, whose families would shed many tears at the hound's departure.

When light was failing and hounds and men were both beginning to call "enough" they would think about the tramp home. Hounds with sterns down and men silent because they needed all their wind for walking, perhaps three

Sept. 22, 1997. Dr. Addis' Warwick Village Hounds with one exception every stern is down. My bitch Slipper (center) shows the full effect of a long and tiring 4-hour morning hunt—she too has her share of swamp earth clinging to legs and belly.

type. This shows itself in their plodding, solemn method, making sure of every inch.

A very different type of mind from the clean, smart, dashing "take-a-chance-and-get-on-with-it" mentality that goes with galloping shoulders, clean neck, smart head and straight legs. Taste and the country to be hunted should decide which kind is the more suitable.

In spite of the fact that many packs were hunted afoot, the Old Southern was often a big hound, up to twenty-five inches, while some were little larger than Beagles.

T. Ivester Lloyd Painting of the Old Southern Hound.

Francis Duckenfield Astley, Esq., and his harriers; by R. Woodman; after B. Marshall.
By Courtesy of Messrs, Arthur Ackermann & Son, Ltd.

Since these hounds in this painting are identified as Harriers, I thought it would be a challenge to the reader to evaluate their ancestors. I believe they are weighted in genetics to the old Southern hound (harrier) and just by chance the sire may be the smallish white terrier running in the middle of the pack. "The heads have it—not the tails!"

His Majesty's Harriers; by R. Woodman; after R. B. Davis.
By Courtesy of Messrs. Arthur Ackermann & Son, Ltd.

Reproduced from the pages of T. Ivestor Lloyd's book *Hounds*, 49-52.

The Western Harrier

AS a boy I saw my first hunting with the old Stanton Drew Harriers.

John Fowler, a farmer well-known in the West, hunted hounds mounted on a cock-tailed hunter with a man afoot turning hounds to him, and rare sport he showed.

While many of the Western packs hunt hare up to Christmas, and, after that, fox, the Stanton Drew hunted whichever got up first, and, as if this did not give them enough variety, finished the season with a deer on the Mendips.

Without viewing their quarry, the old hands knew when they were hunting fox by the way hounds ran, going over that good scenting West

Country as if tied to his brush, and with a different venom in their cry. The way they would burst a fox was rather surprising to anyone seeing them for the first time and remembering that they were *Harriers*.

While in the hound lists, "Old English Harrier" may mean either Old Southern or Western, there is a great difference in the hounds. Most of the West Country Harrier packs are composed of these lighter boned Westerns with their small pretty heads and what used to be called "sweet" expressions, as against "sour-faced." The chiselling under the eyes is more pronounced and the muzzle finer, resulting in a "bitchy" look. They are rather on the leg but well muscled up, and round in the barrel with good ribs and hare feet. It is thought that a hare foot is more serviceable than a cat foot in the rocky coombs of Devon and Somerset as well as on the hills of Gloucestershire. In many parts of these countries there are thickly wooded slopes and stretches of heather where a heavily marked hound would be different to see from a distance.

The Western is a light pied hound, inclining more towards red than lemon, while some are almost white. The men who hunt with them in the West Country swear by them for showing sport there.

One peculiarity in the breeding of these pied hounds is that the usual light-coloured parents occasionally throw a black-and-tan whelp; not

one with some white, but a real black-and-tan.

The Aldershot Drag which hunt fox for two days a week in the Vine country, bought most of the Tanat Side hounds a few years ago. These were Western Harriers, and I was told that the Aldershot people found them a little wild on hares. Considering they were Harriers, this was not hard to understand!

I always think that a pack of Harriers at work is one of the prettiest of sights, particularly when their pace is matched by their noses and taste for real hound work.

Left alone, they will draw a fallow thoroughly and not merely wait for someone to whip up a hare for them. A hare squatting in its form carries little scent, and the hounds, as if they know this, will quest every likely place. Even then, it is very easy to draw over the quarry, and I have noticed that on ploughland, with a small field out, six times out of ten Puss gets up behind hounds. It is as though she lets the vanguard pass, squatting close, and then, thinking the coast clear, slips off in case they should return.

Most hare-hunters are of the firm opinion that the tricks of Puss in evading her pursuers are more numerous and wily than those of Charley.

The last paragraph of T. Ivester Lloyd's chapter titled "The Western Harrier" brought to mind an occasion that one can substitute a red fox for a squatting hare [puss].

Some 35 years ago (1970's) deer hunting season drove us out of our county, so I accepted an invitation to a joint meet with Eddie Vale and Joan Dougherty's Cool Spring Hounds in southern Chester County, PA. Hounds had just jumped our third fox and were flying across this heavy sod field. I was playing catch up to the pack and field.

With thundering hound and horse hoof beats pressing this bewildered fox, it suddenly disappeared. Not until the combined packs over ran this squatting fox did I realize what was happening. What a surprise I had when out of the grass this fox jumps up and high-tails it from whence it came. By this time the fired up pack had turned and caught sight of Mr. Fox. The last image I had was the lead hounds were about to roll this baby. From a distance, the chase suddenly ended with a sure kill. As I approached for the ceremonies there was nothing to be seen but a hole in the ground.

-*H. L. Todd Addis*

T. Ivester Lloyd painting, The Western Harrier.

Reading from Sir Newton Rycroft chapter titled "Les Chiens Blancs Du Roi (The White Hounds of the King)," Sir John Jardine is quoted again: "The chiens blancs du roi have at one time or another influenced most of the French breeds to some extent, and of English hounds the West Country light coloured harriers . . . no doubt owe most to the chien blanc."

Rycroft is further quoted—Mr. Poole in his book *Hunting* wrote, "If I had to choose a single type of hound, I would choose the West Country Harrier; for me it is the rough country hound of greatest excellence."

Warwick Village Ring-side was excused from the 2011 show ring. Perhaps he was too aristocratic looking. Could he be a desendant of the White Hounds of the King?

POITOU HOUND, OUR HOUNDS' ANCESTORS?

Material gathered from Sir John Buchanan-Jardine, *Hounds of the World.*

There was a gentleman living at the time of the French Revolution named Monsieur de Larye. De Larye was a famous wolf hunter in the reign of Louis XVI (1754-1793), and somehow during the forty years or so of his hunting career bred himself a pack of hounds of unusual merit.

The Larye family of Scottish origin when settling in Poitou, France brought some hounds with them. Possibly the Norman hound blood was crossed with theirs. For in many ways the Larye strain were like the Norman to look at, but vastly improved in quality. The Poitou hound stood not more than twenty-four inches. The color being a mix of black-white and tan and/or lemon and white.

The excellence of the noses was quite extraordinary: they could often wind the line of a wolf a half mile away.

His hounds were not exceptionally fast but had extraordinary stamina, were close line hunters but quick, active and intelligent at a check, any one of them alone being capable of following the line of a wolf from dawn till dusk.

M. de Larye himself was guillotined in 1793 and his hounds were dispersed about the country, but a couple or two of pure-bred ones managed to survive the revolution and from these the modern Poitou hound is said to have been bred. Sir John Buchanan-Jardine tells the following story about a Poitou village squire who owned a couple of hounds of this precious breed, and who, during the Revolution, fearing that their aristocratic appearance would get them in trouble, cut their ears and sterns to make them look like cur dogs.

One might rightfully ask what constitutes an aristocratic-looking fox hound?

DOB Jan 2012. DNA Test inconclusive for being Poitou ancestors.

In continuing my search for Penn-Marydel hound material I was attracted to a story included in MacKay-Smith's *Anthology* titled "Dear Old Uncle Mose." When I reached the 9th paragraph on the first page of this chapter I immediately decided this story penned by Samuel J. Henry was for me.

I could not help but conclude that Uncle Mose's lemon and white fox hounds were in all probability ancestors of the Old Western Harrier of England. Thumbing forward one hundred and eleven pages in this anthology, the excitement built. Two wonderful Paul Brown sketches stood out illustrating Old Uncle Mose with his five lemon and white Maryland dawgs.

We must conclude that Alexander MacKay-Smith persuaded artist Paul Brown to read Samuel J. Henry's story and portray Old Uncle Mose with lantern in hand and moving off on the river trail with his hounds.

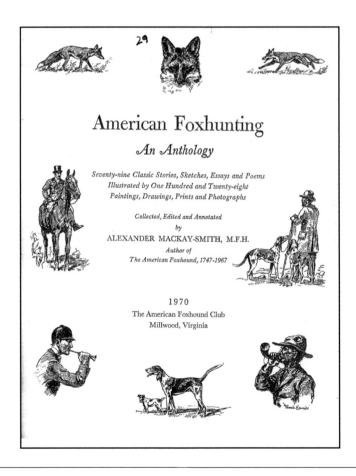

Dear Old Uncle Mose

For a Souvenir

62

DEAR OLD UNCLE MOSE (1933)

by

Samuel J. Henry

AMONG the men and horses and hounds I have known none stands out more vividly than Uncle Mose. Many a pair of puppies he has walked for me which, when taken up around nine or ten months of age, came close to being finished fox dogs. He does not know how old he is nor where he was born. "Reckon Ah'm 'bout eighty," he opines. "My kin were all sold down de river befo' de war when Ah was a chile, en' Ah doan' know where Ah comes from."

His weather-beaten cabin, on the edge of an impenetrable forest, sits well back from the road, and massive trees encroaching from the rear seem to suggest that Nature is about to foreclose on the decaying work of man. But from his porch, screened by the wild honeysuckle, Uncle Mose's bleared eyes look down on rich bottom-land of the serpentine Potomac, where corn of luxurious green waxes high in the humid summer months.

Poor as he is, he manages to maintain, negro style—and that's pretty skimpy—a few dogs, the descendants of a pair of exhausted hounds who, thirty years ago, drifted into his place one cold winter's day and, hound-like, calmly took up their abode. No one ever knew where they came from or anything about them.

Not far from where the ebony patriarch lives is the Woodcote Club, owned by an aggregation of men banded together for the fishing, duck shooting and foxhunting with which tidewater Maryland is blessed.

Even in midwinter there are days upon days of open weather with endless opportunity for sport, and the Woodcote crowd are going pretty well around New Year's. They are a gay, lively set, always out for a good time, and any sort of a lark calls an adventurous group together.

One night in 1933 after a hilarious dinner some of the young bloods bribed the kennel man to smuggle out three couple of hounds for a go with Uncle Mose's dogs. It was midnight when the roisterers reached their destination, and the old man was sound asleep.

"How about a fox race, Uncle!" they called from their cars when he peered out. "We've heard your hounds running of nights and we would like to try them with a few of ours."

Looking up at the sky and sniffing the keen air, the darky replied, "Gent'muns, old Mose glad to go wid you. Jes' let him git some cloes on an' he'll be out in a minute"; proving himself not only a hunter but a sportsman who never dodged an issue. Pretty soon he appeared, hickory staff in one hand and lantern in the other, wearing three pairs of trousers, slouch hat, sweater under a canvas hunting coat, and gum boots. Item: a tightly tied scarf around his neck, said scarf originally white and now soiled, with running foxes discernible on it.

"Have you got any *good* fox dogs?" he was asked. "Any stayers?"

"Yas suh. Ah got some dat gits around a little," he replied modestly, and winding a low, rumbling call on his cow born—it sounded like a steamboat whistle—he proceeded to a shed and released five flea-bitten, scrubby animals, yellow and white in color and badly in need of groceries. Yet so eager were they to greet him that, whining and squealing their delight, they

173

almost smothered him with caresses, expressive of that mysterious bond between negro and animal, which no white man may ever hope completely to enjoy.

With hounds there is an air of good breeding, and after superficial canine greetings the ill-assorted pack preceded the hunters up the shell road which ran parallel to the river; one by one the animals quietly disappeared, leaving the men to proceed alone, guided by Old Mose and the lantern.

"Can your potlickers recognize a fox trail?" teased the kennel man, "or do you start them with a bagged fox?"

"My dawgs air runnin' dawgs, suh," the negro replied, ignoring the taunt, "but Ah doan' know how dey will stan' up wid de Woodcote houn's. Dey sho' is a handsome lot, an' dey might outrun my dawgs, but dey won't bed 'em."

"How would you like to have a nice pair of puppies?" he was asked. "We have some beauties at the Club."

"Well, dat's mighty fine of you all; but Ah jes' doan' feel like changin' de breed," Uncle Mose hedged. "Ah bin a-huntin' dis strain er dawgs now for many years. Ah kinder got used to 'em and dey makes allowances fer me. You unnerstan' how 'tis, Mr. Cecil."

"Perfectly, Uncle Mose," replied Cecil Huntington. "That's the sign of a real hunter—develop your own hounds. There's the old-line Maryland hounds and the dogs of the Walkers, Triggs and Birdsongs—those famous types were all developed by noted hound men—hound families, I might say."

"Yas suh, Ah knows how 'tis," Uncle Mose replied. "Ah hears tell dat de Walkers kills a dawg what comes in from de chase befo' it's over."

"They are ruthless on hounds in the Kentucky country," Cecil replied. "If a hound doesn't make good—and they are mighty strict—they take him down in the woods and all they bring back is the collar."

Far up the river a determined challenge punctured the solitude.

"There he goes, old TRUMPET, he done made de strike," whispered the negro as the hound repeated his deep, throaty cry again and again.

His voice rumbled afar off and seemed never ending; Gabriel himself could find no flaw in this impressive summons. "A big red fox roams up yonder an' if we can git him goin', gent'muns, you'll have a race. TRUMPET is cold trailin' now." Night hunters, like good Christians, see through the eyes of faith.

Arriving at a hilltop, the men built a fire in a stubble field and, seating themselves at the foot of a shock of sweet-smelling fodder, they smoked and listened. Dick Jenkins—a bit under the weather—broke into a ribald song, inelegant parody on Grey's immortal lines:

"Many a jag of whiskey, gin and beer
The sharp deep pains of D. T.'s bear—
Many a hiccough is coughed unseen
To pollute with its vileness the midnight air."

Shortly Dick was curled up asleep in the dry bedding and that's all he knew of the hunt.

"Don't think that TRUMPET is after a rabbit or ground hog, do you, Uncle?" some fellow wise-cracked. "He wouldn't be fooling us, would he?"

"Ah reckon not," the negro replied. "Ah kinder believe he is on de drag of a fox. They'll jump him terectly."

"What do you call that hound-killing fox?" the kennel man inquired. "Is he a red or a grey?"

"He's a red, and Ah calls him de gold-tooth fox," said Uncle Mose, not batting an eye.

"Gold-tooth fox?" pondered the hound man. "Why, that's the most ridiculous thing I ever heard. How come?"

"When he faults houn's, he sits up and grins, an' Ah done seen de gold tooth shinin'," said the negro. He took a chew of tobacco and threw a log on the fire.

Several other dogs now opened up and Uncle Mose grinned with delight. One hound had a gurgling note; there was a musical singing cry; another just howled.

"White folks, Ah believe it's a fox," the negro said, as the tempo slowly increased until every hound joined in the untutored score for a smashing climax. "They've settled on him now. It's dat up-river—Ah mean goldtooth fox—all right. An' he gwine to carry 'em," Old Mose chuckled.

"Hark on TRUMPET, TOOTHPICK, KATE—" he hummed. "Drive him hard—"

And the kennel man replied, "There's WASP-

174

American Foxhunting

ISH and WRANGLER, DUCHESS and DAFFODIL in there, too—Uncle Mose, do you think your dogs can stand it?" as the pace stiffened and became a whirlwind of sound.

"Dey done turned on de heat. Now dat rascal gotta run," the darky replied, noncommittal. "It's gwine take a real houn' to stay with 'im, gent'muns. Hark on, good dawgs!"

The fox circled in five-mile loops; now out of hearing and now back again. It was clear that the hounds had a real job on their hands; it was going to take nose and endurance to compete with this fugitive, for such a fox never does a foolish thing; his labyrinthian trail forces hounds to cover three miles for every two he traverses, and he picks his own route. Tearing briar and tangled underbrush delayed his enemies. Two o'clock merged into three, and four slipped over to five.

At the fire half the crowd, unseasoned to the rigors of night hunting, had passed out.

"Ah specs deys all on de trail," Uncle Mose observed. "Dey bin runnin' back of de Pincushion Swamp—rough country on a houn'."

They drove him hard, but he was a tough customer, this *Gold Tooth*. Sometimes he bore to the right and then doubling, he would swing left-handed. Occasionally dogs would lose him; their momentary silence perplexed the men. "Has he holed up?" they asked, only to be reassured by a burst of music.

Once more the running fox drifted out of hearing, and in the interlude two of the blue-blooded hounds limped in and lay down by the fire. If ever dogs looked beaten, they did. The chagrined kennel man strove to drive them back to the front into the killing mêlée; but they were immovable; no more *Gold Tooth* for them. You could have heard a pin drop. Nobody uttered a word, but the surrender—known as "bedding" —cut deep into the Woodcote men, while in old Mose's eyes there shone a twinkle easy to understand.

When the procession again turned up, the remaining hunt-club dogs were noticeably missing; only the courageous battle-cry of the yellow-white band remained. Dawn came and they made their sixth circuit around the fire, old TOOTHPICK in the lead—slobber roping her chest and shoulders—and with her companions bawling every time her feet hit the ground.

The sun moving up from the horizon shone on four tired men: Cecil Huntington, two other sleepy chaps, and Uncle Mose—all that was left of the party of twelve.

"Aw, fellows, let's get back to the Club," said Cecil, yawning. "This hunt will go on far, far into the day. Uncle Mose, come over to the Club this evening. I want you to tell those foxhunters over there all about your pack—that is if I leave out anything," and he presented the negro with a fine silver flask. "Keep it for a souvenir," the sportsman said, and then turning to his companions he remarked, "Looks like our neighbor has taken us for a ride. Oh, boy, wait till the M.F.H. hears of this! So long, Uncle Mose."

The kennel man long since had departed with the quitters. But old Mose, game as a fighting cock, proudly stayed on, and the last they saw of him was standing on the hill, erect and bare-headed, alert to catch every note of his tenacious pack which, with a desperate skill born of long experience and muscles hardened by nights of punishing contention with old *Gold Tooth*, were working out their problem, a mere handful of country dogs, so to speak, free from the well-meant but often disconcerting interference that their cousins in regimented packs need submit to from mounted huntsmen.

This type of sport, the primitive fox-race, was the job of Uncle Mose's own little band, and right nobly were they acquitting themselves, to the humiliation of the visitors, to be sure, but with obvious satisfaction on the part of their impecunious master.

"Drive on, good dawgs!" he exclaimed, as the Woodcote men passed from the scene. "Stay wid ole *Gold Tooth*. Dis nigger's houn's doan' run no rabbits. White folks, you know it's a fox."*

---

*From "Foxhunting is Different," 1938.

175

Master and Huntsman Jody Murtagh, of Rose Tree Foxhunting Club, showing his pack in the pack class.

Dr. Addis exhibiting his Warwick Village Penn-Marydel Hounds. Question: Are they descendants of the Western Harrier?

MY CRITICS

Jake Carle.

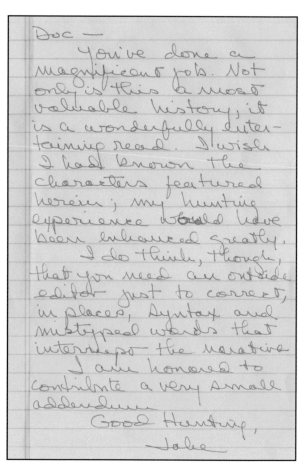

Doc —
    You've done a magnificent job. Not only is this a most valuable history, it is a wonderfully entertaining read. I wish I had known the characters featured herein; my hunting experience would have been enhanced greatly.
    I do think, though, that you need an outside editor just to correct, in places, syntax and mistyped words that interrupt the narrative
    I am honored to contribute a very small addendum.
        Good Hunting,
            Jake

Note from Jake Carle.

My wife, Hampton C. Addis.

Section II

Setting Sail and Arrival

In Section II you will have departed from the ports of England, sailed the Atlantic Ocean and landed 20 miles up-current on the Patuxent River from its junction with the Chesapeake River. With the docking of Sir Robert Brooke's boat the family, indentured servants and hounds moves on shore to the land now called De La Brooke Manor. This 2,000 acres with an additional 8,000-acres plantation is situated in St. Mary's County of Maryland (and occupying the western bank of the Patuxent River).

During the reign of King Charles of England (1625-1649), the First Lord of Baltimore in possession of 5 million acres gave this land to his good friend Robert Brooke. This friendship was so strong that the title of "commander" was not limited to St. Mary's County but you can tack on the assignment of Charles County, Maryland, as well.

So the western shore of the Patuxent River is where I chose to begin.

"Leashed Hounds" was painted circa 1860 by French painter Constant Troyon (1810-1865). Troyon was best known for his paintings of animals and landscapes. He was a member of the Barbizon School of painters, who focused on landscapes and scenes of rural life. This painting is in The John G. Johnson Collection, Philadelphia Museum of Art.

SQUIRE OF COBB NECK
THE LIFE OF ROBERT CRAIN
by Hulbert Footner

Not only do we know that De La Brooke W Foxhounds occupies the same territory that the first recorded pack of Foxhounds (Robert Brooke 1650) landing on southern Maryland soil, I chose to enter an article written by David Raley (Ex. MFH and Professional Huntsman) showing off his Penn Marydels at Cooksey's Store and Mt. Victoria Post Office.

With the arrival of an interesting 318-page biography of my wife's paternal grandfather, Robert Crain, on March 2011 I could not restrain myself from recording some passages.

Robert Crain, 1865-1928, was a distinguished lawyer with offices in Baltimore, Md. and Washington, D.C. His love of land and farming was remarkable so states his biographer. He acquired some twenty separate estates in Charles County amounting nearly to 15,000 acres. These properties' boundaries held nearly 12 miles of river frontage on both the Potomac and Wicomico Rivers.

His biographer says, "however 'much' Robert made he always spent more. He never had to pay for anything at the time he bought it; the banks were delighted to lend money to so obviously a prosperous man."

One of his Potomac River front properties in which I lost my hunting horn on the famous 7-hour Mt. Victoria hunt, 1970's needs further discussion. "Mt. Republic often erroneously called Mt. Republican is a dignified mansion on a lower level, having its own fine views towards the Potomac. It was built in 1790, i.e. in the early days of the Republic; the detail is fine, particularly the entrance doorways, front and rear which are considered among the most beautiful in Maryland."

(The next two sentences in this biography are the reason for the preceding information.) "This house is famous as the home of Francis Weems, who maintained a pack of a hundred foxhounds, and kept a poker game going for forty years."

Until further information appears in writing, we can assume De La Brooke W Foxhounds are number four, following Marlborough Hunt 1936, in the standings of large PMD packs that hunted or are hunting these southern counties of the western shore of Maryland.

———— •-•-• ————

We have read many times that fox hounds from England were introduced to America in 1650 by gentleman, Robert Brooke. Landing on the western shore of the

Patuxent River, we are lead to believe that most of our hounds originated from the boundaries of Maryland.

For the February 2009, issue of *The Friends of the Penn-Marydel Newsletter*, I researched and wrote an article on MFH Wikoff Smith of Whitelands Hunt, Chester County, Pa.

In a November 19, 1938, dinner card that MFH Smith distributed to the Whitelands Members, he begins its history as follows:

"Hunting in the Eastern counties of Pennsylvania is a sport almost as old as the counties themselves. Many a gentleman colonist brought his horses and hounds along on the same ship with his family from England and set up his establishment on the same lines as those he was used to in the mother country. In fact, an ancestor of our first master, Richard M. Newlin, was the first man to run hounds in the (Pa.) Commonwealth."

Unless someone comes forth with another name, the Newlin family and ship may be the only other name known to sail to the colonies. The Delaware River and Philadelphia ports would have been the landing site.

Many pictures of both formal and farmer packs that date back for over a half century are colored with tri color Black-White-Tans. Again I turn to T. Ivester Lloyd's book *Hounds* and dwell on a chapter, A "Stud Book" Harrier.

Not only Lloyd's painting of these tri-colors at work enforce my belief that these harriers may have been on the Newlin ship but his second paragraph in this chapter says it all.

"There may be some truth in the old tale that when dusk had made further sport impossible, a stick was put in the ground where hounds were stopped and that next day they went back to the stick in the hope of again picking up the hare's line!"

-T. Ivester Lloyd

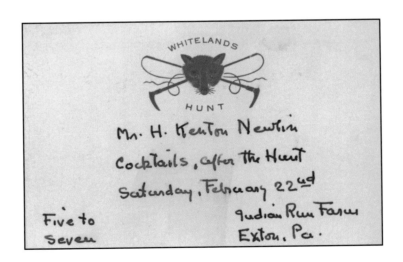

DE LA BROOKE'S JOINT MEET WITH MARLBOROUGH HUNT
by David Raley

(I chose this well written article because it is in the counties to which our first settlers (Robert Brook) brought their old Southern English hounds to the colonies.)

On a bright day at the end of this past January, the De La Brooke Foxhounds W hosted the Marlborough and Commonwealth Hunts at a meet at Yatten. It is situated on the Wicomico River in Charles County, Maryland, and is the home of Mrs. Walter Slowinski and family. De La Brooke and Marlborough each brought fifteen couple of hounds. With one hound from Dr. Todd Addis on its way to his new home at the De La Brooke Kennels. We drew through Yatten on towards Mt. Victoria which is the old home of Happy Addis and the present home of the only reliable red fox in the area. Along the way, we had a lively fifteen minutes, ending with a "treed" cat. Todd Jr. and I endured the collective giggles of three hunts and slunked across the road into Mt. Victoria.

As we drew through the heavily wooded section of Mt. Victoria, Todd devised a plan for us to separate, widely spreading the hounds across the direction we were drawing. I looked upon this plan with some trepidation. Would we not be starting with an already split pack? What if my hounds act like proper imbeciles when away from me? Worse still

De La Brooke Foxhounds W, with Master and Huntsman David G. Raley, Skip Zahniser and Jim Weaver in the summer of 1998.

was the potential scenario that as Todd and the hounds leave on the line of the fox, I end up with a disappointed and surly field! My only hope was to pick the side closer to where we had found the fox before and have the hounds with me hit first.

The hounds closest to Todd struck first. How will I ever get the hounds, the field and myself over to the action? Out came the horn, and what? The hounds had already rushed to the first cry! Thus began a chase which would last for one and one half hours, the fox being viewed four times. I never saw Todd during the entire run, as both of us were up with the hounds at different segments of three very large circuits through beaver dams and old gravel pits. Gaining time on the pack, and leaving the staff in that mess, the fox crossed back into Mt. Victoria and disappeared. It was the powerful voices of the Penn-Marydels which had made this one of the better joint meets at De La Brooke.

DE LA WHO?

De La Brooke had its start in the 1930's as the Charles County Hunt as was recorded in Bailey's Hunting Directory, Volume 64:

> *The Wicomico Hunt finds its origins in the former Charles County Hunt which was organized in 1937 and was disrupted by World War II, the last hunt being in December 7, 1941, when after a particularly successful day's hunting with a long run and a kill close to the kennels, the field returned to find the United States at war.*
>
> *Re-established after the war as part of the organization of a "country club" was not viewed as a satisfactory arrangement by the hunting members and the group formed a separate organization and incorporated it under the laws of Maryland as the Wicomico Hunt, Mt. Victoria, Maryland.*

This new organization incorporated in 1962, with William Zantzinger as Master. Until the early 1980's, this was an important position in that who ever was the master responsible for the hound side of things generally keep the hounds at their home. This might not be a bad thing, except that the masters never lasted more than three seasons.

In the course of seeking recognition from the Masters of Foxhounds Association in the early 1970's, it was discovered that another hunt on Maryland's Eastern Shore had already secured the name Wicomico Hunt. The "new" name De La Brooke Foxhounds W(icomico) was taken from the home established in 1650 by Robert Brooke in what is now St. Mary's County. When Brooke arrived his retinue included a pack of foxhounds. This pack of hounds began many of the bloodlines in the famous breeds of American hounds such as the Walker and July (Newman, H. *The Maryland Dents,* Dietz Press 1963).

Except in a very few instances, De La Brooke hunts on private lands throughout southern Maryland. The pack still runs over the lands of Robert Brooke, as well as The Cage (1652) in Calvert County, Mulberry Fields (1760) in St. Mary's County, and Mt. Victoria in Charles County. De La Brooke also hunts land on St. Jerome's Neck, which is home to the Trossbach family, of whom Linwood Trossbach was the premier houndman in St. Mary's for many years. It is now De La Brooke who continues the pursuit of the fox across a territory that has been hunted for over three centuries.

As De La Brooke developed, it put together a pack of American hounds through drafts from pre-Penn-Marydel Marlborough, Potomac, Middleburg, Bull Run and Orange County. The pack would follow along the bloodlines from these hunts through several Master/Huntsman and professional huntsman until 1994.

TIME FOR A CHANGE

Upon taking over duties as huntsman that year, there were several problems with the pack. The most apparent problem was kennel fighting, deer running, kennel fighting, lack of voice and kennel fighting. In addition our hunt country which contains Calvert, Charles, and St. Mary's County, is hilly and heavily wooded with think underbrush and cut through with large tidal wetlands and swamps. This is not the ideal conditions for fast Virginia hounds. These problems were compounded by an inexperienced huntsman who desperately needed some biddable hounds which were easier to break off deer and to be able to stay in touch with in the inaccessible parts of the county.

To my rescue came the Addis' and the Penn-Marydel Foxhound. Doc Addis has supplied De La Brooke with a constant stream of old steady hounds, and Todd Addis Jr. has sent from the Marlborough Hunt whelps and bred bitches which will be the foundation of our "new" pack. Presently we have about a seventy-five percent Penn-Marydel population.

A JOINT MEET WITH OAK RIDGE

On March 14, 1998, De La Brooke hosted the Oak Ridge Hunt from Virginia. The meet was at John and Cathy McFadden's home in Medley's Neck that is a peninsula between the Potomac River and Breton Bay. The country is dominated by eight hundred acres reclaimed from a gravel operation. It was a sunny day with the temperature around 65 degrees with 25 knot winds out of the west. Rita Mae Brown, Master of Oak Ridge, had requested a fixture along a Tide water shore. What she got was four foot rollers breaking in the beach. It was going to be a tricky day.

Again, the voice of the Penn-Marydel made the hunt, in what would generally be considered poor conditions. We drew first in a large marsh, hoping to find a gray fox to give us nice tight circles that would allow the field to hear the pack over the wind. Instead Addis' Honor '92, who Doc had given to me in the previous season, trailed up a red fox, bringing the pack to her with her urgent chop-chop-chop voice. The pack ran down wind through a half mile of swamp, their notes coming back to us through the breeze. The fox, finding no relief in the swamp, exited into heavy woods. After a mile of woods the fox found that plan insufficient to shake the pack so he tried a half mile stretch of recently timbered land running directly upwind. No dice. How about a wheat field, the fox must have thought to himself. Sorry, but the Penn-Marydel takes "true to the line" very seriously. After three quarters of an hour, the fox had had enough and started back for the marsh in which Honor had first found him. Another fifteen minutes of marsh, and the hounds put him to ground. The field had been able to stay in touch throughout the hour long run. Penn-Marydels sure make you look good at a joint meet.

THE MARYLAND INDEPENDENT, LA PLATA, MARYLAND

Wicomico Holds Traditional Blessing of Hounds

Name changed from Wicomico Hunt to De La Brooke Foxhounds W.

Along The Chesapeake.

For hunting along the Chesapeake
   Began so long ago
I'd have to "back" the calendar
   Three hundred years or so.

Plantation large - or fishing shack
   Each claimed a spotted dog
To hunt a possum, boar or fox
   Or spiney-sharp hedge-hog.

Folks didn't have one dog for fox
   Yet another one for hare -
Old yaller had to do his stuff
   Be it turkey, grouse or bear.

As time moved on and the river-folk
   Chopped out the hinter land
More kin from far across the sea
   Marked their foot-steps on the sand.

If Blue Boy's got a trailin' nose
   And Bugle's got a voice
There's born a pack and a betting man.
   A hunter's got no choice.

There's a tree to fell and a roof to thatch
   From dawn to the close of day.
But the stars on high, in a twilight sky
   Coax out the hound-dog's bay.

A bay from the ridge; deep throat from the glen
   Each hound adds a note to the song
Begging the Boys 'long the Chesapeake
   To "deaf-ear" their "Eve-sup" gong.

     Ann H. Addis 1900 - 1991
       Apr 6th - Apr 6th

A Tarheel's Impressions of Pennsylvania
Fredrick Berry Esq. MFH and Elaine Berry

September, Friday the 13th, 1996. I loaded my hounds and horse to make the annual pilgrimage to hunt with Doctor Todd Addis and to attend the Kimberton Hunt Hound Show.

For 51 weeks of the year, I look forward to the week I spend in PA each fall.

At 8:00 a.m. Saturday morning, Dr. Addis cast the hounds behind his kennel and in less than 10 minutes hounds were running. We were out four hours and I expect hounds were running hard for 3 hours. Hounds ran in and marked two fox, the first in the quarry and the second in a ground hole on a hillside. We believe hounds ran the third and last fox in, but Doc and I were giving our horses a breather and talking and were not as close to hounds as we should have been.

Monday was not quite as good a day from the scenting standpoint, but we still heard a lot of running and saw a lot of good hound work. Saturday, when a hound struck, his cry had authority. Huntsmen with a real ear for hounds could hear the hound's authoritative "follow me". Monday the sound was amore tenuous "I think the fox went this way", but we still had 3.5 hours or so of hard running.

The final day, Wednesday, was very interesting. The early morning was ideal for scenting and hounds ran with tremendous cry. Hounds were cast at Cochrane's at 8:30 and were running hard in less than 15 minutes. Hounds split and each pack ran very well until one pack was foiled by our horses. Beth harked those hounds to the other pack and hounds were together for the rest of the morning. We believe hounds ran this fox in, but as the chase ended in the swamp next to highway 401, no member of the field was close enough to verify that the fox had been denned. About 11:00 or so, scent deteriorated to the point that hounds could only trail. However, that gave us a good opportunity to see a lot of hound work.

Around 12:30, Doc decided to call it a day, and without being conscious of it, gave a demonstration of what a grand hound man he is. Doc has some very strong going, hard hunting hounds. I doubt there are any harder hunting hounds in organized hunting. Yet, when Doc was through, he dismounted from his horse and sat down on the grass under a shade tree. With very little attention from his whips, all of these hard hunting aggressive hounds lay down on the grass around him and waited for the hound/ horse trailer to arrive for the ride back to kennels. A most impressive demonstration of the rapport Doc has with his hounds.

Wednesday, Doc and I witnessed something that scared us both pretty badly. Nina Christianson fell from her horse and after she was on the ground with her pistol under her, it discharged. Doc and I were certain she had shot herself but lady luck was on her side. A good lesson: One should never shoot unless firmly in the deep seat defensive riding position.

I leave PA each year with several outstanding impressions: the hospitality and courtesy shown by all, especially Sandy and Barbara Dunn and the Addis family; the beauty of the PA country; the courtesy of the motorists, who seem to always give way to horses and hounds; and the manner in which the citizens of PA have conserved the land so that their way of life can continue. In NC, the DOT will not pave the narrow lanes as is done in PA. NC DOT requires a full width two lanes so who school busses can meet and pass. Curves much be straightened and shoulders and right of way planted in grass. White and yellow paint lines in the center of the roads are required. So everyone drives 65 M.P.H. right up to their driveway. Not good for foxhounds or mounted hunt members.

So thank you to everyone who made my visits so much fun, and may you all have good hunting.

Sincerely,
Fred and Elaine Berry
Sedgefield Hunt, N.C.

Mission Work in the South
by Elaine Berry

When Red Mountain hired a new huntsman, a young man from Maryland, rumors spread among the heathers. When he brought hounds with him, some might have said they were not the prettiest specimen of foxhounds. However, it didn't take long before the talk was not about how they looked but about their "voice" and "drive". David had begun a mission of introducing other hunts to the glory of the Penn-Marydel hound. Red Mountain participated in joint meets, carried hounds to the Belle Meade Hound trials, showed at the Carolina Hound Show, promoted his best dog hounds for stud, and began an annual Hunt Weekend. The first of these hosted by Red Mountain was in 2002, organizing hunts

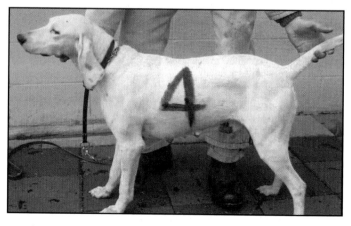

Red Mountain Foxhound's, "Yogurt," helping with the mission work.

with De La Brooke, Shakerag, Sedgefield and Smith Mountain. The 2003 event took North Carolina hunts to Maryland for three days. De La Brooke put on a wonderful hunt on a glorious Sunday morning in March.

Sedgefield Huntsman Fred Berry was the first convert. He was so impressed by the noise, drive and tenacity of the hounds that in the spring of 2003 he decided to make a change in Sedgefield's pack. He wanted to hunt a pack of Penn Marydels. Fred met many of the Denomination's elders at the Huntsman's days in Emporia, Virginia that April. Passing the hat on a trip during the Bryn Mawr Hound Show; Doc Addis, Marlborough, Golden's Bridge, Rose Tree, De La Brooke, Thorton Hill and Red Mountain contributed hounds to the collection basket. Soon a large number of long-eared, loud hounds with slopping heads tool up residence at the Sedgefield kennel. The transformation had begun (and continues).

Sedgefield hosted the other clubs for a 3 day hunt event in December 2003 and in March 2005. The Sedgefield Hunt organized the first Carolina Hound Trail. Red Mountain, Smith Mountain, Moore County, Meckleburg, Sedgefield and Yadkin Valley participated at the hunt territory east of Danville, Virginia. It is worth noting that Red Mountain's Yogurt '02 was the high point winner. She is athletic, loud, hard-driving, and almost unstoppable. She was sired by Addis' Forrester '98 and her dam is Addis' Rosette '96.

Thanks to the Right Reverend David for spreading the gospel. Many thanks also to Doc Addis, Jody Murtagh and everyone else for helping so many others in their effort to create a better pack. Triangle Hunt and Moore County have been influenced by the evangelists and the Carolina Hound Show now has a Penn Marydel ring.

Recently, Fred went to Berryville, Virginia to collect a litter of ten pups from Doc. Transporting them in a sedan turned out not to be so practical. The pups would not be contained in boxes and they were hot and LOUD. A flashing blue light and the sedan could have pulled others over. Using the trunk, the back seat, air conditioning and bluegrass music the hounds were finally lulled to sleep and they made it to North Carolina. So move over Yogurt, choir practice begins in September.

Penelope's pups 05.

TRUE TO THE LINE

(no matter how long the line is)
by H.L. Todd Addis

In the Penn-Marydel foxhound Inc. booklet we read the phrase "True to the Line". However, the founding directors failed to give us any thoughts on how long is this "line" to be honored.

Some recent phone conversations may give the questioner some guidelines on how long their Penn-Marydels should run before they start sending their hours into the Guinness Book of Records.

Huntsman Billy Dodson of Thornton Hill Hounds said he started the meet at 1 pm on February 11th. Hounds jumped their fox at 1:30 pm. The paths, fields and woodland cover were frozen and footing was ugly. Due to the footing, it took some time before the staff and field joined the running pack. At the end of the day three well-seasoned hounds were absent from roll call. Several trips back to the meet failed to retrieve the hounds.

The next early morning recovery did not improve. So huntsman Billy drove to the adjacent hunt country and at about 10:30 am, he viewed two red foxes crossing a

Thorton Hill hounds, "waiting patiently", at Opening Meet, 2006.

meadow. He stopped his engine and rolled down his window to listen if the foxes were 'tonguing'. They were running mute, but the three hounds behind them were not. 'A bird in the hand is worth two in the bush' as the saying goes, so Billy broke them after 21 hours of all night and morning running. "Oh my, they never raised their heads or moved a muscle for two days."

Just maybe Sandy Dunn's Kimberton hounds have out done Billy Dodson's southern hounds. Here is the story.

On Wednesday, February 7th we met at the kennels and moved off to Powder Mill Hill. Little time elapsed from the 10 o'clock meet, when hounds began to entertain themselves on several foxes. Before the pack of 20 couple returned to kennels at 2:30 pm, five hounds were heard crossing Flowing Springs Road. With the temperature in the mid-20's and dropping no staff volunteered to track them down.

One lady called and reported them going through her yard at 7:30 pm. Huntsman and Master Dunn went on a search and seizure mission and heard them running behind the cow barns of Kenny Miller's farm. This 9:30 pm discovery was only about a ½ mile from the kennels. Hunt member Kay Johnson reported in the next morning that her house dogs 'carried on' at 4 am when running hounds passed by. Another resident Pat Calhoun repeated the same story only at 4:30 am.

When they officially stopped running the Dunns do not know, but all arrived at kennels at noon. None staggered but all their sterns were bouncing off their hocks. All were down in the backs and looked 'washed out'. 'Jammed up' is another descriptive term for foot-sore hounds that are just plain beat. Since there was no official timer their 24 plus hours of running a fox has to have an asterisk behind the record.

George Dunn, MFH and Kimberton Hounds.

THE KILLERS
"BRING THEM TO HAND"
by H. L. Todd Addis, MFH

Every time a newsletter is produced I begin to fret about what in the world can we find of interest for the next one. Santa Claus came through when he placed another gift under the tree- a book titled Rycroft on Hounds, Hunting and Country. I gave it extra attention when I saw that it was compiled and edited by my friend Jim Scharnberg, Master and huntsman of the Skycastle French Bassett Hounds here in Chester County, Pennsylvania.

As I read through it, I began to think, why not get back to my college days and try to pull my grade up in English Composition 101, by trying to do a book report. Everything that is of interest in this report is taken from the somewhat warped point of view of a Penn-Marydel Hound enthusiast. Here goes!

The book, as Mr. Scharnberg states in the acknowledgements, is a collection of articles on hounds, breeding and hunting, written by Sir Newton Rycroft and published in Hounds Magazine from 1984 to 1999.

The first subject, 'A Hound's Most Important Quality', which appeared on the second printed page (page 4), really helps divide the 'religions'. The Question: what is the object of hound breeding? Sir Newton states, "This is surely to catch the fox! If this is so, then all the essential requirements such as nose, cry, stamina, pace-cum-drive and all the others become and remain mean to that end. Mr. (Isaac) Bell's advice was to breed from those hounds that 'help you bring foxes to hand'. This is surely as good a definition of a class foxhound as anybody could possibly give."

He also believed that to breed such a class of fox-killers, the hounds bred from should have as few stains as possible in their pedigrees for at least the first three generations. "This has always seemed to me the best recipe, because it is the most certain one, for a killing pack."

From my father's time to the present, nearly a century, American Masters and huntsmen have dug, bought, relocated and even stolen foxes to move them from one place to another to proved the thrill of the chase, and haven't been overjoyed by a kill.

It was only natural over the past few centuries for the English to take the slow, monotonous Southern Hound and experiment with the genes of greyhound, mastiff, terrier, pointer, and bloodhound. Who knows whether or not a disgruntled hunt servant threw his father's favorite mongrel in the breeding pen as well? A Master's reputation as a hound breeder is directly proportional to the numbers killed, so state the English authorities.

Under the subject of 'Change and Non-Change', Sir Newton devotes a few paragraphs on the merits of whether hounds 'turn' with their quarry or 'swing' with him. "In the history of French Stag hunting, the best packs have always been extremely lethal in taking their deer, even the slower packs that may take 4 to 6 hours in doing so. I think all hounds that are bred to hunt will do one of two things when their quarry changes direction. They will either 'turn' with him or they will 'swing' with him. The former to my mind is so important that I think it is about the surest sign of 'class' in any hound. Close turning in fact has the most obvious advantage. It saves time and so keeps them close to their hare and fox, and greatly reduces the chance of their changing. I think this last is easily appreciated by a beagle huntsman in a 'sea' of arable with fresh hares popping up on all sides when every yard his hounds over run must increase mathematically the chance of a change."

When I judged the Western Tour Challenge in April 1999, I saw most of the English and Walker crossbred packs take the 'swing' to the extreme, with heads held high, and change merrily from coyote to antelope.

Under the subject of 'Stamina and Constitution', Sir Newton defines stamina as the ability of a hound to hunt long hours several times a week, but by constitution he is referring more to longevity and the ability to withstand disease and parasites. "No breed of hound or working dog has or ever has had as good a constitution as the best foxhound. The only possible exception here is the husky of the far north," so says Rycroft. It is my opinion that our Penn-Marydel fox hound falls behind the English and Crossbred in constitution, but for the present day foxhunter, they can dish out all the stamina we can take.

There are certain passages in Sir Newton's book that stir my thoughts. On an unknown

The Dumfriesshire's TRIOMPHE, a Gascon-Sainteongeois Hound, from a painting by T. Ivester Lloyd in John Jardine's Hounds of the World, *1937.*

Warwick Village Hound, Work Bench.

Campbell (on left) with the Hounds at a kill.

SALLY, a typical brook bitch, ca. 1903.

Alexander Campbell, MH, hunted hare with his Hailsham Harriers on foot and mounted from 1902 to about 1925. They were the last purebred pack of Old Southern Hounds in England. The photos are from Hare Hunting and Harriers, *1927, and* Horn and Hound, *1903, by H. A. Bryden.*

Note: Many of us have tried to breed out the broad, flat head with not so low set ears. But, those genes, that carry theses characteristics keep popping up. T.A.

date the great hound man Mr. George Foljambe wrote to Lord George Bentinck of the Old Brockelsby:

> *"The pace and the way they run together I was charmed with. In short it was quite a tip top thing, yet the hounds certainly were a mean looking lot. Too seedy to please the eye, you never saw such narrow animals, but the mode of their hunting and running and their style of killing, the way they carry and the pace they go, sets aside all my prejudices, and I am inclined to say that although they are by no means hounds to breed from in as much as they want bone and substance, yet take them as they are, they are one of the most level packs I ever saw and as they are all alike and have a peculiar character, I cannot fail to admire them on that score and for the quickness of their performance and their speed and swiftness they cannot be surpassed. They are ridiculously small in substance and weedy to be sure."*

Could Mr. Foljambe have dipped overseas and witnessed a day on Kent Island on the Eastern Shore of Maryland, and just described a day with the Penn-Marydels?

To continue my amateurish book review I must record the statement of Rycroft under 'The Smaller Kennels': "Quite rightly, we laud and respect the great hounds of such packs as Brockelsby, Warwickshire, Belvoir, Milwn, Berkeley and Duke of Beaufort's so to speak 'bred in the purple'. Yet that most wonderful creature, the modern foxhound, has also benefited greatly from hounds that were bred and entered in lesser known hunts than these."

Back during the Second World War, our "sportsmanlike" Pennsylvania Game Commission put on an intensive campaign to kill off all predators to enhance the small game population for the returning service men. To counter this vermicide, my father communicated with Albert Smith, a gentleman and a likeable chap of English birth, who was then hunting Amory Haskell's Monmouth County Harriers in New Jersey.

Dad acquired 10 couples of these harriers and released some Kansas Hares in an attempt to generate sport.

The only names I remember of the lot were Hatbox and Hurry, and we named three young entry Champion, Spark, and Plug. As I can picture them now, I would consider them to have been typical of the modem Harrier type. Sir John Buchanan-Jardine in his book, *Hounds of the World*, states that "the modem harrier bears no greater resemblance to the one in use fifty years back, than the hunter of the present day to that ridden by our grandfathers. In fact, he is now nothing less than the foxhound in miniature, which it is the endeavor of all breeders to have him. Before the old fashioned harrier, the hare had time to play all sorts of tricks, to double on her foil, and so to stain the ground that she often escaped by such means; whereas the modern hound, if the scent be too terribly good, forces the hare from her foil to fly the country.

Several wonderful pictures appear in the Rycroft book, one showing a 1906 picture of the Holcombe Harriers, and another of Alexander Campbell, Master of the Hailsham Harriers 1902, 1917 with his Old Southern Hounds. It was the last pack of pure Old Southern Hounds hunted in England. We must conclude that if the old Southern Hounds hunted fox it was a foxhound and if it hunted hare it was a harrier.

The few remaining New Jersey harriers were part of the merger of the Perkiomen and the Whitelands Hunts in the early 50's. Huntsman Room Inductee, Albert Crossan, tainted with Penn-Marydel faithfulness, soon weeded them out of the pack. A few crossbreds did survive and did well. The last surviving crossbred, Axle, was drafted to MFH, Richard Harris to help build his private 'deer proof' pack. Richard Harris then took over the Mastership of the Huntingdon Valley Hunt in Bucks County, Pennsylvania.

In closing, I would like to pay tribute to a hound named Triomphe, a Gascon-Sainteongeois hound of Sir John Buchanan-Jardine's. A picture taken from a painting by T. Ivester Lloyd appears in Sir Newton's book.

Since this hound is so typical of our Penn-Marydel hound. I wish to quote what Sir John wrote about him in his book, *Hounds of the World*.

"Without being very fast they are still very much faster than the old Gascon breed, while yet retaining his magnificent voice; in constitution they are not quite first, class either, but their wonderful gameness and tenacity keep them going when other hounds would have given up or gone home, and their perseverance on a cold or twisting scent is marvelous. I speak from experience as I have had several individuals of this strain, and still have one now (1935). He is a dog called 'Triomphe' and is of the Gaston color, i.e. blue mottled but is of course Gascon-Sainteongeois in breeding. He hunts with my foxhounds (Dumpfriesshire) regularly and though never in the lead on a good scent, he manages to keep with the body; and on a bad scenting day, with a twisting fox or on a line down the road, he makes himself very conspicuous indeed have often seen him tired, but I have never seen him drop his stem or show signs of 'throwing in his hand.' He has, too, a magnificent voice. I have never seen a hound fonder of a piece of a fox."

FRENCH HOUND PACK BRED WITHIN FOR 50 YEARS
by H. L. Todd Addis

I found the following in one of Judy Harrison Addis' (my sister-in-law) books titled *Bridle and Brush* by George Denholm Armour, 1937.

Under Chapter X Family Matters and some notes on French Hounds. (Not quoted exactly as published.)

Armour along with a friend visited France for the purpose of seeing some old breeds of hounds. Many packs were reduced almost to vanishing point. There apparently was a great reduction because of the French Revolution. This visit was in 1914 one year before WWI or the anticipation of WWI. "We chose those (kennels) which showed none or little English cross, our intention being to see as many purely French types as possible. When we addressed the hunt servants in most villainous French, we were graciously received everywhere. The various breeds of hounds we saw was all bred with the same object and same qualifications. They must have cry."

"The last of some 20 packs were visited were rather remarkable from the fact, which Monsieur Levesque, the Master, told us that they had been bred form the same stock for fifty years without introduction of any new blood; they derived originally

Victor (front and center) had the exact markings described by Monsieur Levesque. Dr. Addis' Warwick Village Hounds.

from 2 hounds, one French and the other French-English cross. In color this pack were peculiar, being pure black and white in about equal proportions, with small lemon tan markings about the eyes and on some cheeks but not elsewhere?

Could it be that some of the genes that made up Monsieur Levesque's hounds carried along with the blue ticks until the right odd's developed?

My dog hound Victor pictured center-bottom had the exact markings so described in my Monsieur Levesque. Never before have I had such coloring on a hound.

- H. L. Todd Addis
Warwick Village Hounds

THE WASHINGTON'S HEADQUARTERS STORY
by H. L. Todd Addis

The Eventful Years, by Thomas R. Thompson. On one of my wife's compulsive buying sprees during Christmas shopping time, she picked out his little blue pamphlet.

It is not my intent to give a history lesson to our fox hunting readers, but a little back ground will help you understand why I was impressed with one important statement. Read on!

The Battle of the Brandywine here in Pa. was arguably the largest battle of the American Revolution with 29,000 combatants.

In spite of the American defeat, the public awareness of the Battle of the Brandywine received a major boost when a young, history loving school teacher, Christ Saudnerson, began residing in the Old Ring house or Washington's Headquarters in 1906.

While teaching in a one-room school house in Chadds Ford in 1905 he wrote his mother, Hanna Carmack Sanderson, that the east wing of Washington's Headquarters was for rent.

Mother Sanderson combined with son Christ from 1906-1922 and help made the headquarters a national shrine.

Throughout their sixteen years of occupancy, Chris and his mother never once tried to commercialize or benefit personally from the tremendous number of visitors to the headquarters.

The Sandersons were tenants of Dr. A. H. Cleveland and Mr. Richard Atwater who jointly owned Washington's Headquarters and on Dec. 31, 1921, Chris was notified that he and his mother would have to vacate their home by April 1922.

Chris was so hurt by this 'eviction' notice that he had cards printed for his friends and acquantances.

For 16 years mother and I allowed the stranger as well as friend to visit our private home which I rented the Washington Headquarters of Chadds Ford, Pa. Over 21,000 did so during the past 3 years and 9,257 during 1921.

The owners claim they want it for relatives, whether the public will be allowed to enter, remains to be seen. Others are reaping the harvest, which I have been sowing for all these years. So, to go away is like leaving the old homestead. With S. B. Read I can exclaim: "Oh, ye who daily cross the sill, Step lightly for I love it still."

The pamphlet at its beginning list the eventful years
1777 The Battle of the Brandywine
1906 The Sandersons move to W. Headquarters

Washington's Headquarters. Credit: "The Washington Headquarters Story" by Thomas R. Thompson, Curator Emeritus of the Christian Sanderson Museum, Chadds Ford, PA, Copyright 2002.

1910 The Bronze Marker installed
1922 The Sandersons leave the Headquarters
1927 The 150th Anniversary Program
1931 Washtingtons Headquarters destroyed by fire
1952 The Dedication of the Rebuilt Headquarters.

Near the end under a paragraph titled [Parties] is what caught my attention:

> *"During the time we lived there we (the Sandersons) had many parties. Many schools in buses and in winter time country schools participated on an old fashion sleighing party. Twice we had great fox hunts on Washington Birthdays, one in 1910 we had over 400 riders from 32 Hunt clubs and from 4 states {Pa., Md., Del., and N.J.}"*

Penn-Marydels you can bet these hounds were the ancestors of our present-day Penn-Marydel. The friends cannot leave out N.J. in our title!

Washington's Chadds Ford Headquarters courtesy of Chris Sanderson Museum Curator, Charles Ulmann, Musuem phone number 610-388-6545.

OWNER AND PREACHER.

A Little Church Near Chadds' Ford That Is Owned and Conducted by a Colored Woman

Down over the hills southeast of Chadds' Ford stands a little church in which the colored residents of the neighborhood worship. There is nothing peculiar about this, only in the fact that this little old building, formerly a school house, is owned, as well as the graveyard adjoining, by a colored woman named Archer, who is also the preacher in charge, and has been for many years. Here the good colored folks gather from Sunday to Sunday, to listen to the Scriptures read and the sermon preached by this good woman, who is known far and near as being the only colored woman minister in this section of the country. Mrs. Archer does practically all the work there is to be done about the place, even to the care of the church and taking up the collection. She is strictly honest in her dealings with her fellow man, and acts as Secretary and Treasurer. In order to be repaid somewhat for the work, she charges the colored brethren a certain amount for allowing them to inter their dead and is also remembered to some extent by the collections taken at the several services. She attends to all the repairs needed, taking all the responsibility upon herself. Auntie Archer, as she is commonly known, is a great favorite among the children, both, white and colored, and is daily visited by some of them. This remarkable woman, who is now getting far advanced in life, is happy in her chosen work and greets all visitors with a pleasant smile and says that she is waiting and watching and is ready to go when the summons of the Master shall call her from earthly scenes. She is very fond of singing and one of her favorite hymns while going about her household duties is "I Shall Know Him."

THE CHRISTIAN C. SANDERSON MUSEUM
CHADDS FORD, PENNSYLVANIA 19317

Copy from: _____

_____

WASHINGTON'S BIRTHDAY,
"Washington's Headquarters."
THE CHADD'S FORD HUNT
Cordially invite you to be present at a
Drop Fox Hunt.
To be given at WASHINGTON'S HEADQUARTERS,
The home of Christian Sanderson, one mile east of
CHADD'S FORD, on
TUESDAY, FEBRUARY 22d, 1910.
Breakfast at Chadd's Ford Hotel at ten o'clock A. M.

The "Headquarters" will be open to Visitors.   Bring your friends.
Pen dogs at Headquarters barn.   Drop at 11 A M   Owing to quaran-
tine the dogs of C. H. Wright will not be present at this hunt.

Christian Sanderson   Chas. H. Wright   F. J. Stackhous

Yourself and friends are cordially invited
to attend a
Drop Fox Hunt
to be given at the home of Wm. Ring,
1-2 mile West of Chadd's Ford,
on Thursday, February eleventh, 1909,
at eleven o'clock A. M.
Lunch served at Chadd's Ford Hotel
at ten o'clock.
Bring dogs and pen at William Ring's barn.
C. H. Wright.   F. J. Stackhous.

Wyeth Portrait of Sanderson Hangs in Museum
by Gene Pisasale

The Brandywine Valley has become associated over the years with many famous artists, most notably Howard Pyle and N.C. Wyeth. Wyeth was later to become his best known student.

When N.C. Wyeth set up his studio in Chadds Ford after the turn of the 20th century, he gained recognition for illustrating many popular novels, including "Treasure Island" and "Robinson Crusoe." Wyeth's home was not far from Washington's Headquarters within what is now known as Brandywine Battlefield Park. Chris Sanderson and his mother lived in that house from 1906-1922 and became good friends with the Wyeth family.

Chris and his mother posed for many portraits by Wyeth and members of his family. N.C. Wyeth's gifted son, Andrew, painted a large portrait of Chris in 1937, welcoming him and his mother back to Chadds Ford after they'd moved away from the area. Andrew invited Chris and his mother, Hanna, over to his home for dinner on April 30, 1937, to view the portrait. Hanna later wrote that the painting was "so absolutely perfect that my astonishment knew no bounds . . ."

The painting shows Chris (around the age of 55) standing dapperly in a brown suit, holding a map of Chester County in the foreground, green rolling hills in the distance. Bucolic countryside wrapped around isolated houses, a woman in Colonial-period garb working in the fields, is overshadowed in the upper right hand corner by dark storm clouds, rain beginning to drench the area. This may have been subtle symbolism by the artist, as storm clouds were gathering over Europe, Hitler having invaded the Rhineland in 1936.

Christian Sanderson as painted by Andrew Wyeth.

Standing before the painting, the viewer is drawn both to Chris' finger—which is pointing to the map of Chester County—and his eyes, piercing the scene, which seem to be telling us "Pay attention . . . important things happened here . . . The young Marquis de Lafayette fought alongside George Washington's troops at the Battle of Brandywine, the largest land battle in North America up until the Civil War . . . Artists have painted our beautiful countryside, which holds many treasures for you to find . . . Come and enjoy what we know here . . . You will learn much about our heritage and find a sense of history . . . your history . . ."

The portrait of Chris Sanderson by Andrew Wyeth is just one of many paintings within the museum by members of the Wyeth family, Peter Hurd, John McCoy and others who knew and loved Chris. Their work—portraits, landscapes and still lifes—is a testament not only to the beauty of this region, but also to the inner beauty of this man, who preserved these and other priceless artifacts for all to see.

Visit the Sanderson Museum—A Man's Life, A Nation's History at 1755 Creek Road (old Route 100) in Chadds Ford, just north of Route 1 or on-line at www. SandersonMuseum.org.

SOME WRITERS CAN JUST SAY IT BETTER
JUST WHAT THE DOCTOR ORDERED, A PRESCRIPTION ON HUNTING

Highlighting random thoughts and memories
recorded in Eric Morrison's Fox and Hare in Leicestershire, 1954

Eric Morrison was a doctor by profession and a hunting man for sheer love of the sport. He has kept both hare and fox hounds for a very long time in a variety of circumstances. The author served over seas during the last 5 ½ years of WWII, being on of the original members of the famous 7ᵗʰ Armoured Division (the Desert Rats). He may have not shoveled dog turds in this kennel but he sure was there to see them deposited. The first three sentences that I quote could be challenged, but the experiences can only add to one expertise.

"Hare hounds should be your first love. No one should be allowed to ride to hounds until he or she has first run after them.

For the lover of hound work, too, hare hunting is the choice and, of all hare hunting that with Basset Hounds is the caviar."

This hound (the basset), originally imported from France, is in several varieties there, and it was because the 4ᵗʰ Earl of Onslow imported the crooked-leg specimen into England that people say, "This is the basset." They forget the other varieties in France. The crooked-leg sorts were never intended to chase a hare. Their duty was to put the game out of the thicket and then stop so that the guns could take over.

The beagle, if it is good enough to produce good music, will be so fast that when a hare is put up the pack will disappear in a burst of music and a cloud of dust and the foot-slogger is left high and dry, and may as well go home. Music is all important to the foot-hunter because nothing imparts that imperative urge to be with them? The man and horse like good music. Chopin (composer) cannot produce action like Rachmaninoff, and so the good music has to be of a special variety. If it is too 'thin', it does not produce the same determination that the richer, or, shall we say, more National Anthem variety does.

Now for the basset and when I say basset, I mean the second, straight-legged hound. With this hounds you are able to keep the size and consequently the voice, and still see the battle going on if you are a good runner or a canny one. The music will be such that you will run faster than you normally can; in foot you will probably run more with bassets than with beagles because you will see so much more of the hunting and your urge to be with them will be increased. Pennel Elmshurst (Brooksby) once heard a pack of bassets running near Northampton, and this is what he wrote:

On Tuesday, October 27, 1896, I had the opportunity of seeing a form of hunting
altogether novel to me, viz., the chase of the hare by basset hounds, The Messrs. Cooper having

brought their pack from Delapre Abbey. I confess that I was charmed. There was something so sporting in seeing these little hounds (to all appearance just cross between a turnspit and a fox-hound) driving along in grass that almost hid them. Their music—as compared to fox-hounds—was as a peal of church bells to a tune upon glasses. The roar of the nine couple would have drowned the combined dog packs of Pytchley, Grafton and Warwickshire. As they circled Eston Neston House, and went round and round the park, I cannot but think Her Ladyship's horses in stable must have deemed themselves victims of some horrible nightmare, and when next they have the honour of carrying her with fox-hounds they will image a rivalry of hobgoblins is again in store. The thought is rather alarming.

As I sifted through Eric Morrison's book I find myself mentally substituting the Penn Marydel pack for the straight legged basset hound.

So the reader, no matter, what your religion, can join me in my joyful conceit of this remarkable PMD hounds that need not be tampered with in their breeding.

To continue with Author Eric Morrison's pen—on a bad scenting day there is infinite enjoyment in watching them, as it has to be a very bad scenting day, such as seldom occurs, for bassets not to be able to hunt on at a fair pace. A close-scenting hound is required for such a day, and the basset, unlike many hounds, never seem to get tired of working. For the lazy huntsman, and consequently probably the good one, this is the hound to hunt, as he does it all for him.

Rabbit in the brush.

LAKE OF TWO MOUNTAIN'S RESPONDS
by Julian Allard, MFH

I would like to thank the "Friends of the Penn-Marydel" association for introducing me to this fantastic breed of hound!

It all started when a friend and fellow hunt member Michael Sinclair Smith arranged a meeting with 16 masters who hunted Penn-Marydels. In 2005 I met Fred Getty, MFH, who gave us four beautiful puppies on our first encounter. Needless to say we were thrilled. (Even though they were not blue ticks we love them!) I then got the phone and started begging my new contacts for more hounds.

Sandy Dunn gave me an old bitch "Oatmeal" who no longer hunted and promised to breed it for us. A couple of weeks later my son-in-law, our huntsman, Francios and I drove to Pennsylvania, to pick up Oatmeal, where Sandy met us with 4 more and took us to the Radnor Hunt where we obtained another seven. Doc Addis, who is now a great friend, gave us an additional four hounds-a total of 16 hounds! (Doc had some awesome puppies about 6 weeks old at the time I tried to wheedle from him. He said with a smile "over my dead body." Oh well!) Oatmeal surprised us with 8 beautiful tri-colored puppies that have all started hunting this fall and are showing much promise. As for Oatmeal, she somehow wormed her way into our hearts and into our HOUSE! She is now our resident couch potato!

I have been keeping in touch with Doc Addis ever since and learning something every time I talk to him. During one such conversation, Doc reminded me of the puppies I had begged for. He said that if I liked he would give me four of them, not because they were not good but he had been given some that he liked even better. I was thrilled! I WOULD LIKE EVERYONE TO KNOW THAT THE FOUR DOC ADDIS PUPPIES ARE ALMOST ALWAYS AT THE FRONT OF THE PACK! (What a treasure of a man!)

On September 13th, this year, I found myself hunting the hounds alone, as our huntsman was away. I lost my whip, my daughter, early on as she had to help a new member in trouble. At that point the pack entered a corn field and the entire field roared through an adjacent property causing some damage. I had to stop and calm down a very angry farmer! I could hear their cry but had lost the entire pack. The music was fantastic and went on from 10:00 a.m. till 4:30 in the afternoon before I could finally round them all up and bring them home.

Wow! I have been hunting for 41 years, with English, Cross-breds, and Welsh hounds, but never have I heard voices, seen scenting ability or the capacity to pick up checks, the way the Penn-Marydels do. Many of our members love this new hunting experience and although most have hunted in Europe and various other places, have never experienced such thrills!

So thank you Mike for introducing me to these wonderful people! Thank you to Mary Anne and Fred Getty, Barbara and Sandy Dunn and Happy and Doc Addis for your kindness, patience and help in rebuilding our hunt.

Thanks again.

Julian Allard, MFH, Lake of Two Mountains Hunt, Ontario, Canada (Oatmeal says thanks too!)

RED HERRING

On August 17, 2011 at 2:30 pm my wife Happy, who is addicted to murder mysteries, of course was helping the detective solve the murder. As the naked corpse (genitalia not exposed) lay there the 'actor' pathologist discussed a false clue and as he picked up a few hairs with his forceps remarked, "that it may be a red herring." He expanded his dialogue by explaining that back in the 15th century a huntsman would first train his hounds by laying a drag on salted Red Herring and in due time challenged the hounds on a live fox trail.

The act was to divert attention of the hounds from its trailing the intended quarry.

All of you readers who already knew the meaning and origin of the term red herring may I congratulate you.

-H. L. Todd Addis, August 17, 2011

———•·•———

I was sent a copy of an essay written by Theodore Roosevelt about <u>An American Boy</u>. Teddy at one point states:

> "So at home time the Persian Kings had to forbid polo; because soldiers neglected their proper duties for the fascination of the Game. We cannot expect the best work from soldiers who have carried to an unhealthy extreme the sports and pastimes which would be if indulged in with moderation, and have neglected to learn as they should the business of their profession. A soldier needs to know how to shoot and take cover and shift for himself-not to box or play football. There is, of course, always the risk of thus mistaking means for ends. Foxhunting is a first class sport; but one of the most absurd things in real life is to note the bated breath with which certain excellent fox-hunters, otherwise of quite healthy minds, speak of this admirable but over-important pastime. They tend to make it almost as much of a fetish as, in the last century the French and German nobles made the chase the stag, when they carried hunting and game-preserving to a point which was ruinous to national life. Fox hunting is very good as a pastime, but it is about as poor a business as can be followed by any man of intelligence.
>
> "Certain writers, writing about it are fond of quoting the anecdote of a fox-hunter who, in the days of the English Civil War, was discovered pursuing

his favorite sport just before a great battle between their lines as they came together. Of course, in reality the chief serious use of fox-hunting is to encourage manliness and vigor, and to keep men hardy, so that if needed they can show themselves fit to take part in work or strife for their native land."

Harriet, shown by Whipper-in Nina Christiansen.

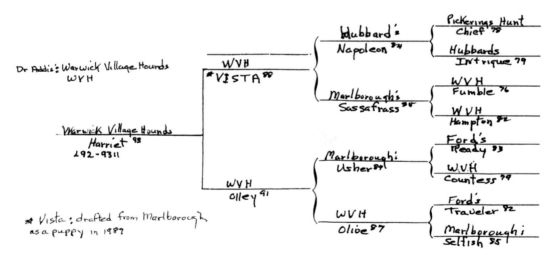

Some folks expressed themselves in that they wished I would feature a number of hounds and their pedigrees. With one exception I resisted. Because this picture was exploring the female bond between hound and her handler Nina Christiansen, I thought this would be an opportunity to record the one and only pedigree in this book. -The Author.

DISTINGUISHED ANCESTORS OF OUR PENN-MARYDEL HOUND
by H. L. Todd Addis

Taken from the pages of a book *A Sporting Family of the South*. A hunting story was told by Frederick Gustavus Skinner that he participated in a century and a half ago. This story is about the origin of the Washington Hunt, Washington, D.C.

"For many years before the organization of the Washington Hunt, a quiet genial old fellow named Steward had a kennel of some 7 to 8 couple of Native (American) breed which was located across the Avenue opposite what is now Willard's great Inn. The old man hunted regularly three times a week through the season. He was not a bold nor hard rider, but thorough was his knowledge of the country, his dogs and his game that he always kept within hearing of his founds and rarely missed being present at the death of a fox.

"Next to a good run, old Stewart's greatest delight was at night, seated before a cheerful fire with a journ of screeching hot punch at his elbow, to relate to his companions all of the minutest incidents of the chase and to comment on the individual conduct of each of his dogs, as if they were so many human companions.

"The late John S. Skinner (father of Fredrick Gustavus Skinner) then owner and editor of the *Turf Register and Sporting Magazine*, and postmaster at Baltimore, who was frequently in Washington on official business was induced by a Washington based General to ride to the Steward hounds, and was so delighted with the sport that he proposed the organization of a regular fox-hunting club on an extensive scale.

"A British Minister of State and a retired foxhunter, Sir Charles Vaughan along with numerous members of his legation, espoused the cause with greatest enthusiasm and in a short time the club enrolled among its members many of the highest dignitaries of Washington, D.C.

"With a full treasury, the club succeeded in gathering together a pack of 80 to 100 hounds the best that could be found in Maryland, Delaware and Virginia. The hounds were hunted early in the morning. The foxes were trailed step-by-step through their wanderings of the night. A glorious burst of music would commence and moved onto the heels of the fox."

Fredrick Gustavus Skinner goes on to describe the scene at one infrequently held drop hunt. On this occasion a local native fox is run to ground and then dug out. He or she is then put back into his native surroundings at an advertised time.

"The 'meet' was announced for 11 A.M. at the Eckington Gates. The fox was given a 15 minute start and then the hounds were laid on its trail. They went off on a burning scent. Anyone with a horse within miles came forth for the excitement. Horses excited beyond control ran away with their helpless riders and these might be seen in all directions, hatless and powerless, clinging to their horses manes like so many monkeys at a circus: The story continues with the following land-marks so masterfully entwined in the direction of the chase. Blandensburg, Riversdale, direction of the Potomac, Arlington, right branch of the Eastern Branch, Congressional burying ground, between the Navy Yard and Capital Hill. The fox was killed on the river bank of the East Branch.

"The carcass was used for a drag by the Englishman Buchanan and he chose a path to return directly to the starting point of Eckington Gate. It so happened that the Capital, with Congress and Supreme Court, then in session, was in direct line of the chase. The witness to all this F. G. Skinner with descriptive words such as: cyclone of yelping hounds, clattering horsemen, sudden invasion, sacred precincts, legislative and judicial, assembled wisdom. These words were skillfully used and ended with this last thought.

"In a word, functions, legislative and judicial, of the greatest nation under the sun were paralyzed by this mad freak of the irreverent and run-man foxhunters."

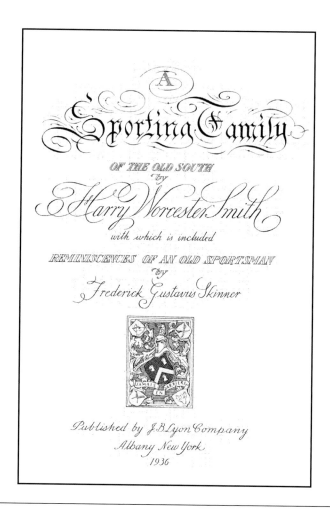

WHAT IS A GREAT DAY OF HUNTING?
by Elizabeth Addis Opitz

One of my great hunting days happened about a month ago. My parents came to visit my husband, kids and me in Northern Virginia. As they usually do, they came with their pack of Penn-Marydel hounds. This time with no horses, as I have enough (too many) to mount them. For a mid-March hunt, it was unusually cool, sunny morning for our Friday joint meet.

My kids were disappointed that they couldn't take the day off from school, but my husband Erwin did take off from work. Hounds struck soon after starting, but I missed the first few minutes of hound music—I was making the just-in-case they go West ride—of course they went due East.

I knew my Dad was here, because when I finally did catch up with hounds, the level of cry that came from the combined pack, was a level I was not used to. Our pack is loud, but with the added 13 couple of Penn-Marydel's, the intensity was palpable.

It was a great day because I was galloping, almost the whole time, with my Dad in front of me. Just like it used to be for the first 26 years of my hunting life. My Dad has slowed a little, because now I can keep up with him. (Of course when Dad read this his comment was, "What the hell do you mean I'm slowing down?!")

The hounds had to work at times, as did the Huntsmen. It was great to ride with my Dad again. I was cheating, riding with him, not whipping-in but, I just wanted to be there as he thought out loud. Where he thought the fox went? Which hounds he thought show real promise?

Sometimes when I'm hunting without my Dad I'm afraid I'm losing my "touch"-as a student of the "hound", or as a whipper-in, because I don't have him there to teach me. It's been more than four years since I have hunted with him on a regular basis, sometimes I do think I've lost my "touch". Who knows?

The greatest moment of the hunt came when I was out ahead of the hounds, who were slowly working the line over the other side of a hill. The hilltopping group was nearby, so I decided to join my mother. She was helping with the intense gossip. We could hear hounds in the distance start to pick up speed and volume. We stood very still, as they were headed our way. The noise level of the combined pack became so loud that at one point we thought it was a place or train coming our way. In fact, it was so loud, it caught my mother and me speechless. (And if anyone knows my mother...)

The hounds went on to run hard, not many checks and hounds running as a tight group. It was a great hunt because I knew my Dad, in my opinion, is still the best at what he loves to do. (The huntsman I follow now, Billy Dodson I should point out, is not far behind.) There are few other feelings that rival that of hounds running great, and sharing it with kindred spirits. And lucky for me, it happens to be with my family and hunting friends. (That evening I had to be careful how I told my kids the hunt went, as they are a lot like me—they don't want to miss a great hunt.) Thanks Mom and Dad for a great day.

Beth Addis Opitz hunting her father's Warwick Village Penn-Marydels, 1989.

KEEP THE FAITH, BABY
by H. L. Todd Addis

(I sent this article to Ms. Marion Maggiolo, publisher of the sporting magazine In and Around Horse Country. *It remains un-published and apparently went to the the 'trash.')*

Sometime during the age of eighteen I was struggling with a course at Ursinus College, Pennsylvania titled *Philosophy of Religion*. An 'in class' assignment by my vitamin deprived professor was to write a composition on faith. Of course, I had no exposure to any religious instruction, consequently there was no coherent beginning with this assignment and with an ending very near the beginning my mark was less than that needed for a passing grade.

Not until 56 year later March 17, 2008 did this word faith and that troublesome assignment really flash in my mind.

It all started in late November 2007 when family, friends, and 15 couples of my Penn-Marydels joined Virginia's Thornton Hill Hounds at Mike Massie's Crossmolina. The day was wintry (just right) and both packs joined like kennel mates. Huntsman Billy Dodson drew the thickets near 211, the road to Warrenton, and I drew a wooded knob. We all were pumped when the packs started a handsome Rappahannock red.

The fox made a tight circle and passed back over the rolling meadows giving the car followers a long view. On we galloped and glided over Googe Mountain, Round Mountain, and Aaron Mountain down the other side and up again to (maybe) South Googe Mountain. We all made it to the hound crossing, but late we were. We then galloped on, changing sea level with every stride.

I know now that Billy had some thoughts about what this 25 couple of Penn Marydels were running. He had several couple of older hounds following at his horse's heels. The pack had split on some challenging knobs. We soon intercepted over 15 couple but several of Thornton Hill hounds and 10 of Warwick Village hounds were gone. Somewhere after Googe Mountain we speculated that a pair of coyotes threw in their 'lot'.

Billy had all of his hounds by late afternoon retrieving the last at the abandoned Mt. Salem Church at the end of Long Mountain. For the next two days I drove, called, and talked. All were kenneled by Sunday evening but my handsome lemon and white bitch Wishful. Finally, after a month there was a sighting near the historic Virginia town of Washington. It was only a mile off the path that coyote and hounds had taken. So Happy and I took a quick trip south and spent 2 days calling for this phantom bitch. During my Flint Hill visit, I shared a birthday celebration on January 3rd with my grandson, Bennett.

Another month went by before several sightings were made. Bill D. and my daughter Beth raced to the areas, seeing the hound but calls only made her move on. My next plan for recovery was to take my trailer with a token number of hounds and park it at the meadow where she was sighted. Sounding my horn brought forth Brooke Miller's scattered beef-herd, what an audience, weanlings, yearlings, and mature cows gathered at the base of my horn like the fans at Woodstock. No luck after 2 days and nights.

Since she was sighted on several occasions on the medial strip and sides of dual highway 211, I knew she must have had Obama's God looking down on her.

Before my brain shut down at bedtime, I would design a hound trap that would surely capture her. Using three 6'x8' wire screens and attaching them to a s 'slam drunk' drop gate was the last best hope. The drop gate was held up by a lever that anchored a slim rope that crossed over the back screen and fed through a small pulley. It had to be baited with meat that she recognized. It had to be tough and somewhat resistant to decay. What else but a good old healthy bovine windpipe (trachea) with a portion of esophagus, vena cava, aorta and some lung tissue attached. I also took a bag of old hound bedding from the benches for scent and a 'bed'.

Three weeks after setting up this "fool proof" catch pen on March 17, 2008 my son-in-law Erwin Opitz, while driving to his work-site took a look at 'the cage'. With eyes wider than normal and a dropped jaw, "Damn" there she was! He immediately called for backup and daughter Beth raced over. As she approached, Wishful made a jump to escape, but immediately turned around and approached her with thankful eyes and wagging tail. Three and half months! "Keep the Faith, Baby!"

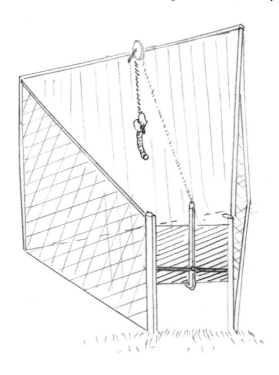

The Perennial Philadelphians
The Anatomy of an American Aristocracy
by Nathaniel Burt, 1963

At a recent July 4th 2007 poolside picnic, I was introduced to the *Perennial Philadelphians* just for a quick glance. I was lucky enough to convince the lady to place it in my hands for a few days in order to make some copies of pages that dwelt with foxhunters—aristocratic foxhunters to be more precise.

The loan-er Sarah Emlen said she could not leave the book because it was on loan from a friend of hers.

Now as the loanee from the double loaners I will attempt to digest its material under a chapter titled "The Unspeakable and the Uneatable" Page 28-296. —In part—

Sports are no more an individual affair to Philadelphia than any other aspect of life, since to indulge in most of Philadelphia's most characteristic sports one has to belong to some sort of club, and then often to a team within a club. This of course involves being eligible, preferably, or course, by heredity, and involves too, the boards and committees and officers, the banquets and dances without which no Old Philadelphian activity can be properly undertaken.

First and foremost in the regard, mythology and history of Philadelphia sports are its fox hunts—

The Gloucester Hunt (1st organized fox hunt 1766) is no more, and the country it once hunted over is a melancholy wilderness of suburban New Jersey slums about Camden.

The members led by Christian Sam Morris, the clubs first Master of Foxhounds, were all Philadelphia city men.

Benjamin Chew, MFH of Radnor around the 1st World War wrote:

> *The members of the Gloucester Foxhunting Club, most of whom were members of the Old State in Schuylkill, the oldest club in the world with a continuous existence, formed, in the early days of the Revolution, the now famous First Troop Philadelphia City Calvary, which has distinguished staff in every war in which this country had ever engaged. A great majority of its members have been foxhunters, and the lessons of the hunting-field have been without doubt in camp and field of battle.*

Of the really large American cities, certainly Philadelphia is still and always has been, the most fox-conscious. Baltimore would be the only other contender. William Penn himself hunted over his Irish acres.

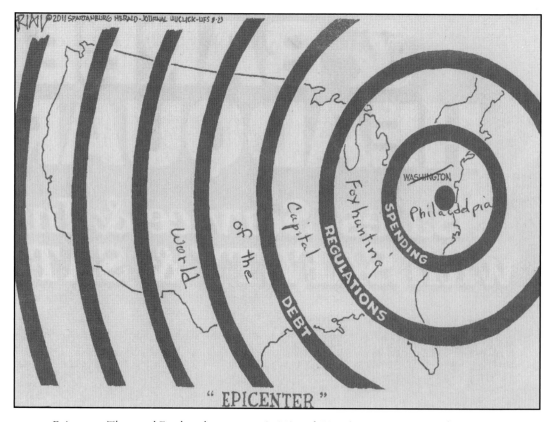

Epicenter—The actual Earthquake center was in Mineral, Va., August 23, 2011, 1:40 P.M. Est.

Philadelphia's really expansive foxhunting days, however, coincide with its industrial and social expansiveness after the Civil War. From then till the First World War, Philadelphia and its surrounding countryside contained more packs and more hunts, private or organized, outlaw or official, than any-other section of the country. At the turn of the century the landscape was crawling with hunters; it was not uncommon for a combined meet of some dozen of these clubs to put into a field well over a hundred riders and three hundred hounds.

The author, Nathanial Burt makes one powerful statement:

"This is certainly the way God and nature meant to cultivated countryside to look." He goes on with his description: "Most of them are Philadelphians, driven out of their . . . On the Mainline by over-building. They live mostly in the kind of remodeled stone farmhouses that is the peculiar charm of such farther reaches of Philadelphia, but many also in somewhat grander and more pretentious manors, surrounded by fields and patches of woodland and post-and-rail fences, with wide horse-trails along both sides

of the roads, "set-backs", a sure sign one is in hunting country. It is a most beautiful and beautifully kept landscape, groomed and curried, and a powerful argument for ownership of the land by fox-hunting gentry."

"Following the 1907 organization of the Masters of Foxhound Association some Recognized Hunts considered another pack hunting in their "sacred precincts" as "outlaw packs"—groups of sportsmen recognized neither officially nor as a rule socially. Sometimes these 'bootleg' organizations have gone to great lengths to attract publicity: the most spectacular feat, which made the 1919 front pages of the local papers, being a foxhunt by airplane, a fox was let out of a bag with a white streak painted from his head to tail, and was followed by a field of airplanes, each flown by a war ace and containing one socially prominent lady.

"Many of most of our hunting paths have been macadamed over or have been criss-crossed with foundations of suburban home; however, a few monuments were erected—the body of former Jesse Russell was buried in a standing position at his request on Rosetree's country, Hunting Hill, so that the 'cry of the hounds might ring in his ears until the end of time.'

"There are other monuments: to animals, such as horses and hounds. J. Howard Lewis of the Rosetree buried his fourteen-year-old hound Slasher with ceremonies and a Latin inscription. At the funeral poems were read, tears shed and toasts drunk. The wake lasted for three riotous days. Oddest of these memorials was a dinner given in memory of Pandora, famous and favorite mount of Dr. Rush Huidekoper (1st Dean of University of Pennsylvania Veterinary School) of the Rose Tree Hunt. Pandora, who had survived unscathed a betting jump over a barrier of bayonets, finally rode for the last time and had to be put away. A memorial banquet in Pandora's honor was given at the Philadelphia Club—where Pandora was served up to old friends in the form of steaks–not his."

-H. L. Todd Addis

Pickering Hunt Celebrates 100ᵗʰ Anniverary
by H. L. Todd Addis

Although actually having begun hunting several years earlier, the Pickering Hunt received its charter as a Pennsylvania Corporation on March 17, 1910, making 2010 its 100ᵗʰ Anniversary. I was happily invited to their anniversary celebration by Ex MFH Dr. Don Rosato. What follows here is my response to Dr. Rosato's invitation:

Dear Don,

Your invitation to Pickering's 100ᵗʰ Anniversary is very generous. The only thing that I can do to contribute to this Anniversary celebration is to dwell on some experiences that I had with its Huntsmen.

As you know, I researched and visited the families of three of your Huntsmen and have published their stories in the Friends of the Penn-Marydel Newsletter.

Early on William Clothier was a member of Radnor Hunt but frequently hunted with a sizeable farmer's pack in southern Chester County. Orville Roberts hunted the hounds during the first decade of the 20ᵗʰ century while his two brothers Pearce and Harold whipped in. Clothier not only enjoyed hunting with this pack but contributed heavily to them. Eventually, he coaxed Roberts and his brothers to come to Phoenixville with their hounds and merge with the local pack.

Robert's career lasted to 1939 and whipper-in Edward Mooney assumed the position. Rumor was spread the Mooney's constant criticism (back biting) of Orville to Clothier lead to his dismissal.

My father was a great friend of Huntsman Roberts and not only procured hounds from him, but also frequently traded hounds. Roberts and his family, son, Ellis, and daughters, Bertha and Ada, moved to his new farm on Merlin Rd. outside of the village of Kimberton. He established his own private pack of hounds. Bart Higham, frequently a member in the field, kept a diary of the Roberts' Hunts after leaving Pickering.

Orville would frequently visit our farm near Collegeville and I would load some excess offal to feed his hounds. My stomach muscles were often left strained from laughter due to his story telling. He was such a gentleman and well thought of that Ed Mooney named his second son Orville.

Well known horseman Harry King and family were great friends of the Roberts family so a new arrival, a son, drew the name of Orville Ellis King. Many of us know his brother, Huntsman and Master of Virginia's Bedford Hunt, and Ex-Huntsman of Radnor Hunt, William (Billy) King, to whom I just sent a brood bitch.

The lead article in one of the Friends of the Penn-Marydel Newsletters featuring Orville Roberts, led me to present his nomination to the Huntsman's Committee of the

Museum of Hounds and Hunting. The committee accepted him for induction and I had the honor of presenting him.

Edward Mooney followed Roberts as Huntsman. Much of his time hunting hounds was in the war years and also when the deer population became more of a problem. Ed's oldest son Bill Mooney stepped in to help his Dad hunt the pack. Upon retirement Ed Mooney would occasionally hunt with me in East Nantmeal Township. He either kept or borrowed a horse from his daughter Sylvia Booker who lived on Rt. 401 just west of the Township building.

Milford Mills' long time farmer and hound man Guy Mercer was engaged to hunt the Pickering Hunt hounds. Guy was well aware of their thirst for running deer. He merged his own 6 couple of hounds with the Hunt.

Guy recruited George (Reds) Albright to come on board to whip-in. Reds hunted his own fox and coonhounds in the northern hills of Chester County. This period spanned the fifties. From all reports Reds Albright gets the credit for breaking the hounds from running deer by the use of a pistol backed up by birdshot.

Guy loved to tell hunting stories. One was about the earlier days of his working with the Pickering pack. One day after hunting, he made a 10 p.m. kennel visit to check on the return of the hounds. With most of them back home he loaded the pack in his truck and drove them to a spot about 5 miles away. They were dumped out and Guy went home to bed. When he got back to the kennels the next morning all the hounds had returned. Horses were saddled, and a "hunting we will go." Needless to say, Guy's own hounds were fresh and ready to go, while the Pickering hounds were tired, jammed up, and limping in a long line behind their huntsman. They were hunted as much as possible until every deer was given a stare as it passed by. Guy and Reds were now ready to declare them "deer broke."

Guy Mercer

Albert Crosson

Ever since my first encounter with Albert (Pud) Crosson in 1948, I was in awe of his riding skills and aggression in following hounds. I gained much hound sense while following Albert hunting the Whitelands pack from 1949 to 1960. John Barnes Mull, ex-Pickering member, had hired Albert as farm manager and then took the Mastership of Whitelands in the late 1940s. So Albert assumed two duties as farm manager and Whitelands whipper-in in 1948, and then huntsman from 1949-1960. In 1960 MFH Josephine Betner coaxed Albert over to hunt the Pickering hounds.

In April 1958 I invited Guy Mercer (Pickering), and Albert Crosson (Whitelands), to bring their hounds to hunt at my father-in-law's farm at Mt. Victoria, Charles County, MD. Never in the 300 years of foxhunting in southern Maryland did the red foxes have to move so fast and so long as those touching that sandy soil that day.

I had the pleasure of visiting widow Gladys Crosson in Damascus, MD and her brother-in-law Donald Bracken in Lancaster County, PA to gather material for yet another story in the Friends of the Penn-Marydel Newsletter. Unbeknownst to Marion and Roger Scullin, Gladys kept a scrapbook of Albert's hunting dating back to whipping-in employment at Rose Tree in 1939 and then hunting their hounds until he was drafted into the Navy in 1942.

Using this colorful article Marion Scullin and Pat Theurkauf presented Albert to the Huntsmen's Room Committee at Morven Park, VA.

Albert Crosoon 50's Whitelands Tr.

HOUNDS, GEORGE, AND LA FAYETTE
by H. L. Todd Addis

The time, as best as I can determine was 1786-1787. The source was the author Brand Whitlock, who collected every bit of information on Marquis de La Fayette and published two volumes in 1929 titled *La Fayette*. I am quoting page 289.

"The correspondence between the Marquis (La Fayette) and George Washington was constant, and they were always exchanging presents. The Marquis sent him, by John Jay, a painting of himself and his family. But Washington had not as yet received the promised jackass, and having written to Harrison, the Minister at Madrid, to send him one. Washington sent word to Admiral Suffern to procure a jackass and two females."

The Marquis also procured from the Count d'Oillamson some of the famous foxhounds of Artois and sent them to Mount Vernon, for Washington wished to improve the breed of his pack, and when the Countess d'Oillamson heard of the transaction, she sent her own favorite bitch to the General.

The Marquis sent pheasants and red partridges, and Washington sent more hams and some ducks, but the poor ducks were dead on their arrival at Havre.

Top hound is Legionaire and bottom is Laffeyette. Warwick Village Hounds.

Picture taken by Dottie Wambold from a museum in up state New York near Genesse Valley. Looks like a French painting of French hounds, Old Southern hound or just our good old Penn-Marydel.

So what did Washington get in order to improve his pack? Sir Walter Gibey, in his book *Hounds in the Old Days*, 1913 says "The hounds of Normandy, Artois and Picardy—The Northern provinces of France—had much in common with England's Southern Hound, and the frequency with which the Kings and Nobles of England and France exchanged presents of hounds makes it certain that the breeds of the two countries were much intermixed."

Lounging on a hot summer day.

In Sir John Buchanan-Jardin's book *Hounds of the World*, 1937 "The hounds of Artois were once a distinct and separate breed. They were rather compact, thick-set hounds, about 18-20 inches, team and white or badger pied in color and looking rather like a big, course Beagle. They were considered very good for hare hunting.

This type has long since vanished; the disappearance having been accomplished not by extinction but by being freely crossed with Norman blood.

The modern hounds of this breed reproduced fairly closely the type of the old Norman bounds, but on a smaller scale; The excellent nose and fine voice of the Norman has been handed on to them, together with the strong inclination to dwell on the line and hang about at a check. They have, also like their ancestors, great stamina and good constitution, but they are, I am told, never fast, and certainly all that I have seen, were very slow indeed, probably a little faster than Bassets; this characteristic of their motion may be partly due to their heavy build, and often loaded shoulders.

Some points of interest listed in the official type:

Skull—Pronounced dome; the occipital peak often showing.

Ears—Set on as low as possible, well folded.

Stern—Well set, rather long; scarcely any feather; carried like a sabre.

Color—Black-white-tan, lemon and white, or badger pied, ticking not desired.

Washington was hunting the grey fox: Did these hounds and their crosses improve his pack? What do his diaries say?

THE FIRST TIME
by Wm. Todd Addis, 9-15-07

The first time my Dad let me hunt his pack of foxhounds I learned a few lessons. React to your instinct because inaction can lead to events that can spiral out of control. Back in 1980 I was 20 years old. Having hunted beagles as a kid I thought I was ready to hunt the pack—40 foxhounds. (My dad had to make a presentation to the PA Game Commission, therefore would not be able to hunt the pack that Sunday. The prior month we had 10 hounds caught in traps and found another 20 traps. We found them in a 10-acre block on one hunt. We thought trapping was a little out of control. Fur prices were in their heyday. The Game Commissioners had a little surprise when he dropped a garbage bag full of traps on the floor. Anyway, that is a little off topic.)

The morning of the hunt my Dad said to watch out for 3 to 4 young dogs. On the prior hunt they had pulled down an injured deer. So Sunday morning I took the hounds up into the hill. They found a fox and ran him along the ridge, crossing a blacktop road. Further down ridge I noticed the cry of the pack starting to decrease. At the end of the ridge there was a strand of round wire that blocked us from accessing the next hard road (on horseback). We found a stick to prop the wire and galloped down the road. I looked up the road to my left and saw an angry landowner and the pack racing away parallel with the road at top speed. He yelled the hounds were on a deer. I told him they couldn't be, because this pack was deer-broken.

As I galloped up the road, a little voice of doubt started to whisper in my ear. Hounds were just crossing this road as I got there. Only 3 hounds were tonguing; the rest were "observers". At that point there was an impassable swamp and then the PA turnpike. On the map it is between the Downingtown and Morgantown exchanges. The hounds swung to the left. I thought that maybe if I was lucky I could catch them crossing the power line 2 miles down the road. I galloped for all I was worth. I could barely hear them but I knew they were going to cross the power line. Down the power line I went; however, I was too late. They crossed. At that point the hounds swung directly towards the turnpike. I galloped down to where the power line and turnpike met. I looked down the turnpike only to see the deer crossing, with 40 hounds only 10 feet behind the deer. I jumped off my horse and handed it to the guy with me.

I ran down, crossing the turnpike with my .22 in hand. Traffic on this 4-lane highway is nonstop. When I reached the hounds up on the bank they had the deer pinned up against the fence, biting away. I fired the .22 (birdshot) into the pack 4 or 5 times. The hounds started to scatter but I was able to corral them so they wouldn't cross back over the highway. The deer got up and went down the fence line and then crawled under the gap. At that moment I realized I needed to get hounds out of this predicament.

1993 Oatlands VA Houndshow—2nd Place Pack Class—Marlboro Huntsman Wm. Todd Addis and his sister Elizabeth Addis, Whipper-in.

I thought the best thing to do was stop traffic and re-cross, because I wasn't sure if any backhounds would come. I started to wave my arms for traffic to stop but every time the car slowed down, the instant they saw the gun in my hand they sped up with wild looks in their eyes. They thought I was Patton without medals. I decided to throw the gun back across the highway. Hounds were still sitting on the bank. I started waving my arms again and this beautiful longhaired blonde stops her car and gets out. No problem, everybody stops, both lanes. I called the hounds to come on, and retrieved the gun just as the state policeman was pulling up. He made sure the blonde was okay, and trotted off with the pack. It was a miracle that not one hound was lost. It was a lesson I will never forget.

French Staghound. Alfred Barye (c. 1870). Reproduced by permission of The Chronicle of the Horse.

Some Things Never Change
by H. L. Todd Addis, MFH

The Past: Mr. J. Stanley Reeves' journal heading, Cubhunting and Early Season 1941-1942, is a good introduction to my story of March 12, 2007. Mr. Reeves writes- "Several of our old friends, however, have been decidedly out of luck of late. First on list was J. Charles "Dick" who had the misfortune to break is collarbone and a couple of ribs early in September; then William J. (Bill) Clothier, Master of Pickering, had a smashing fall and fractured a vertebra in his back, after which pneumonia developed, thereby confining him to the Bryn Mawr Hospital for weeks and weeks. Robert E. (Bob) Strawbridge, ex-MFH Cottesmore, fell over a chicken coop quite recently and he is out for six or seven weeks with a broken collarbone; then, to cap the climax, last Saturday, the 22nd November, the Master of Cheshire, W. Plunket Stewart, came a crashing fall over a fence just as hounds were settling to the line of a straight-running fox. He was thrown fully twenty feet beyond the fence and the situation looked so serious that hounds were stopped and sent home and the days' hunting was cancelled. An ambulance from Kennett Square took our injured Master to the Chester County Hospital, where he regained consciousness after eight and a half hours, and from last reports is making strides towards complete recovery."

He continues on, "Brandywine's turn came, but, fortunately their Master missed it. However, five of the field galloped smack into a low strand of electric wire fencing in a corn field and side by side turned upside down. No serious results for the humans, but their equine conveyances were rather badly cut up."

The Present: Saturday, March 10th, 1 pm meet 2007. Warwick Village Hounds met a James/Billy Cochranes' farm. Our guests included William Todd Addis, MFH Bright Leaf Hounds, of Lothian, Maryland; his daughters, Jennifer and Hampton, on college spring break, and Beth Addis Opitz and children, Bennett and Elida, from Flint Hill, Virginia.

As our newly jumped fox circled Bill Gross' vineyard, we received the messages over the 2-way radios that Mary Ann Burns' mare had slipped on the ice and the rider was lying there unconscious.

Just then a very expensive looking helicopter passed overhead. Numerous sirens could be heard in several directions. Word then arrived over the radio that a large, red fox was viewed crossing James Mill Road and entering our friend's open country.

At that moment hounds came to a check at the vineyard's electric fence. My decision to take hounds to the viewed fox, only took from the time I pulled the horn from its case to pushing it to my lips. As I arrived at the fox's crossing, the helicopter passed overhead with Mary Ann's body. The thought raced through my mind "if she is dead",

Children and Grandchildren of Todd and Happy Addis; l to r, Beth Opitz, Elida Opitz, Jen Addis, Bennett Opitz, Todd Sr., Todd Jr., Jamee Emlen and Hampton Addis.

should the hounds be lifted in respect to the deceased or should we gallop on and avoid the bad news. Being a ruthless foxhunter I chose the latter.

The fox moved over the manicured Bentley property, clipped the old Lester Orr farm, crossed an unknown named road into Warwick Furnace Farms. They glanced Ring Neck covert, along with ninety-five to one hundred and ten deer, which did slow the pack. They then broke out and raced past Ebenezer Church to Wambold's Hollow. It seemed like twenty seconds was the duration that they spent getting through this mile and half covert. Finally, I reached the pack in the backyard of Warwick County Park headquarters. By the way, my son-in-law, James Emlen, gave me his horse after my big grey suddenly came up lame (this transfer took place during the first run).

The Penn-Marydels came off the top of this 2-mile long Park land woods and went to the north branch of the French Creek. The fox then returned to the Park office covert and down to the Knauertown thicket and swamp.

I just knew this was his home territory.

Wrong again, the car followers, with an element of panic in their voices, said, "they just crossed" the 23,000 car volume Route 23. I galloped west bucking traffic and side-stepping drainage grates with fair-ease. As I pulled up to cross the highway, I was rear-ended by my four grandchildren, son Todd and daughter Beth, whipper-ins and numerous discards. We now bush-wacked into the big covert called the Falls of St. Peters.

The packs' foot prints were soon seen on a snow covered path. We are now immediately above St. Peter's Village. The Village and its well-known Hotel & Inn is now owned by Mike Piazza [Hall of Fame bound Dodger or Mets catcher] and its investors.

One ambulance, two fire engines, one helicopter, and 25 cars with flashing blue and red lights, managed to save the fallen foxhunter. The silly patient (Mary Ann) never thought to ask the pilot to follow the hunt; at least she would have had some joy out of her $12,000 ride!

LETTER FROM JOHN BROWN OF GETTYSBURG, PA

Sounder sired by Marlboro's Unido and dam my Swan became for a few years a great strike hound and had a tremendous deep voice.

He was used as a stud dog and produced some very good 'fox-dogs'.

Doc and Happy,

We can't thank you enough for Sounder and Greta. No one has even looked at a deer since they have been with us. We have been exclusively hunting our home county, which is comprised of our place and about 1800 additional adjacent acres. We have plenty of fox and are surrounded by low-density suburbs on three sides. The fox don't seem confronted in running through backyards or crossing the one busy road in front of our house so we have a nicely contained operation. Also, we have a nicely wooded bottom and large stream in the middle of the country in which we usually find and into which the fox always return. We have not drawn blank or failed to have at least one view since Sounder and Greta have joined us.

As you know we are basically a family hunt and our usual is to get a leisurely start after a light breakfast on Sunday mornings. We are generally out for about three to three and a half hours. I think our pace has done wonders for Sounder. He is completely "sound" now and seems very happy. Danny inducted him into our kennel's exclusive order of "House Hounds" an honor which contributed greatly to his new outlook on life and confidence. He is top dog here and he knows it. When he is returned to the kennel Sunday evening after an afternoon of football, people food, and being chased by Danny's

John Brown's Monocacy Valley Hounds' Carmen, won first in the Female Puppy Class.

radio controlled toys he graciously allows everyone a sniff of the house scents he has acquired. They all seem dully impressed.

We have one slight problem with both Sounder and Greta. They are obviously accustomed to going out for a lot longer than three and a half hours. When Liz, Danny, and I and the rest of our people for that matter are ready to quit, they are not. I have to get in front of them, get off my horse and literally tackle them as they come by and get their attention.

I know we are on their mailing list, but they are not on mine as in I can't find a newsletter, etc., so I have enclosed a donation for stamps etc. for the Friends of the Penn-Marydel, which I am sure you can get to the right person. Thanks again for all your help.

- John, Liz, and Danny

A pair of Penn-Marydel bitches in Luzerne County, PA owned by Robert Cragle. Whether hunting or not, they should have had their noses to the ground. They joined a pack of PMD's that helped bag 48 coyotes this season 2011-2012.

CHARACTERIZING THE PENN-MARYDEL:
YOUR CHOICE—TENACITY OR ASSIDUOUSNESS?
by H. L. Todd Addis

My favorite word best describing one of the attributes of a PMD foxhound is tenacity. Lo and behold, that may have been topped by a new word that I must admit I had to look up in the Webster's Dictionary: assiduousness. It is defined as "constant personal attention."

Alexander MacKay-Smith, in his American Foxhound 1747-1967 book, quotes W. Newbold Ely as follows: "They run on and on and stick to their fox-like grim death. In fact many times, when it appears scent has failed and the run is over, their never failing assiduousness suddenly pays dividends and they are off again as hard and fast as though they had just left kennels."

Who was Newhold Ely? Even though Mr. Ely's hunting country was adjacent to my father's Perkiomen Valley Hunt country in Montgomery's County, Pennsylvania, I never had the opportunity to meet him. His hunt was recognized in 1931 and was maintained until his death in 1947. At this stage I was only 13 years of age [at the time of his death] and confined to the house, lawn, barn, and kennel.

Every one of us who has a long tooth in our mouth remembers Mr. Ely's famous crossbred bitch that welped 24 puppies and was handsomely displayed in *Life Magazine*. Eight bitches and the rest dog puppies all grew up to be entered in 1945. Anyone who has bred hounds knows to get 24 healthy one-sized live puppies is a falsehood.

Knowing Mr. Ely's country and kennel based in Ambler, Pennsylvania, it was difficult for him to produce sport. He however, promoted himself well among the many prominent masters with his writing skills. He was editor of the national comic weekly Fudge. He volunteered and served as foxhunting editor for The Sportsman, the official publication of the Masters of Foxhounds Association. Soon after the founding of the Penn Marydel Association, he began serving as secretary whenever Mrs. Jackson was unable to get to its meetings. "His task in foxhounds was eclectic," so says MacKay-Smith, "his pack at different times included English, Welsh, American, Penn Marydel and various cross-bred hounds."

The index of the American Foxhound 1776-1976 book lists 17 pages with New-bold Ely's name. MacKay-Smith continues to write "In trying to win greater acceptance for the Penn Marydel hound among masters of organized packs, its promoters were faced with the necessity for improvement both in working qualities and in conformation. In 1912 Harry Worcester-Smith wrote: "In Pennsylvania there is the tall, black and tan with rattail, high peak, long ears and long cry-wonderful trailers, but with not enough speed to account often for his quarry."

Newbold Ely put it another way: "The old Penn Marydel hounds had a marvelous deep voice and very tender nose, but a tendency to dwell and to 'tail out' when running."

Judge Thomas J. Keating, MFH Corsica Fox Hounds 1927-1933, prepared "the most complete exposition of the qualities of the Eastern Shore hound" in 1946 for The Chronicle but never submitted it for publication. On the sixth paragraph of this very lengthy discourse, Judge Keating discusses "tailing out" and how it was handled many decades ago.

"Gameness (or bottom as it is called) has always been the other important quality for which Eastern Shore foxhunters have bred. A hound that quits while other hounds were running committed an unpardonable sin. If persisted in this behavior the punishment most frequently was death. Thus, the huntsman was saved the ignominy of having such a hound trot at his horse's heels; and it was made sure that the particular individual should not pass his fault on to any progeny. This rather inhumane method has been abandoned in later years in favor of more modern techniques."

> *"It is the writer's [Keating] experience that in the matter of conformation discipline, and disposition a great deal can be accomplished in a few generations by careful selection of the hound to be mated. I believe this experience is borne out by others who have used Eastern Shore strains as foundation or outcross for their packs of Penn Marydel hounds, notably the late M. Roy Jackson, when Master of Radnor, Messrs. Wm Ashton and Joseph Neff Ewing with their Eagle Farms Hunt, the late George Brice, himself an Eastern shoreman, when hunting the Essex Foxhounds, the late John B. Hannum Jr. of Chester, Pennsylvania and a number of others. The packs developed by these gentlemen improved in these particulars to a marked degree in the space of a comparatively few years."*

Keating's last paragraph, though lengthy, will serve to finish my article with an articulate description of our hound:

> *"And coming now to the last, but by no means the least consideration, the ground may be slightly controversial. This is the question of drive. Those who are accustomed to hunting English hounds and the Virginia strains of American hounds are prone to feel that the Eastern Shore hound lacks drive. If we accept, as a standard of excellence, the ability to run a fit fox the longest distance in the shortest time, regardless of weather, and do it three or four days a week, without suffering from lameness, fatigue or condition then the Eastern Shore foxhound does not merit this criticism. They will only lift their heads and fly when scent and the terrain over which they are hunting permit. They can-*

not be induced to burst away on a 'hot' fox when scent is bad or is lying very close to the ground. On such occasions they prefer rather to run close to the line, making sure of every turn hardly checking at all. In such conditions, they will thus give long, if somewhat slower hunt and frequently account for their fox on many days when other hounds would 'run out of scent' after the first two or three fields. But on days when scent is good they will drive with such determination, eagerness and foot as to hold their own with a pack of any other strain or breed. And it is then that the crushing crescendo of their cry will drown the voices of most other hounds."

All mouths are open.

A MORNING WITH DR. ADDIS
WARWICK VILLAGE HOUNDS
CHESTER COUNTY DAY, OCTOBER 2009
by H. L. Todd Addis

Early on, recorded American history tells us the wealthy English settlers loaded their ships with household goods, horses, hounds, indentured servants and on occasion, the English red fox. They, the red fox, did not spread as fast as the swine flu, but they began to share the countryside with our native grey fox.

From the first 1650 date we move on to a marvelous article published in the November issue of the 1902 ERA Magazine. It was published in Philadelphia. The lead article titled Fox Hunting In Pennsylvania was written by Edwin Fairfax Naulty. He Naulty, interviews some prominent folk primarily in Delaware and Chester Counties. Football, baseball, and tennis as not yet invented could not be part of our outdoor recreation. The hound, whether foxhound, beagle, coon hound, bear hound, or hare hound took man, woman and child to the wilds.

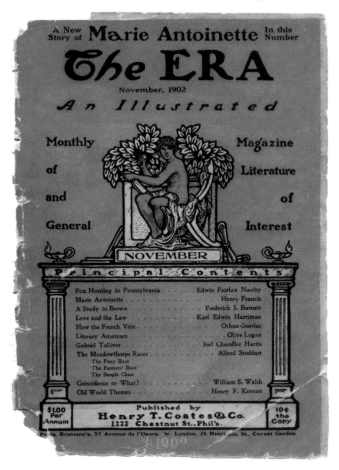

Could you know when you drive east on the Schuylkill Expressway and pass the Gulf Mills Exit, that you just passed former farmer, fox hound owner and foxhunter, Gulf Mills. Did you know that he was one of 200 farmer pack owners comprising some 10,000 hounds in Delaware, Montgomery and Chester Counties?

King of Prussia, formally Reeseville, was the hub for the well known Chester Valley Hunt. If you found their hound along a dirt road, call E. Brooke Norristown Telephone #1621.

Even my father, Clarkson Addis, got the bug. If you

would have found his Perkiomen Valley hound you would have called Collegeville #250.

My recently published memoirs, *A Backward Glance,* reveals that Dad bought the Chester Valley pack in 1922 and named me Todd, after one of its fine hounds. Is it any wonder that my family, wife Hampton (Happy), son Wm. Todd, daughters Ann and Elizabeth love the sport of the chase. To bring along all six grandchildren the daughters spiced the chase of the cottontail with their fine beagle packs. Even the sons and daughter-in-laws were vacuumed up and ride on with the best of us.

No guns, no shooting, we love to see our wildlife again.

Thank you Warwick County park for hosting this event.

Dr. Addis' seventh time exhibiting his Penn-Marydel Foxhounds at Chester County Day 2004, Warwick County Park.

PRESIDENT DR. BUD FACKLEMAN
SPEECH TO THE BLOOD HOUND ASSOCIATION 4-28-79
by Dr. H. L. Todd Addis

I should be honored giving a speech on the subject of smell. Now that I think of it, the speech will probably stink. I noted one interesting thought taken from the PA Game News—imagine that if we could have a sense of smell just as keen as most animals. If you took a walk down a wooded trail you could detect the presence of a nearby grouse or rabbit or maybe your lover hiding behind a bush.

Actually, by the latest survey on teenage pregnancy, I suspect our young male generation can sense the young lady behind the bush.

Scent comes generally from glands. Anal glands, interdigited foot glands, glands between the hooves of deer, breasts of opposums and facial areas of rabbits.

In man it's probably sweat glands. My wife says it comes from my shoes.

Temperature, humidity, and wind have enormous effect on scent. Ground conditions such as dryness, very frozen ground- frost, whether forming or melting- powdered snow or melting snow.

Conditions mask scent even though scenting conditions are good. Auto exhaust, general air pollution, burned over woodland, or grass fields soiled with horse, cattle, deer, or turkey tracks will challenge the best of hounds to sift out the desired scent.

How do we train a hound or dog to follow the desired scent first? It is most advantageous to have the animal bred for centuries to follow a particular scent trail. The canine must have the desire to follow his companion. Some new entry will follow a scent immediately when it avails itself while others gradually 'catch on' when continually exposed to the desired scent trail.

A hound must adjust its speed via patience to follow the scent trail and not continually over running.

A hound usually reaches the 3rd or 4th year before its most acute scenting powers manifest themselves.

A hound is most reliable when they have maximum exposure to the desired scent trail and maximum exposure to the scents you wish them to reject.

A hound works best when he honors his pack buddies and is slightly tired. He must be 'settled' down.

Behaviors of hounds as individuals or in a pack are similar to children. They must love you and they must have a sense of fear if they range outside of the boundaries you have set for them. You cannot call 'time out' and sit down and reason with them.

Punishment is most effective during the act of misbehavior and a return to the task so desired as soon as possible.

If you encounter a Red Herring that is because back in the 15th century the huntsmen would train their hounds to be honest to the game intended by dragging a salted Red Herring across the scent trail to see if they could be fooled.

Bellwood hounds, hot on the line. Don't miss the hound in the shadow. The scent was not on the rock, 2002. (Photo taken by Karen Kandra Wenzel.)

Remembering a Foxhunting Friend of Maryland's Eastern Shore
by H. L. Todd Addis

On July 17, 1996 a large gathering of family, friends and foxhunters came to mourn and show their respects for Joseph Quimby Sr. at the Centerville United Methodist Church.

This is the first funeral I have attended that one third of seats were reserved for foxhunters. Mr. Joe, as he was known by his close friends, was a simple, ordinary farmer that directed his energies not only to the normal farming activities, but was also active in his church, Lions Club and many conservation organizations. He served as county Sheriff and had considerable influence in regulating the protection of the fox. As a matter of fact, only two counties in Maryland enjoyed red fox protection, Queen Ann and Cecil County.

Joe was the patriarch of foxhunters for generations. Sharing and cooperation of hunting country was Joe's gentlemanly way of hunting. I was privileged to have taken my pack to his hunting country during our most severe winter weather. It was a thrill to ride in the "field" of foxhunters, pickups all jockeying for position to see that red cross the road or fields. When the fox did cross, it was as if a phantom flag was dropped, trucks quickly moved up four abreast to witness the crossing spot and the who, what, where, when of the hound situation was.

How I enjoyed being teased by the Eastern Shore Boys, that those Pennsylvania "dawgs" were choking on mud thrown by the Maryland "dawgs". One could never get an old Eastern Shore Foxhunter to recognize the Penn-Marydel strain of hound, there is no such thing, only Maryland "dawgs".

If Mr. Joe and his friends had recorded all their hunting stories over the years, their memories would displace a set of encyclopedias.

At the end of the ceremony all the foxhunters were instructed to line the walkways upon the arrival of the hearse and following the services, and to line the path from hearse to the grave site.

Not to be disrespectful to the services conducted by Pastor Thomas Hurley, the highlight of the service was a poem written by a life long friend.

TRIBUTE TO MR. JOE FROM SMOKEY
Author Unknown

Many years ago as a wee small lad,
I met this man who I learned to love as dad.
One of God's many blessings bestowed upon me,
He sent me Mr. Joe, a wonderful friend he would be,
Always there for smiles and tears,
A beacon through the years,
To show and to share,
The years have passed in loving care.
And though this man has gone away,
His love for his family is here to stay.
To conclude at this point would be remiss of me,
For my most memorable times shall always be,
Of the pickup loaded with the dogs, to begin our daily ride,
We would leave Needwood Farm with pride,
To gather with huntsman from all over the country,
Laughing, joking, gossiping and awaiting the bounty.
Finally over the horizon, the sly old red boy would appear,
Dogs turned out and running; sweet music to the ear.
Eyes focused in a stare,
Excitement filling the air,
Trucks rolling along the roadsides, passers-by gazing,
What in the world is so thrilling about this, is quite amazing.
The chase underway, through the woods and across the fields.
In great anticipation of what this chase will yield.
Success or defeat, which will it be,
It really does not matter, they all agree.
After a while, the tired hunters round up their strays,
And with reluctance, call it a day.
Proud dogs with their tails wagging,
Weary hunters on their C.B's bragging,
Planning for the great hunt tomorrow,
When shall we return and start the chase again.
So as we gather today to express our loving farewell to you,
Mr. Joe, and I salute you dear friend, with our final
TALLY-HO

CELEBRATION OF THE PENN-MARYDEL HOUND
THE PENN-MARYDEL ASSOCIATION, INC.
AND ITS INCORPORATION, 1934
by H. L. Todd Addis

In the last year or two we have heard the word 'surge' used many times in the conduct of the Iraq Way. Us old timers have recently witnessed another surge called the 'Penn-Marydel Surge.'

The year 2007 brought the Masters of Foxhound Association its 100 year celebration and my thoughts carried over to the hundreth anniversary celebration of the Penn-Marydel Association, Inc. Unfortunately, many of us will not be able to make the year 2034, so the next best time to celebrate is the 75th Anniversary, which happens to be now, 1934-2009.

Thirty years in the making, *The American Foxhound 1747-1967*, by Alexander MacKay-Smith (#633 published 1968) landed on my library shelves and is a store-house of entertaining history of American Hounds. Naturally, my interest immediately focused on chapters XXII, Penna. and Eastern Shore Strains Before 1934 and chapter XXIII, Penn-Marydel Fox Hounds, Inc. 1934. MacKay-Smith writes, "The Eastern Shore Hound has changed very little during the past two centuries. He is, in fact, remarkably similar to what were undoubtedly his immediate British ancestors-the type known as the Southern Hound of England." Sir John Buchanan-Jardine believes the Southern Hound to be descended, not from the Talbot hound of Normany, but from the Gascon Hound of Aquitaine in south-western France, ruled by the Kings of England from about 1150 to 1450.

MacKay-Smith reveals in his Preface that following his resignation from the Federal Government's low-cast housing program, he assigned an 'unemployed' assistant, Charles B. Conner, to read through the files in the U.S. Dept. of Agriculture Library of the 19th century magazines devoted to field sports, including the *American Farmer, The American Turf Register and Sporting Magazine, The Spirit if Times, Turf, Field and Farm, The American Field* and others. Every item on fox hunting was typed, photo stated in triplicate and catalogued. MacKay-Smith supplements his stories of the Penn-Marydel hound with such testimony—the pre-Revolutionary diaries of Jacob Hiltzheimer of Phila, Pa. a January 4, 1828 publication in The American Farmer: a description of three days hunting in Newcastle County, Delaware. Fox hunting on the Eastern Shore of Maryland by Hanson Hiss including Talbot, Dorchester, Somerset, Queen Anne's and Wicomico Counties published in Outing Magazine, March 3, 1898. Obviously, author MacKay-Smith was mesmerized by Felix R. Sullivan, Jr. Dec. 26, 1908 account of an Eastern Shore hunt in American Field. He reproduced this hunting account in his *Anthology of American Fox Hunting 1970* in Chapter 41. Because of space, I will pass along a few sentences that Sullivan wrote that cause us Penn-Marydel enthusiast to pound our chest!

> *Being a great devotee of fox-hunting, it has been my good fortune to have hunted with a great many of the best packs of hounds in this country and after having studied the hounds and huntsmen, whom I have hunted with, I hark back to a pack on the Eastern Shore of Maryland in Queen Anne's County, as the best and surest pack I have ever followed. These hounds are larger and heavier than the hounds usually seen in the recognized packs in this country and are purebred hounds, the original strain of which was imported to Maryland from England many generations ago. They have great earage and evenly marked bodies, black, white and tan, with good bone and notes (voice) that for clearness and beauty of tone I have never heard equaled. These hounds are run five and sometimes six days each week from November until April every year and my last hunt with them was January 1908.*

Long before the Penn-Marydel Association was formed various organized packs used the established Maryland and Delaware hound. The Rose Tree Hunt 1859-the present; The Radnor Hunt 1883-1893, 1929-2000?; Kirkwood Kennels 1929-1944; West Chester Fox Hunting Club 1871-1990?, Pickering Hunt 1911-2009 and counting; Glen Moore Hunt 1915-1917 name change to Eagle Farms Hunt 1917-1980?; Huntington Valley 1914-2009 and counting; John B. Hannum, Jr. 1917 moved to Md 1936-1942; Newbold Ely's Hounds 1929-1947; Perkiomen Valley 1923-1956; Golden's Bridge; Essex Hounds 1913-1935; Mr. Jefford's Hounds, Vicmead etc.

With the marriage of Mr. Roy Jackson to Almira Rockefeller, the

Richard Harris, MFH and Stephen Harris, MFH, President of the PMD Association, at the Huntington Valley Hunt.

establishment of his elaborate Kirkwood Kennels and the Mastership and huntsman's duties of Radnor, he propelled himself into the leadership role; and together with Mrs. Jackson and John B. Hannum, Jr., he organized and incorporated the Penn-Marydel Fox Hounds, Jan. 23, 1934. Mackey-Smith writes "Mr. and Mrs. Jackson asked John B. Hannum, Jr. to join them as the third incorpator partly because he was a good lawyer." "He, Hannum, was able to render major assistance in the compilation of the PMD stud book, one of the prime objectives of the new organization. Certainly, it is most fitting that his daughter Miss Christine Hannum has since 1948 been secretary-treasurer and keeper of the studd book."

Positioning himself well, MFH Jackson named himself President, MFH John B. Hannum, Jr, Vice President, Almira Rockefeller Jackson, Secretary-treasurer; Directors, Walter M. Jeffords MFH and William H. Aston MFH.

On May 10, 1934, a meeting of the officers and directors was held at Mr. Walter M. Jefford's Kennels at Andrew's Bridge to look at hounds with the view of selecting in both dogs and bitches the best type to fill the specifications of the Penn-Marydel Foxhound. As a result of this and subsequent meetings at other kennels, a standard was compiled which is printed in full in the Appendix of Alexander MacKay-Smith's book *American Fox Hound 1747-1967.*

In the September 1936 issue of *Horse and Horseman*, John B. Hannum, Jr. wrote "Good Hunting—Some Observations Upon American Fox hounds and Fox hunting." It reads in part:

> *"What qualities should you seek in a hound? My thought is that he should have courage or gameness, good sense, good voice, good nose, and good constitution— good fox sense—how to determine it? By expression and conduct, and what are the indices of these? Well, you look for expression at its source and expression in a hound is ascertained from his head, his eyes, his ears, his general countenance and his tail. I know that the average, indeed the great average, will tell you that he must have good feet, well sprung ribs, a certain kind of loin, hock, bone, etc. and so he should, but he doesn't hunt the fox with his feet, his loins, his legs or his ribs. He hunts it with his nose, his head and his heart, and while these other attributes should not be disregarded, get the proper countenance first. The easiest thing in the world to breed is feet, ribs, bone, etc. and the hardest fox sense without cunning, good cry, good nose and gameness."*

The readers of this article may questions 'how much of this story is in my words and how much is in the words of Alexander MacKay-Smith?' To be honest, give him much of the credit.

Few specific dates are given but MacKay-Smith chose to give names and credit to those many farmer packs that were willing to 'let go' of sold to many budding affluent hunts that lay north of them. The hounds names and owners are matched to the recipient hunt. From 1936 to 1967 five counties in Maryland supplied 90% of these long eared hounds to the like minded hunters to the north. Men like Walter Hill, George Brice and Ben Funk (Pa) went with their hounds.

For the record I have chosen the names of houndsmen and their state of origin, who over the last century, have by necessity (financial) or goodwill have shared their 'true to the line' hounds with us. In 1975 we organized some thirty (30) packs of hounds in Chester County, Pa. and still are active and enjoy a summer picnic.

Many, but not all these names were contributed by the pedigree records in Alexander MacKay-Smith book.

Claude and Hill Anthony	MD
Howard Bowers	MD
Harvey Brice	MD
George Brice	MD and NJ
Duland Clark	MD
Frank Coleman	MD
D.C. Collins	MD
Ben Coppage	MD
Silas Crosson	PA
Leland Credick	MD
F. Durborow	PA
Ben Funk	PA
Ralph/Andrew Ford	PA
Chalres F. Davis	PA
Walter Hill	MD and PA
Carney Hobbs	MD
S.W. Hyde	MD
James Hollingsworth	MD
J. Urie Jones	MD
Raymond Jones	MD
Samuel Kirk	PA
W.G. Little	Del.
Merrit Lynch	MD
Guy Mercer	PA
Wm G. Merion	PA

Webster Moore	MD
Jack Nickerson	MD
J.C. McCoomb	Del.
John Perry	MD
M. Pencoast	PA
Charles Quinby	MD plus
Joe, Jim, Bill, Fred, Charlie	
Rouse Story	MD
B.J. Show	MD
Jennings Smith	MD
Lee Smith	MD
Clinton Stayton	MD
Earnest Stillwagon	MD
J.W. Sours	MD
W. Stackhouse	MD
John W. Talley	MD
William Tomlinson	MD
John Voss	MD
Authur E. Webster	Del.
H.K. Wingate	Del.
Willet Yerkes	MD
Orville Roberts	PA

Albert Crosson, son of Silas, Orville Roberts, George Brice, Redmond Stewart soon to be or inducted into Hunstman Room at Morven Park, Va.

Chalfant
Upland Road
Unionville, Chester County
Pennsylvania 19375
February 23, 1979

Dear Dr. Addis,

That was a very good letter of date February 15ᵗʰ and I enjoyed reading it, and shall write Mr. Bowers, Dirctor of the Game Commission, in my role, as a one time secretary for 32 years, and presently treasurer of the Penn-Marydel Fox Hounds Corporation.

I have a paper written by my father, John B. Hannum, Jr. Esq. in 1936, entitled "Some Observations On Foxhunting," which I believe to be one of the most authentic on the subject, I have ever read; no doubt, daughter prejudiced, he was an able lawyer and an excellent huntsman—with a voice, as big as Justice Owen J. Roberts which really carried—terrifying women and children when he hunted his hounds at night. He, with Mr. and Mrs. H. Roy Jackson was one of the three (3) Incorporators 1934 in Delaware of the P.M.D.F.H. Inc. and had much to do with setting up the Bylaws and Standards and establishing the Stud Book, to preserve the purity in the blood lines of that species of American Fox Hound bred and hunted for generations throught the south eastern sections of Pennsylvania, Maryland and Delaware. For years his kennels were in Delaware County at Elwya, then they widened the Baltimore Pike and he moved the hounds to Theodore, Maryland where he had bought a farm. His pack, as you probably know was never recognized—reason: quote, unquote, "I don't like people in my hip pocket!", though a good horseman, he rode to hunt, not the reverse—his great pleasure after a long day at the office, or in court was to kick the kennel door open, after supper, on a moon fit summer night and enjoy all that lovely music, he knew each hound by their cry–and would say "listen", then identify a hound—then pater quergme, I'd take wild guesses—like, Tango, Flirt, Random, Chase, etc.—I was usually wrong—the wrath! Then are, they coming toward us or going away? Was usually wrong there too—so then with disgust he'd tell me to go to bed!

When he was rising three (3) my grandfather took him to a circus on the parade grounds at the Pennsylvania Military College in Chester—a block from where they lived, he saw a small, attractive pony which was part of the circus, when it was time to leave—he refused, roaring with rage and grandfather had to buy the pony. Then all docility and smiles, he led the pony home to their stable; so you can see he was a very determined and strong minded boy, grandfather was strong willed too—I was always grateful I missed that confrontation by 32 years.

If it would interest you to read the article, I should like to send it to you. I only have one copy, so will ask you to return it after perusal—let me know!

Sincerely Yours,
Christine P. Hannum
Telephone: 347-2486

John B. Hannum, Jr. with his hounds.

WASHINGTON TIMES

WASHINGTON, D. C.

July 13, 1934

Dear Sir:

Once again this year, on or about September 1, the Washington Times will publish its annual SPECIAL FOX HUNTING EDITION, the only edition of its kind in the world.

You, and members of your Hunt, cordially are invited to contribute to this Special Edition .

As you probably know from last year's SPECIAL FOX HUNTING EDITION, this annual is intended to be OF, BY and FOR fox hunters. ALL articles appearing in this edition are written by men and women who are every-day devotees to the sport. News-paper reporters are NOT employed for this edition.

Each Master is urged to send in, NOT LATER THAN AUGUST 15, an article of about 200 words forecasting events of the 1934-35 hunting season. This article may be in the form of a letter to

> THE EDITOR,
> SPECIAL FOX HUNTING EDITION,
> WASHINGTON TIMES,
> WASHINGTON, D. C.

In this article or letter, the M. F. H. should endeavor to reflect for fox hunters of other sections activities in his own section, so that the fox hunter in Maryland or Virginia will know something of the conditions, methods, etc., prevailing in Colorado, or Oklahoma, or Massachusetts.

SPECIAL ARTICLES of interest to fox hunters are ESPECIALLY solicited from MEMBERS OF ORGANIZED HUNTS. These articles, too, should be in the hands of the Editor of the Special Fox Hunting Edition NOT LATER THAN AUGUST 15, 1934. SUCH ARTICLES SHOULD HAVE THE STAMP OF APPROVAL OF THE MASTER.

For the information of fox hunters, this annual Special Fox Hunting Edition has a fourfold purpose:

(1) To call to the attention of Federal and State authorities the ECONOMIC IMPORTANCE of fox hunting and to urge upon those officials the necessity of NOT building hard-surfaced roads in fox hunting countries;

(2) To give the general public a better knowledge and understanding of the sport;

WASHINGTON TIMES

WASHINGTON, D. C.

-2-

(3) To aid in the movement to eliminate class hatred by spreading the gospel of good sportsmanship; and

(4) To bring added prestige to the sport of fox hunting and its devotees.

Poems of fox hunting; accounts of unusual incidents of the hunting field; specific observations of interest to fox hunters; pictures; and other data of interest to fox hunters are solicited. ALL PICTURES WILL BE RETURNED.

The annual SPECIAL FOX HUNTING EDITION of the WASHINGTON TIMES is NOT a commercial enterprise in any sense of the word. While it is true that advertising for this edition is solicited, the revenue so derived is devoted to turning out an edition of which devotees of the sport justly may be proud.

The edition is planned TO REFLECT THE SPIRIT OF THE CHASE. Contributors are NOT paid for articles appearing in the edition. Nor does the Editor of the edition receive extra remuneration. The monetary motive is wholly absent, thus assuring an edition that lives, absolutely, to THE CODE OF FOX HUNTING.

Enclosed you will find an editorial, "Sport and Wise Spending". This editorial appeared on Page 1 of the 1933 Special Fox Hunting Edition. It gives you some notion of the ideas of the Washington Times in relation to this annual special edition.

This newspaper, its executives and its staffs, solicit your aid in making the 1934 Special Fox Hunting Edition one that will aid in placing the sport of Riding to the Hounds in its rightful category as one of the Anglo-Saxon's greatest pastimes, if not the greatest.

The annual Special Fox Hunting Edition of the Washington Times, just as The Hunt, is primarily dedicated to the wholesome and invigorating sport of Fox Hunting; reflects traditions of the sport which have survived for centuries; and, is retained, not as a passing hobby or a commerical enterprise, but rather as an inspiration for sportsmanship and a medium through which community interests may be fostered and developed.

Will you please respond to this communication, as soon as possible, informing us if we may expect your assistance?

Sincerely yours,

Harry Costello

WASHINGTON TIMES

per: Harry Costello, Editor,
Special Fox Hunting Edition
Washington Times

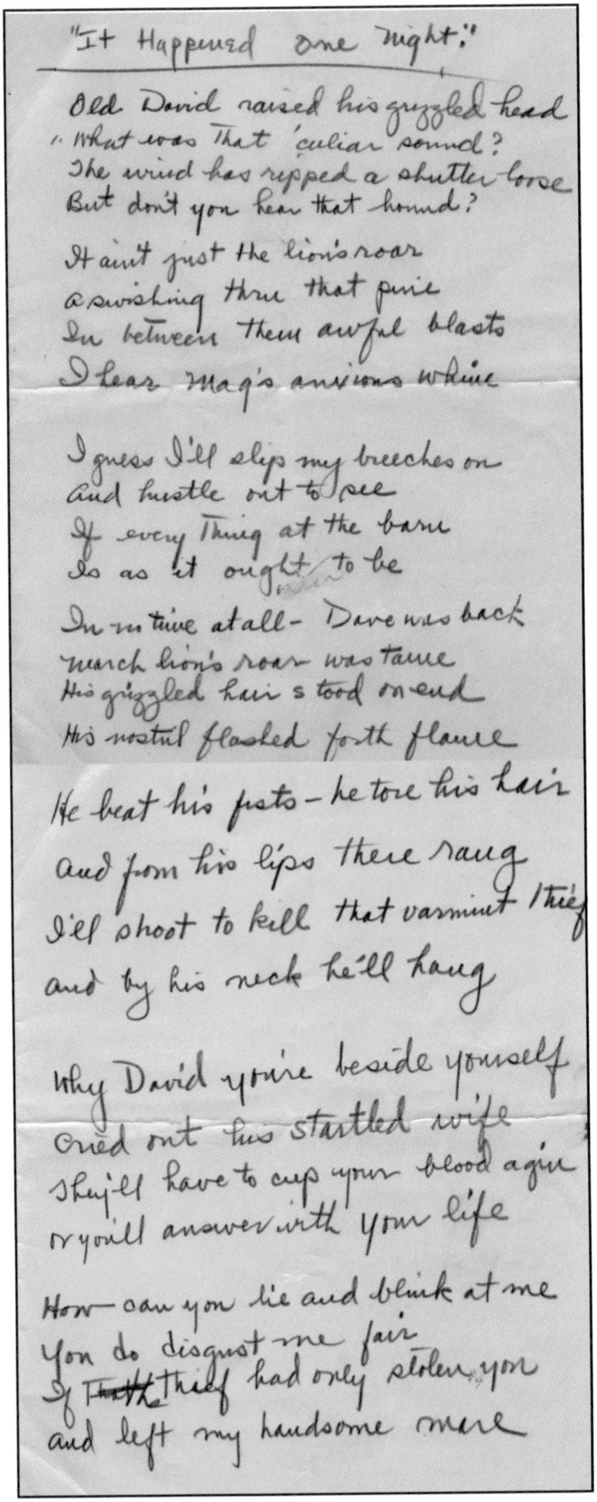

"It Happened One Night."

Old David raised his grizzled head
". What was that 'culiar sound?
The wind has ripped a shutter loose
But don't you hear that hound?

It ain't just the lion's roar
a swishing thru that pine
In between them awful blasts
I hear Mag's anxious whine

I guess I'll slip my breeches on
and hustle out to see
If every thing at the barn
Is as it ought to be

In no time at all— Dave was back
march lion's roar was tame
His grizzled hair s tood on end
His nostril flashed forth flame

He beat his fists— he tore his hair
and from his lips there rang
I'll shoot to kill that varmint thief
and by his neck he'll hang

Why David you're beside yourself
Cried out his startled wife
They'll have to cup your blood agin
or you'll answer with your life

How— can you lie and blink at me
You do disgust me fair
If the thief had only stolen you
and left my handsome mare

IT HAPPENED ONE NIGHT

One of dozens of fox-hunting poems written by Ann H. Addis born April 6th, 1900 and died April 6th, 1991. This poem was never published and not written in response to The Washington Times' *request.*

WASHINGTON TIMES

WASHINGTON, D. C.

July 18, 1934

Mrs. Ann Addis,
c/o Dr. Clarkson Addis, M.F.H.,
Perkiomen Hunt Club,
Collegeville, Pa.

Dear Mrs. Addis:

    Once again this year The Washington Times is putting out a special Fox Hunting Edition. Won't you come to our aid again this year with a good poem on Fox Hunting?

    We expect that this year's special Fox Hunting Edition will surpass last year's in every respect.

    May I hear from you in the near future?

                    Cordially yours,

                    Harry Costello

LETTER TO THE EDITOR
by Sean Cully MFH

Thought I would share with you my use of a few Penn-Marydel hounds I run with some mixed breed foxhounds around the central Pennsylvania and upstate New York area.

About 3 years ago a friend of mine that hunts a farmers pack of Penn-Marydel's on horse back, asked if I would like to raise a litter of his hounds and keep the ones I wanted for my own use. He explained to me that these hounds would be the smaller faster type and might mix well with my current hounds. I was interested in giving them a try, so I brought his bitch home to raise the pups. I ended up keeping three of them and got them started with my older hounds at about 6 months of age. These pups were the first I have ever raised and started myself, so I really worked hard to make them a success.

Other than continually putting them in places where the correct game was, they were naturals and developed well. Now my one worry was what I have always been told about the Penn-Marydel's and that is not being able to keep up with the Walkers and Julys that I am accustomed to. I had raised these pups through late winter and worked them hard through the summer months. Putting them out with the older dogs from 6 months on. They got to run a lot through the summer. Their first winter came and I took them every time I went. I was doing some coyote hunting in upstate New York over their one-year birthday. We had about 8" of fresh snow and a nice sunny day at about 25 degrees. We found a pair of fresh coyote tracks and put four older dogs on them. They quickly jumped a coyote and were driving it hard. Within minutes they had crossed out of the block I was in and with me on foot, it was up to the guys in the trucks stay with that race. As I was sitting and waiting for their return, a stray coyote came back through the woods towards me. This was the chance to see what these pups could do. I made the twenty minute trek back to the truck, unloaded the three pups and we made our way back to where this stray had gone through. They quickly picked up the line and by themselves quickly went out of hearing. One of the guys on the road heard them coming his way and saw them cross the road not too far behind the coyote.

I stayed where the hounds had left me, about an hour went by and I began to hear the three pups coming. I was grinning ear to ear as I could hear each one of their voices, as I had learned them well over the past summer.

Well this day we were not far from the farm that was having trouble with the coyotes killing their sheep, so orders were to kill. About fifteen minutes later that coyote about knocked me down as he came by and I ended the chase with one shot of number four buck. About two minutes later the pups showed up right on his track and got the petting down of a lifetime, as well as a little tug at his hide. Had many other runs on both coyote and fox that winter that really helped the pups develop.

The start of this past winter my pups were about 20 months old and up to the level of an experienced hound. I could cast them at the right spot and they were more than capable of cold trailing and jumping their own quarry. One day early in the season they really showed me what they could do.

I had put some older dogs out into a large forest on one side of the road. There was no action after about 30 minutes so I went with two of the Penn-Marydels out into some brush patches on the other side of the road. Within 20 minutes they had jumped a coyote, as I saw it several times cross the open fields around the brush. Well this was at about 9 in the morning. One of my older hounds on the other side of the road got over to this chase and made a grand pack of 3 hounds. Well things really started heating up and they must have been getting close to the coyote. The chase left the block we were in. We pursued in pick-up trucks for the next six hours and ended up about eight miles from where they had jumped him. They had crossed a strong upstate New York river a few times and had headed into a remote section of forest with only one road that stops in the middle. We got back into the hounds that luckily were only a few hundred yards off the road. From the road we could hear the chase had stopped, but the hounds were still causing a ruckus. I walked in and they had caught the coyote. He was standing in a small stream under an overhang and looked pretty tired. The two Penn-Marydels and the Walker had been chasing for over six hours, and had caught their game. When they saw me there they decided it was time to finish the coyote and that they did. The coyote was a large male and weighed in at 45 pounds. That was early in the winter and was just the start of things as the young hounds repeated this performance all winter long.

Thanks for reading, Sean Cully MFH

HAL-LE-LU-JAH
by H. L. Todd Addis

On occasion during a Sunday hunt my hounds have stirred my thoughts on spirituality when in pursuit of the fox. The East Nantmeal Baptist Church's parking lot, cemetery and surrounding stone wall is something used by Mr. Fox to cause hounds to check. The congregation sometimes leave the front entrance door open on a warm morning. It seems to attract the curious new entry to poke their head in to either listen to or get a stern sermon.

My guilt of not being a church goer evaporated when I read an article under "Religion" of the *Daily Local News*, Jan. 30, 2004.

Diana L. Gruerrer, animal behaviorist and therapist in Big Bear Lake, California, says "Animals serve as a line to the intuitive and to the devine." She goes on to say in her new book *What Animals Can Teach Us About Spirituality*, "They can compel us to pursue a connection to the spirit without the need for a religious or denominational approach."

Now that I have reached 76 years of age and sometimes inquiring about the "here after," I am substituting Hal-le-lu-jah instead of Tally-Ho.

My daughter Ann and son-in-law James watching over granddaughter Kemper Ann posing in front of the East Nantmeal Baptist Church, Elverson, PA, 2005.

SECTION III

IO

'DISCOURSE ON HORSEMANSHIPPE'
GERVASE MARKHAM
1568–1637

The Music of the Pack, 1593

*I*F you would have your kennel for sweetness of cry, then you must compound it of some large dogs, that have deep solemn Mouthes, and are swift in spending, which must as it were bear the base in the consort; then a double number of roaring and loud ringing Mouthes, which must bear the counter tenor; then some hollow plain sweet Mouthes, which must bear the mean or middle part: and so with these three parts of musick you shall make your cry perfect: and herein you shall observe that these Hounds thus mixt, do run just and even together and not hang off loose from one another, which is the vilest sight that may be; and you shall understand, that this composition is best to be made of the swiftest and largest deep mouthed dog, the slowest middle siz'd dog, and the shortest legg'd slender dog. Amongst these you may cast in a couple or two small single beagles, which as small trebles may warble amongst them: the cry will be a great deal the more sweet. . . . If you would have your kennel for depth of mouth, then you shall compound it of the largest dogs, which have the greatest mouths and deepest slews, such as your West Countrey, Che-shire and Lanca-shire dogs are, and to five or six base couple of mouths shall not add above two couple of counter tenors, as many means, and not above one couple of Roarers, which being heard but now and then, as at the opening or hitting of a scent, will give much sweetness to the solemnness and grave-ness of the cry, and the musick thereof will be much more delightfull to the ears of every beholder.

22

Taken from A Fox Hunter's Anthology.

27

' MASTER OF GAME '
EDWARD DUKE OF YORK
c. 1400

A True Hound

A HOUND is true to his lord and his master, and of good love and true. A hound is of great understanding and of great goodness, a hound is a wise beast and a kind one. A hound has a great memory and great smelling, a hound has great diligence and great might, a hound is of great worthiness and of great subtlety, a hound is of great lightness and of great perseverance, a hound is of good obedience, for he will learn as a man all that a man will teach him. A hound is full of good sport; hounds are so good that there is scarcely a man that would not have of them, some for one craft, and some for another. Hounds are hardy, for a hound dare well keep his master's house, and his beasts, and also he will keep all his master's goods, and he would sooner die than anything be lost in his keeping.

72

33

'MASTER OF GAME'

EDWARD DUKE OF YORK

c. 1400

The Perfect Hound

OF all hues of running hounds, there are some which be good, and some which be bad or evil, as of greyhounds. But the best hue of running hounds and most common for to be good, is called brown tan. Also the goodness of running hounds, and of all other kinds of good hounds, cometh of true courage and of the good nature of their good father and of their good mother. . . . A running hound should be well born, and well grown of body, and should have great nostrils and open, and a long snout, but not small, and great lips and well hanging down, and great eyes red or black, and a great forehead and great head, and large ears, well long and well hanging down, broad and near the head, a great neck, and a great breast and great shoulders, and great legs and strong, and not too long, and great feet, round and great claws, and the foot a little low, small flanks and long sides, a little pintel not long, small hanging ballocks and well trussed together, a good chine bone and great back, good thighs, and great hind legs and the hocks straight and not bowed, the tail great and high, and not cromping upward. Nevertheless I have seen some running hounds with great hairy tails the which were very good.

The best sport that men can have is running with hounds, for if he hunt at hare or at the roe or at buck or at the hart, or at any other beast without greyhound, it is a fair thing, and pleasant to him that loveth them; the seeking and

79

the finding is also a fair thing, and a great liking to slay them with strength, and for to see the wit and the knowledge that God hath given to good hounds, and for to see good recovering and retrieving, and the mastery and the subtleties that be in good hounds. For with greyhounds and with other kinds of hounds whatever they be, the sport lasteth not, for anon a good greyhound or a good alaunte taketh or faileth a beast, and so do all manner of hounds save running hounds the which must hunt all the day questeying and making great melody in their language and saying great villainy and chiding the beasts that they chase. And therefore I prefer them to all other kinds of hounds, for they have more virtue it seems to me than any other beast.

34

KING JAMES I
1566–1625

Royal Support

*I*CANNOT omit heere the hunting, namely with running houndes, which is the most honourable and noblest sort thereof; for it is a thievish form of hunting to shoote with gunnes and bowes, and greyhound hunting is not so martial a game. . . .

80

Under an Abner Garrett painting by F. B. Voss from 1923, we read he was huntsman for Upland Hunt 1900-1909, Rose Tree Hunting Club 1918-1930, and Mr. Jefford's Hounds 1922-1928. I must conclude that the picture of the Rose Tree Hounds at Sycamore Mills in the 1920's shows huntsman Abner Garrett on the Grey. Unfortunately, a picture of George Schrivery was not forthcoming. Picture from The Rose Tree Families.

MR. JEFFORD'S HOUNDS

The third section of this book will feature a number of distinguished huntsmen of the Penn-Marydel foxhound. I chose to concentrate on these huntsmen that ushered in the first half of the twentieth century. Their accomplishments, if not already lost, will soon vanish if not committed to paper.

Needless to say Alexander MacKay-Smith and his book *The American Foxhound 1747–1967* helped immeasurably in providing positions of not one, but three huntsmen employed by Walter M. Jeffords Sr. I have a vision of the podium at the winter Olympics with three recipients standing tall with medals laying on their chests. As a make-believe judge I place huntsman Abner Garrett with the Silver, George Shivery with the Gold and Haines Kirk with the Bronze.

The Gold went to George Shivery because he accepted the position of huntsmen from Mr. Jeffords Sr. when the pack was moved to Andrews Bridge in Lancaster County, PA. His services were appreciated for a period of 32 years, 1927–1959. Not being fired, his retirement suggest of a man with a pleasing personality, loyalty to his master and exceptional talent in hunting his hounds and directing a kennel that dominated the Penn-Marydel show ring for decades.

Present-day Andrews Bridge huntsman Steve Hill (2008) said he went to work for huntsman George as a kid and grew up with him helping with hounds and kennel duties. Always present, was a personality absent of temper and bad moods. Huntsman Hill says huntsman Shivery loved to use his voice while hunting his Black and Tans and only sparingly un-pocketed his horn.

I chose the Silver medal to be awarded to Abner Garrett not because of a lesser ability to hunt hounds, but because of a "dual" or "rambling" employment. MacKay-Smith reports that in 1900 a Mr. Edward Crozer organized and founded the Upland Hunt in Delaware County, PA. His hounds came from a branch of his family dating back to 1830. Abner Garrett hunted the Upland pack 1900–1909.

The Upland Hunt was disbanded in 1918 and Samuel D. Riddle of Man-O-War thoroughbred fame gathered a pack that hunted the country that Mr. Crozer hunted.

Mr. Riddle's joy of hunting his hounds was short lived and Walter M. Jeffords Sr. took over the Riddle pack in 1918. Mr. Jeffords not only took on the mastership of Rose Tree Hunt in 1918, he also maintained his private pack employing Abner Garrett as his huntsman, 1922–1928.

Jeffords Sr. resigned the mastership of Rose Tree in 1928 and Abner Garrett went on to hunt Rose Tree hounds from 1918–1930. No dates are given by author MacKay-Smith, however he states that Garrett at sometime hunted hounds for a James C. McCoomb of Claymont, Delaware.

The senior Jeffords thought enough of Abner Garrett to produce a grand portrait of him cheering his pack on. The painting was commissioned by F. B. Voss, 1923, and reproduced on page 256 (d) of *American Hound 1747–1967*.

After reading these pages several times in MacKay-Smith's book, I came to the conclusion that at one time or another Abner Garrett may have been hunting three packs of hounds at one time

Haines Kirk came on as whipper-in for George Shivery in 1954 and then was promoted to the huntsman position of Andrews Bridge in 1959. Haines continued the successful breeding of the Black and Tans for many years in the second half of the 20th century under the mastership of Walter Jeffords Jr. and Robert Crompton.

Hopefully the family of Haines Kirk is "looking after" his well-earned Bronze medal.

Huntsman Haines Kirk and three of Walter Jeffords, Jr. children.

ALBERT CROSSON—TRUE TO THE LINE
A SHORT BIOGRAPHY BY H. L. TODD ADDIS, MFH

Whatever success I have had breeding and hunting hounds I should give credit to my father. Realistically I know I 'learnt' from Albert Crosson.

It seems when the great huntsmen of America were recognized at the Foxhound base camp at Morven Park, our Pennsylvania huntsmen were ignored.

Those who rode behind Albert were not cheated on experiencing the finest hunting that America had to offer.

In my feeble effort to bring the life of Albert 'Pud' Crosson to the Friends of the Penn-Marydel reader, I thought it best, to start with an interview with Albert's widow, Gladys.

I arranged an overnight visit with Gladys' daughter and son-in-law Marion and Roger Scullion, so all three of us could coax as much history as possible from Gladys after all these years.

Much to our surprise, Gladys searched her apartment and produced a scrapbook with all sorts of pictures and articles of his hunting career.

Practically all of our great huntsmen gained their knowledge and instincts, not from reading a book, but from following the path of their father. Sure enough, in Gladys' scrapbook was a 1984 calendar produced and distributed by the Kennett Area Senior Center. The August calendar page shows a 1933 picture of Silas Crosson (Albert's father) on stage holding some of his blue ticks and tri-colors. The cast of characters was giving a performance of the story of Kennett. The story of Kennett was written by the distinguished author and foxhunter Bayard Taylor.

On this same calendar page another foxhunter stood on stage holding his Penn-Marydel hounds. It was not until I interviewed Albert's brother-in-law, Donald Bracken, that I was able to identify this mystery foxhunter as Melch Becker of Kennett Square. He played the part of Sandy Flash, the local outlaw, who was hung by the neck for his misbehavior.

My other fact finding mission was a visit to 94 year old Bill Fenstermacher of Unionville, PA. Gladys accompanied me to the interview. Bill was Albert's brother-in-law (married Gladys' sister Betty) and also his uncle. Albert's mother was Bill Fenstermacher's sister. Think about it, I'm still confused.

With much searching, during the interview, Gladys and I were able to find the 94 year old's hearing aid. With great difficulty he was able to find a small screwdriver, placed it in the strategic hole in the hearing aid and made a much needed adjustment. After much shouting we gathered that Albert's first hunting experience away from home was hunting hounds for the Cedar Croft Hunt. That pack was kennelled in the Cedar Croft Farm and School, owned by Anita Edge. This was also home for the old Baynard Taylor Hunt, near Kennett Square.

Albert then went on to accept a job as whipper-in at Rose Tree with Edward Quigley as huntsman in 1939.

Albert moved from his 1st whipper-in position to that of huntsman on February 4, 1940, when Edward Quigley resigned.

Edward Quigley continued his farming career, while retaining a private pack of hounds. Putting two and two together I interpreted a letter that he [Quigley] wrote to the Chronicle of the Horse, dated July 23, 1943. The former Rose Tree Hunt huntsman Edward Quigley, states "First it has been the custom of hunt clubs, particularly of late years to elect as Master one who has the most money or leisure, or both, in which to conduct duties of MFH. It should be very clear that by this method the club may have an excellent MFH or it may not." Other points in the letter suggest that he (Quigley) was unhappy with his master and resigned. After his resignation Quigley continued hunting with his own private pack. Quigley remained on good terms with Rose Tree Hunt, as was shown in a paragraph of the following article initialed P.G.G. and published in a 1941 issue of the *Chronicle of the Horse*.

Dated January 3, 1941. "Hounds met at 11 o'clock at Jay Mills, Happy hunting ground of other years. Huntsman Crosson being ill with pleurisy, huntsman Quigley took over for him, hunting his [Quigley's] and Rose Trees' hound together in country many of us love. It was like old times to be starting off over the set in [jump] and onto Willcox's."

P.G.G. writes, in a separate article, a wonderful account of a Rose Tree Hunt, which was also published in the Chronicle.

"On Saturday Feb. 14 1942, The Reule Farm at 11am and what a valentine a stout-hearted red fox presented to Rose Tree and their Radnor guests! A beautiful day, frozen ground, it is true but blue sky and yellow sunshine. The weather helped us give a warm welcome to Radnor- a field of 75 followed Albert Crosson and hounds also Radnor's huntsman Jimmy O'Neal, through chestnut sprouts into the field beyond. Here cries of Tall-ho rose to the blue sky for two foxes sped out of the briars at the foot of the hill. Hounds followed the latter as he sailed along the crest of the hill his beautiful brush brightened to gold in the shining sun.

Behind chorusing hounds we galloped to Providence Road where we hopped over the set-in across the Moran fields to Gradyville Road, past a spilled gentleman getting first aid, his horse, it seemed bolted, he lost a stirrup, and then came a cropper-up the road, through the pines into Black Oak Farm woods whereof speedy but chicken-hearted pilot ducked in.

Promptly, therefore, huntsman Crosson led hounds towards Hunting Hill to pick up the line of the other fox. Instead of following the field to the meadow I circled the woods on a hunch that the fox would take a line across the open hill and field beyond. For once, mirabite dictu, I guessed right and had the joy of seeing hounds

The Rose Tree Hunt with Edward Quigley as huntsman, and Albert Crosson as whipper-in. Photo taken between 1939 and 1941.

come out of the woods and pick up the line. From then but for two momentary checks we were galloping on behind hounds with a drive I'll remember when I'm dead and gone. Rose Tree hounds! Ye Gods, They deserve a Valhalla all their own! Across the road into Mendonhall's Road, though Simmons to Locksley Mills, up past the stone quearry. In big country now, they led the field over a 4'0" barway and onto Brinton Dam to Baltimore Pike. Here at Chadds Ford the stout-hearted pilot went to hole.

Or did he? At this point I can record only what I hear. (I hate to admit it, but I missed the last 15 min. I pulled out because I was all in. To Jane Bug's [P.G.G.'s horse] complete disgust-never did I feel such a "panty waist". But sometimes even bellicose medicos are right!)

My husband's comment 'What a fox! He outran the steadiest hounds in the world!' Huntsman Crosson: 'I'm not saying what that fox did. There was a big hole there in the woods but hounds weren't noticing it'. Albert started to cast on ahead and Mr. Reeves roared out 'What are you doing? Don't you see we're damned near dead. Turn hounds near home for God's sake.' MFH Sellers, 'Don't you think he went in after a 12 mile point!' Albert replied, 'I think he did-Maybe!'

There was much more to P.G.G.'s article that vividly entertains the reader, space forbids me to re-tell.

However great Albert Crosson was a huntsman, P.G.G. was just as great in recounting Rose Trees' hunts and religiously sending them to the Chronicle for the subscriber. Polly Goodwin Griffin (Mrs. Hastings Griffin, MFH Terry Griffin's grandmother) the Chronicle needs you again.

The best of Rose Tree ended for Albert when he was drafted into the Navy in 1943. He reported for duty when daughter Marion was six months old. He spent his time in Guam, and returned in 1945. While he was gone, his father continued hunting the hounds in Gum Tree, Chester County. Old Silas worked the night shift at Ways Greenhouse in Kennett Square. This left time to hunt during the day.

Another old gentleman who shared hunting the Crosson hounds when Silas's legs and body were wearing down as Scrap-Iron. No one seems to know his real name but we can all imagine his occupation. Betty (Albert's sister) said Daddy would get so furious at his old friend, Scrap Iron, because he never seemed to blow the hunting horn until he was under someone's bedroom window.

Albert was the oldest of eight children, following him were Christine, Oscar (huntsman at Mr. Stewart's Cheshire Foxhounds and Vicmead), Jackie, Iva Jane, Margret, Betty and Silas Jr. All of Albert's relatives and home grown friends called him Pud, because his mother said he looked like a fat bowl of pudding as a baby.

Albert took a huntsman's job at Huntingdon Valley Hunt in Bucks County after the war, but left after three years. Little was recorded about Albert's hunting adventures at Huntingdon Valley. We do know that H. Douglas Paxson was MFH.

Albert's brother-in-law Donald Bracken came to whip for Albert during his second year. I asked Donald why he only stayed three years.

His answer was that after hunting each day and after the horses and hounds were cared for we would be invited to the master's house and we would party too long. He said once he could remember Albert passing out, in among the leaves next to the stone wall.

Donald Brachen also recounts: "On one exceptionally good hunting day the pack split and the one group got away from us. We went back to the Paxson's for their vehicles to search for hounds but the Mrs. had the keys and all the vehicles were locked up. So we took my old '37 Plymouth coup. We gradually picked up the unchaperoned pack and loaded them in the front and back in the rumble seat. When we headed home we came through Doylestown and were stopped by the police. Then they took Doug Paxon, Albert and I to jail." I asked Donald what were the charges. Donald said "I guess drunken driving." Mrs. Paxson finally arrived and bailed them out. Of course the men had no idea whether the hounds were jailed or held to wait for the next of kin to pick them up.

Donald said Mr. Paxson was a great rye and soda man. Maybe this is where Albert began to drink 2 or 3 cups of black coffee in the morning. I believe Albert ended his drinking when the Huntingdon Valley position ended.

After Albert left Huntingdon Valley, he took a job as Farm Manager for B.J. Nice in Hatfield, Pa.

Possibly home sickness and magnetic attraction to hounds and fox, moved him back to Chester County, where he took another job as farm manager for John Barnes Mull. Hearsay. Many years ago it was rumored that handsome Mr. Mull was a little too smitten with the ladies, among the Pickering Hunt ladies and was politely excused from the club. He then took over as MFH of Whitelands Hunt in 1948. Albert was summoned as the last whipper-in to huntsman George Hill. Huntsman Hill died in the summer of 1949 and Albert then took over as huntsman.

The second of three articles printed in the Archive, Downingtown 1949 by Jane McIlvaine [Sullivan], titled Distinguished Chester County Huntsmen, has a paragraph quoting old George Hill. One of the best hunts he can remember took place last year early in the season when hounds met at the Grove and ran around what is called the Southside for five and a half hours, before darkness necessitated calling them off. Only Hill, Albert and Clarkson Addis Sr. from Collegeville were in at the end of the day.

My early memories of hunting in Chester County were first with George Hill, with Albert as whip. Then Albert took the horn in 1949.

By all accounts deer were becoming a major interruption in all hunting countries. Albert began looking in the shadows of the small foot and mounted farmer packs on his days off. These associations gained him many bootless foxhunting buddies in the rugged hills of Northern Chester County.

One red-headed, ex-paratrooper of World War II, who became Albert's side kick throughout his years with Whitelands, was George (Reds) Albright. Reds was extremely good natured, happy go lucky, fellow, who became the whipping-post of the teasers.

Before Reds teamed up with Albert, he, Reds, had already accumulated a conglomeration of good hounds that he managed to deer break.

This he did by himself, using bird shot in his 22-35-or 45, and possibly some surplus hand grenades were thrown too! (Just kidding.)

With constant scolding Albert managed to break two young hounds from rioting on deer, before the application of the pistol. Grappler and Glamour were the two. Whenever the pack would strike deer, these two sensitive hounds would inevitably return to Albert. Albert's horn would then alert the staff and truck followers of the riot. Stones would fly, the pedal to the metal and the ammunition would be activated and gun smoke would clog the noses of the pursuing hounds. Old Smokey Joe Swarmer was Albert's best 4-wheeled whipper-in. Finally it worked.

To the best of my knowledge, this was the first pack of hounds that were deer broken in the United States.

Whitelands hunted two days a week, but many of the hounds saw five additional days tacked on by hunting with the farmer packs.

My veterinary schooling years were most difficult with classes occupying six days of the week. However, truck hunting on Sundays was a treat. Oh, what hunts did we have! The meets on Sunday were chosen from the best of Whitelands and Eagle Farms Hunt counties.

We never hunted a cover just to check it out. We hunted covers that bedded foxes that would hold the packs for the entire day.

Needless to say there were some great Penn-Marydel hounds in the field and Albert never missed a chance to breed to one of them or draft a puppy or two from them. Only a priest listening to Albert confess would know the correct breeding of his hounds.

Not only did I find a beautiful young lady from Charles County, Maryland to be my wife. I also found a new hunting country. Mt. Victoria, the farm where, my wife, Happy, grew up, and father and stepmother still lived at the time, encompassed 1300 acres. Currently, Mt. Victoria is the hub for the De La Brook Foxhounds.

The year following the death of my father, I coaxed Albert to bring some Whiteland hounds to my father-in-law's farm in Maryland. I also coaxed a few of Albert's neighboring farmer packs to join us. No one that lived in the Mt. Victoria area, could tell me what fox species was predominant, or even if there were any foxes.

The last weekend in April 1959 was the date. Friday night was the arrival time, with hounds kenneled in a box stall. Anxious hounds did not wait. Four hounds dug out and were nowhere to be seen on Saturday morning. I told Albert there was no point looking for them, start hunting and they'll join in. The blind began leading the blind. But not really, because, any seasoned huntsman uses his instincts and seeks out the thickest place or most natural place a fox would lay.

It did not take long. Hounds struck. Adrenalin flowed. A tingling feeling raced up everyone's back. Two foxes running abreast. All thirteen and a half couple of the best Pennsylvania had to offer, pounded Maryland's holly bushes for five hours without the slightest hint of a check.

My father-in-law, Bennett Crain, mounted his '52 Plymouth coup and followed that PA hound noise until he became hung up on a stump. Of course, his door was luxated when he failed to close it in time, while wildly backing up next to a tree. Bud Linderman was sitting in the back, slouched down and holding on with a broad grin on his face.

The pack was taken off, including the four escapees, because, there weren't any fresh hounds available for the next day's hunt.

Swan Point, also owned by my father-in-law, was a 900 acre peninsula on the Potomac River, that was about four miles away from Mt. Victoria, producing hunting thrills that would fill volumes.

Albert Crosson while he was huntsman for the Whitelands Hunt in 1957.

There were so many exciting hunts at Swan Point that they seem to all run together in my mind.

This piece of timber land was long and narrow, and had one extremely muddy lane down the middle. As you entered the main entrance gate a short lane turned left going back about 300 yards to the Potomac River and a duck hunting shack. The duck hunters used this shack in November and December. Mice and dormant wasps (during the winter) lived there also. The mice had no shortage of food with there being a leftover bag of shelled bait corn stacked on the first floor.

When the Pennsylvania foxhunter's arrived in April and lit the fires, it rejuvenated the mice and hatched the wasps. At one point I tried to interrupt the mice sprinting across the room by placing a box of lead sinkers in their holes. Then we tried quick eradication by the pistol bird-shot method. Little success. The mouse story is capped off by Pickering huntsman Guy Mercer putting on his coat, in the morning, and when his hand went in pocket for his pipe, the mouse jumped out.

The first Saturday of hunting, of our third year down, we were rained out. Or so we thought. As evening approached, Chester "Whitey" Ortlip with his dozen hounds decided to give it a try before packing up and going home. This river bottom point had lots of standing water. Every hole at Swan Point had to be flooded, in spite of this, Whitey was lucky enough to jump a floating grey. Whitey's big, old Penn-Marydels (7 of them by Pickering's Leo) settled in on this grey nicely. Albert couldn't stand it, so he jumps in his truck and heads to Mt. Victoria to load his hounds. When he arrives back, this little grey was running tight circles crossing both the shank lane and the point lane. Albert frantically backed his truck in the right position and dropped the tailgate so they could hark directly to Whitey's hounds. Unfortunately Whitey's last hound disappeared before Albert's first hound saw it. They immediately harked to where they thought they were, hitting the line backwards.

If Albert were a general we all would have been court marshaled, for letting them run it backwards, and that is after a good chewing out. This is serious business you know. Needless to say they were harked to the pack. At 11 o'clock that night no one had witnessed a check so far, nothing else except a smile on Albert's face. Five hours of heavy pressure on a grey kept everyone in Maryland for the next day.

For the next several years Guy Mercer, huntsman for Pickering and Albert with Whitelands and the few other farmer packs returned in April to hunt Mt. Victoria and Swan Point.

Many of the readers of this newsletter have attended hunt balls, weddings, bachelor dinners, hound shows, races, funerals and more at Mt. Victoria. To have experienced a great fox hunt across the fields and lawn of Mt. Victoria is to have visited a little bit of hunting heaven. Albert experienced that little bit of heaven.

Those of us who whipped into Albert knew that he could fly off the handle and give you a piece of his mind. Don't call a hound if he can be driven. There was only one huntsman in Albert Crosson's hunt, and don't you forget it.

Albert saw greener pastures in 1960 when he was offered the huntsman's postion at Pickering Hunt.

He was able to reduce many road miles at Pickering, plus, it had a more affluent membership. The hunting country was well paneled and gentler.

Before leaving Whitelands his daughter Marion joined the hunting field and became a great help in getting horses and hounds to the meet.

After graduating from Veterinary School I was forced to accept a commission in the Army Veterinary Corp. My up date was at the end of August in 1959. I had no idea where I was going to be stationed, so Albert, feeling sorry for me, lent me 14 of his most trustworthy hounds to hunt for a week at Mt. Victoria.

I almost killed one of them running it to death on a hot muggy morning. What trust he had in me.

The Army bent to my wishes (Ha Ha) and I landed duty at Walter Reed Institute of Research in Washington D.C. Needless to say I spent every weekend at Mt. Victoria and began to acquire hounds. Albert drafted three old stubborn bitches, (Dee, Doris and Rattle) and four puppies. A great start.

Even though I saw little of Albert during his years at Pickering, many of his hunting buddies would keep me well informed of the many notable hunts.

After I was discharged from the army and settled outside Warwick Village in Chester County, my friend Reds, who was now whipping for Albert at Pickering, turned his well bred hounds over to me. One litter of six was sired by the great Eagle Farms' Dante.

Pickering had enjoyed numerous hunts on a great running bob-tailed fox, that when viewed looked like a Welsh Corgi. Being that Albert never entered a joint meet without being prepared, he wanted to make sure this fox was available for an up coming joint meet with Vicmead Hunt.

When the time neared Albert, Reds and Donald Bracken went back to find this wide ranging fox. It took hunting him three days straight before they were finally able to put him to ground. The dug him out at Diamond Rock Hill, which overlooks Valley Forge Park.

Old Smokey Joe Swarner was given the duty of dropping this fox in Powder Mill hill near Birchrunville, as Eastwicks was the fixture.

This fox was a good 8-10 miles from his home territory. Albert and Reds were ready on their best mounts, while Oscar Crosson (Albert's brother), huntsman for Vicmead, could do nothing but follow.

Albert soon laid them on.

Fox and hounds went home hell bent for election. And when the hunt was over, back in the fox's home territory, only the three aforementioned individuals had stayed with them. Some Vicmead crossbreds needed to be found, because they were strung out for miles. The masters and field must have choked on the dust. None were seen at the end.

Another wild hunt Reds Albright tells, is when a fox was unkenneled at Mifflin Largess. Reds, a whipper-in for Albert at the time, can remember the hounds at the end of the chase hunting down the in going tracks at the Paoli train station while the out going train was passing west. Maybe that was a dug fox who could not remember his direction home.

Albert always had some great hounds everyone seemed to know. Cowboy, Frankie, Chief, Leo and Flirt. Flirt, on one occasion treed a raccoon, consequently Albert took her coon hunting at night. Leo was bred by Leo Swisher of Wagontown and had a super deep draw voice. Pickering's Chief sired puppies of Hubbard's Kent County hounds. One of Chief's grandson's came to me, years later, by way of the Marlborough Hunt. Needless to say this was an incredible hound. Good genes bred to good genes, equals good genes.

Roger Scullin, a distinguished equine veterinarian and MFH of Howard County-Iron Bridge Hounds, married Albert's daughter, Marion. It can be said not only for love, but for her knowledge of hounds and hunting.

A long standing bond developed between Pickering and Howard County-Iron Bridge Hounds, that still continues today, with annual joint meets.

Marion Crosson Scullin was so proud with one of these joint meets at, what was then, Howard County Hunt. Marion was delighted to have recorded this memorable day and now we are delighted to finally have it published.

Both are dead now, but "Johnny Bill" Linton would have said his crossbreds showed the Penn-Marydels some smoke. Albert, on the other hand, would have said, if it wasn't for those Penn-Marydels, there wouldn't be a hunt. So here is the double agent Marion to give you the truth.

"A chill in the air and partially frozen ground a foot eight hearty Pickering members and staff present for a joint meet with Howard County Hunt at Doughoregan Manor on January 31, 1973.

"The host huntsman "Johnny Bill" Linton and Pickering's Albert Crosson each selected 10 couples of hounds to combine American-Crossbred and Penn-Marydel talent which resulted in showing the field of 81 riders one of the finest days of sport in the fox hunting history of Howard County.

"Mr. Hazel Welsh MFH of H.C.H. injured his back and right leg on a previous hunt and appointed Mr. Howard Sheaker field master. Pickering's joint masters, Mr. Harry Nicholas and Brig. General Edgar R. Owens were also present for the occasion. Other Pickering members included Mrs. Owens, Mrs. William Hopkins, Dr. and Mrs. Edward Theurkauf and whipper-in Nancy Darling. Other guests were Charles Owens from Marlboro Hunt, Gerald Vesper, New Market, Warren Streaker, Goshen Hunt.

"The hounds were promptly roaded down the Manor Lane to the first covert. No sooner had the field cleared the woods and headed to the open wheat fields

Huntsman Albert Crosson (left) of the Pickering (Pa.) Hunt and his brother Oscar Crosson, right, the huntsman for the Vicmead (Del.) Hunt with their combined packs at a joint meet.

behind the mansion. The hounds made a very brief check and recovered the line with a beautiful cast. The field then galloped down the slippery cart path only to find that the hounds had already passed the pasture, Manor Lane and adjacent cornfield and were running hard in the far woods. When staff and field finally broke from the heavy thickets, they then discovered that the pack had split in two directions. A third fox (grey) was then viewed, but ignored. The huntsmen quickly calculated which pack had the strongest line and harked the other group on to open fields. MFH Hazel Welsh and whipper-in Roger Scullion both viewed the fox crossing back over the Manor Lane and it treated the hill toppers to an exciting view. Away we went again to the wooded country and icy paths. At the next check the field had a chance to give their horses a breather and watch some brilliant hound work. Two foxes again broke from this cover and whipper-in Nancy Darling harked the second pack to the gone-away call of the huntsmen. As the packs became one, Doughoregan Manor was alive with the sweetest music on earth- fox hounds at full cry. The field moved off quickly, galloping on to the Chimney's when they were met by the staff. They were abruptly ordered to do a reverse. Reverses Oh- yes- galloping on to Carroll Mill Road- hounds just-a-flying. They appeared to be headed to Homewood Road- they did. The next big coup we encountered ended tragically for ex-MFH Oliver Goldsmith. His beloved hunter "Jake" died in mid-air and the unconscious and delirious Oliver Goldsmith was then waiting for the ambulance. After crossing Homewood Road they went on to Benedict, Sally Watson's bottom. By this time the 80 riders were spread out from the Manor to Homewood, everyone, everywhere proclaiming, "I've never seen two packs work so well together." As we waited for hounds to work the line, Renard once more, but moving a little slower, came into view of the field going across the Knolls back to the alfalfa fields again and into the woods right by Homewood Road. Again, but with only a handful of hunters left, the hounds ran into Watson's bottom and crossed Route 108 onto Colombia Golf Course. A turn about brought them back across Route 108, Watson and on to Benedicts. Hounds were lifted at 4:15 p.m., while at a check. It was a long hack back to the vans. The field was treated to a hunt breakfast back at the Howard County Club House. After a five hour hunt we at Howard County are sure of one thing, Pickering will return."

"It is difficult to bring this biography of Albert Crosson to an end. Albert was spared a lingering death for he was stricken with a fatal heart attack while following his glorious pack of Penn-Marydels."

Huntsman Albert Crosson

WHIPPING-IN FOR ALBERT CROSSON
by Nancy Darling Fellenser, May 1998

Back in the late 60s, I graduated from college and was asked to join a large, local computer company. I felt quite smug toward all of my jobless, commune dwelling hippie friends.

However less than a year later, one of the projects was cancelled and I found myself among the ranks of my unemployed hippie friends.

Someone told be that Pickering Hunt Club was looking for someone to exercise their staff horses. I figured that would tie me over until the computer company realized their mistake in letting me go and call me back.

So I accepted the job.

I had barely been there two weeks when Albert Crosson, Pickering's huntsman, walked up one morning and handed me a whip, a .22 pistol and a hunting horn.

None of which I had a clue as to how to use.

It seemed my job description had expanded to include whipper-in.

And I hadn't a clue a to what a whipper-in was. Nor had I any idea what happened to the previous one.

Only a few weeks into this new job, on a cold a blustery day, the hounds found well northwest of Phoenixville and ran toward Valley Forge Park. Now it certainly wasn't unusual in those days for a fox to run from one end of the country to the other. Nor was it unusual for hounds to be PERMITTED to pursue a fox for such a distance UNIMPENDED. What WAS unusual was for a computer geek, just recently appointed whipper-in to happen to be in the right spot at the right time.

And so it was.

At 4:30 on a winter's afternoon, I found myself all by myself at the farthest corner of Valley Forge Park with 30 hounds. Either they had lost the fox or it went to ground because at that point they were going off in thirty different directions.

And I hadn't practiced blowing one note on the hunting horn.

I was desperate! Where was old Smokey with the hound truck?

It was getting dark. So I pulled out the horn and attempted to blow. It had to have sounded like a cow choking on its cud. No hound was going to listen to that!

However I KNEW A NAME. I knew the name of one of those thirty hounds.

So in total and complete frustration without a hound in sight, I blurted whatever I could get out of the born, called the only name I knew and headed home.

Every hound followed me 4 miles in the dark, all the way back to the kennels...

In the years that followed, I learned so much from Albert about foxhunting and foxhounds.

Hounds not dogs.

Tonguing. Not barking.

It's not speckled. It's a blue tick.

If I had to use birdshot on a hound rioting on deer, I dared not miss! Albert expected to see blood.

His job was to call hounds. Mine was to drive them. He didn't allow me to forget that.

Nor was I ever to get between him and his hounds.

I learned the names, personalities and voices of every hound.

I could be in the right place at the right time through experience and not just luck.

And I learned how to blow the horn.

I especially enjoyed working with Albert's very fine pack of Penn-Marydels foxhounds. They were friendly, eager to please, relatively easy to discipline, worked so well together as a pack and their voices could be heard all over Chester County.

Seven years later, the computer company called to see if I'd like my job back.

It was the same year that Albert Crosson died.

It has now been 28 years since that day in Valley Forge Park and I still remember the name of the only hound I knew at the time. CRAFTY. And her blood still flows in some of the finest Penn-Marydels today.

In Memory of Albert Crosson
Written by Nancy Fellenser 11-30-76
Submitted by Gladys Crosson

His hounds were running in full cry.
His horse was standing by his side,
        the moment Albert Crossan died.
The fox had safely found his hole
When doors of death freed his soul.
And stunned riders upon the knoll,
Cried...

A finer huntsman we never knew.
His hunting wisdom upon us grew
And now we only question'
Why?

And pray to God that he may be granted immortality,
Forever present where we may see and listen...

Hark to the heavens!
Lend a sharp ear!
Isn't it Albert's horn you hear?
And deep within the Valley below,
Echo of hounds,
A cry,
Tally – Ho!

GEORGE BRICE OF THE ESSEX FOX HOUNDS
by H. L. Todd Addis

Every once in a while the out of doors duties and animal needs seem to be satisfied and the urge to record a little history seems to reach a level of being a pleasure and not a chore.

So, what in the world is a little history of Essex Fox Hounds doing in the Friends of the Penn-Marydel Newsletter? J. Blan van Urk in his Volume II of the *Story of American Foxhunting*, skillfully devoted 26 pages of history, starting by detailing the beginning of the Essex Fox Hounds with the Montclair Equestrian Club. This led to the Montclair Hunt, 1878, the Essex County Hunt 1880 and ending in name only in 1888.

One of the best known gentleman of its one hundred plus membership, was Charles O. Pfizer, Esq. To quote a paragraph from van Urk's chapter on Essex Fox Hounds, "Before the Essex County Hunt ceased to exist as such, Mr. Stewart (Master) has time to take the Essex hounds to Southampton, Long Island, for some early season sport in September, 1890. Later in the same year Mr. Charles Pfizer became owner of the hounds immediately dropped the word County from the title, calling the (by this time private) pack the Essex Hunt."

The reason for the change in name, was the removal of hunting operations by Mr. Pfizer from Essex County to Morris and Somerset counties.

From the preceding pages I gather the 1878 New Jersey hunters started with a small pack of beagles. During the season of 1879 fox hounds were bought from the Queens County Hunt. "Interest was not only kept up, but increased by supplementing 'drag' for genuine fox hunting."

Reading between the lines, I have to believe that drag hunting was very much part of the scene since 1881 spring season and a 5th season fixture cards practically all Saturday

MFH Todd Addis and Ex MFH David Kendall holding a 1923 print painted by artist Alf Haigh and signed by artist. The Essex Fox Hounds showing George Brice on Boteas and Master A. F. Hyde with Penn-Marydel pack. Kendall purchased print at Wilbur Hubbard's dispersal sale at Sotherbys in NYC and kindly gave it to Dr. Addis, Dec. 2009.

George Brice, Amateur Huntsman, of the Essex Fox Hounds, going to covert.

and Wednesday meets began at 3:30 or 4:30 P.M. An off day November Tuesday was at 7:30 A.M. Hackensack and a Christmas Hunt was listed at 11:30 A.M. Bloomfield.

Reporting in two sporting magazines, "Mr. Munn of the (Scientific American) has purchased from Mr. Allen of Montréal, the Ardgouran fox hounds, a pack comprising of thirteen and a half couple, over half of which were imported from England." We can assume from this history that the make up of the Essex County hounds that Mr. Pfizer acquired were predominantly made up of English hounds. Also, that many of the good runs that were recorded were from drop hunts. It was reported in a November 1881 run as follows, "The Essex County Hounds had a very fine run yesterday, Nov. and killed twice, the first fox being a wild one, whose line the hounds struck while running through a cover, the second a "bag-man" who, however, gave the pack a good burst of three miles before they "broke him up." (Ten to one both were dropped- Just my opinion- T.A.)

There is no disclosure in van Urk's research what the circumstances were that led to Mr. Pfizer's purchase of the Essex County Hounds. The pack was kenneled at Pfizer Estate at Bernardsville and then moved to Gladstone in 1896.

Continuing in 1896 and probably through Charles Pfizer's Mastership continued to 1913. We all know and are indebted to his pharmaceutical company. The men recognize the great worth of the antibiotic Penicillin and the women recognized the great worth of the drug Viagra. There are many others that have contributed to our health, but none have done so much to preserve a marriage. The hunt was then incorporated as the Essex Fox Hounds in 1913.

Prior to 1913 some followers of the 'drag', notably Masters William Larned and Arthur Fowler, had made annual excursions to Chestertown on the Eastern Shore of Maryland to hunt foxes with the privately owned pack maintained by Mr. George Brice. They were so enthusiastic that in 1913, upon founding the Essex Fox Hounds and assumption of the Mastership by Masters Barney Schley and William A. Larned, the first move was to persuade Mr. Brice with his family and hounds to migrate to New Jersey. I continue to quote from James S. Jones *Early Days*:

"Mr. Brice with his family and hounds migrated to New Jersey. They moved into the house at Larger Cross Roads. Besides George and Belle Brice, the entourage comprised their three daughters, the blue tick hounds, a team of mules, various horses, carriages, chickens, both fighting and domestic, and a flock of ducks."

Mr. Brice began to show good sport at once, but after the first year Masters, Schley, and Larned resigned in favor of A. Fillmore Hyde of Morriston, who took over for the 1913-14 season and carried on in great style for the next 15 years.

Early Days, author Jones, described a picture painted by Alfred Haig, hanging in the club house. "When on the road Percy Picton, K. H. (kennel huntsman) and first whipper-in came first on Doughboy. He was followed by Geroge Brice, smoking a good cigar and surrounded by some thirty couples of the blue ticked hounds."

To return to van Urk Volume II, he says, "The newly named organization- Essex Fox Hounds- hadn't been in existence very long when the fox hunting gentleman from Maryland, George Brice, Esq. galloped his own pack of thirty-eight couple of American hounds to, through and over the Essex Country. Essex' first season behind the Brice hounds was such a revelation to everyone, that the club soon arranged 1914 to purchase the Brice hounds, with the understanding that their former Master should remain in the club as a gentleman huntsman. And long will the Brice name live in the memories and accounts of fine Essex hunting."

Leaping over a post and rail fence with her mount is Virginia Brice, daughter of one of Kent's most popular people, George Brice. Miss Brice hunted with clubs in New Jersey, was an instructor in horseback riding; and took part in horse shows all over the East. We believe she appeared in shows at New York's Madison square Garden. Reprinted from the History of Kent County.

Mr. Joseph Thomas, Ex-MFH, in appraising American Huntsman said about this man:

"A huntsman who has given much pleasure to more than one generation of enthusiasts is George Brice, who has hunted the Essex Fox Hounds of New Jersey for a score of years. Descended from a long line of fox hunters from the Eastern Shore of Maryland, Brice thoroughly believes in Eastern Shore hounds and in the style which rarely permits hounds to be lifted, whatever the provocation."

Joe Thomas goes on to state Brice was one of three great huntsmen in the U.S. The others being Jack Smith of the Brandywine and Charlie Carver of Virginia. *Polo Magazine*, December 1934.

Further testimony was revealed in A. Henry Higginson and Julian Ingersoll Chamberlain's book, Hunting In the United States and Canada (1928). "Neither of the authors has hunted with the Essex Fox Hounds, but from what we can learn, this pack, which now numbers something over forty couples, has no equal for cold trailing and persisting in sticking to a fox, once found, until he is either put to ground or killed." "These hounds, which had been bred by Mr. Brice's family for many generations, differ in several respects from the ordinary type of American hound used in Maryland and Virginia. In color they are mostly "blue tick"; good looking, big boned, sturdy hounds, with very deep voices and excellent nose, but lacking somewhat in drive and speed."

With the help of Nancy Hannum of Unionville, PA, and John Ike of Millbrook, NY, some old timers of Essex Fox Hounds were called to gather more facts on George Brice. Mr. Oliver Tilly, Far Hills, NJ, Mrs. Screven Lorillard, Far Hills, Phillip Fanning, Unionville, Mrs. Lewis Murdock, Pea Pack, NJ and the most rewarding one was to Mr. Joe Wiley Jr., Bedminster.

We may assume his daughters were accomplished riders, one losing her life while showing. Virginia never married and stuck by her father's side until his death. Belle, his wife, died early on and George, being a tall, handsome man with a degree of polish, became more popular with the ladies, especially when their husbands had to return to New York for office duty.

George Brice was very popular with the membership and was included at many of the social gatherings. Mr. Jones goes on to say, "The period of George Brice with the blue ticks was a long and happy one for the Essex Fox Hounds. The many followers were violently enthusiastic in behalf of Mr. Hyde and his Maryland huntsman. My father carried in his wallet this little verse."

> The Belvoir Tan is gallant and bold
> On scent you can cut with a knife-breast high
> But to sing on the fallow when scent lies cold
> You must trust to the old blue pie.

Mr. Hyde gave up his Mastership in 1929 and Kenneth B. Schley, ESQ. accepted the Mastership. George Brice stayed on as huntsman for few years, says author Jimmy Jones. Mr. Schley, a real country squire was joined in 1934 by James Cox Brady, Jr. now owner of Gladstone. Jones continues to write, "during this period 1934, there was a big "push" to introduce Welsh hounds in this country. Watson Webb at Shelbourne and Harry Peters of Meadowbrook hounds were high on these rough coated hounds. A welsh imported hound, Ringwood, was presented at a raffle at the Master of Foxhound annual dinner- was won by MFH A. F. Hyde of Essex and hunted with Blue ticks for a year- "but not with much enthusiasm."

James Brady as Master purchased, as an experiment, the entire pack of Mr. Erastus Tefft's Welsh pack plus engaged the huntsman 'Gladwin' as well. After a short time Brady decided they wouldn't do and he "got rid of the lot." With George Brice in retirement.

Mr. Brady in 1935 gave up on the Eastern Shore Blue Ticks and hired Charlie Carver of Virginia. Aspiring to gain standings at the hound shows, it was decided to change to the show hounds of a Triff Virginia strain in 1935.

My copy of the *Foxhound Kennel Stud Book of America Volume VI, 1931-36*, list Bella Donna 1928 being sired by Mr. Harvey Brice's, Wringer out of his (Essex) Queen and Nita 1928 sired by Harvey Brice's Richmond out of his (Essex) Violin. 1929 Winder was sired by H. B.'s Wringer out of his Speedy. This was apparently the last trip south for stud services and 1933 is the last entry for the blue ticks in Volume VI.

George Brice's popularity and social standings apparently did not waver following retirement. Joe Wiley of Bedminster reveled that in 1946 he became George and Virginia Brice's neighbor. Belle Brice is now deceased. As the stories go, it seems that George would not leave the dinner parties very early.

I read the other day in a magazine that a man is not considered drunk if he can lay flat out and does not need to hold on to something.

Mr. Wiley said to the best of his knowledge that George Brice was always a gentleman at these parties and left with complete control, however sometimes his Ford convertible, that he was fond of, had trouble staying on those slippery roads. Joe said one morning while leaving his house early he came upon this red convertible that slipped into the ditch—George was in full formal attire and sound asleep. On another occasion while winding his way down this long lane from the Boise Mansion, George did not navigate the last sharp turn. Many rows of tombstones bordered the lane. George and his little convertible had a peaceful and thoroughly restful night mired among the graves.

To analyze one's personality and stature without ever having met them, is not always easy, but from the following story told by Joe Wiley he must have been charismatic.

While a student at Washington College in Chestertown, MD George rode to classes on horseback. Several days a week he would take his hounds to class with him and kennel them in the adjacent box stall. Of course, he would hunt them on the way home. One day he was met at the entrance by the President, Charles Wesley Reid "Dutch", (who was president of Washington College in 1889 to 1903). He said to George "This is a bad day for classes and a good day for fox hunting" so he promptly cancelled the classes and accompanied George and his hounds on the hunt.

Usilton's History of Kent Country 1980, shows a 1891 picture of Washington College's football team. George, the tall one, was standing on the right side of the squad and the caption singled George and a teammate as 'outstanding players'.

I thought this 1891 football team picture would certainly narrow his date of birth, however another humorous tale by neighbor Joe Wiley could add two more years to his age.

After graduating he would return to college in the fall to help with the coaching of the 1893 football team. The team severely lacked some big boys on the line so the head coach coaxed alumni Brice to suit up. So much for rules. So, when George positioned himself at the line during a serious rivalry he raised his head and looked his opponent squarely in his eyes. To his amazement there too kneeled another graduate playing for the opposing College team.

Joe Wiley said George loved his ducks; he kept a flock through out and would never consider locking the foxes out from their nightly feast.

One can only imagine the emotions that George Brice experienced when Mr. Brady sold his pack to the Spring Valley Hounds. Author James Jones Early Days, became the huntsman of these popular blue ticks at Spring Valley, banished to be a drag pack. I end with Jones' statement:

"When I was able to swing the hounds onto the line we were "gone away" behind the pack which threw back the tremendous cry for which it was famous."

I was curious what Masters William Larned and Arthur Fowler had experienced when they visited Chestertown, Maryland to hunt with George Brice prior to 1913.

So, with my wife, Happy and friends, the Traphagens, we set sail on August 13th to visit the Kent County Historical Society. The Society's house was a beautifully restored house filled with period antiques. We then walked one block to a restaurant on the Chester River. We passed by Wilbur Hubbard's riverside home White Hall.

The new owner just spent three million on its renovations; they apparently gutted the entire structure and reinforced it with a steel skeleton.

A Fillmore ESQ., MFH 1914 with George Brice, ESQ., Huntsman

After satisfying our wives with several antique shop visits we set out to find George Brice's homestead. We just could not resist going by Arthur 'Hound dogs' Brown's home so we stopped for a chat. Remarkably, this 90 year old Kent County huntsman had a perfect mind, but like an old horse his joints were unforgiving. We asked him where Brice's Mill Road was and the old homestead. He said "turn left at the driveway, go half a mile and it's on the right." It was there just as pictured. George's father John purchased the 160 acres property in 1882. The farm was passed down to George's brother Joseph in 1900 and remained his until his death in the 1930's. We don't know where George and Belle lived and kenneled his hounds during his first two decades of building a family.

Perhaps, the Kent County mounted hunters enjoyed the blue-ticks of Mr. George Brice's Kent County hounds and then followed the great sport of Mr. Hubbard's Kent County Hounds.

LETTER TO THE EDITOR
AUGUST 29, 2003
by Jos. B. Wiley, Jr.

Dear Dr. Addis:

Thank you for sharing with me your write up about George Brice. He was a most colorful man and you are great to have undertaken the task of putting on paper some of the interesting aspects of his long career.

By the time these lines reach you, I will have been in touch with you concerning your visit to the EFH club on Sunday August 17.

As you may know, the late Jimmy Jones, the moving spirit of the Tewksbury Foot Bassets from its organization in 1953, until his death a couple years ago, had a knack for the written word, and a tremendous interest in country activities, most particularly hunting.

This interest was obviously inherited from his father, Frederick Jones, who had grown up in the Millbrook, New York countryside; later moved to New York City in connection with business and then came within the orbit of Mr. Pfizer during the time when the Essex Hounds (or Essex Fox Hounds) were his private pack in this countryside.

I mention this only by way of preface to the following: Jimmy Jones' story was that the move out of Essex County took place because that area around Montclair, in Essex County New Jersey, continued to be built up to the point where hunting became impossible there. Jimmy's story was that those who took part with the Essex Hounds (in Essex County) finally, and reluctantly, came to the conclusion that they had to give the whole thing up; and it was at that point that Mr. Pfizer stepped in, bought the whole kit and caboodle, and moved it out here to Somerset County.

But back to George Brice. Now for a couple of very minor thoughts. Referring to the last paragraph on your page 7, and specifically to the third line from the bottom, "a degree of polish". I would say that it was significantly more than a "degree". He was a charmer; very witty; sparkling eyes; a great sense of humor; a wonderful conversationalist, and his conversation with attractive ladies could not really be described as flattery (I am not suggesting that you use that word); he did not "flatter" the ladies in the sense of some sort of artificial conversation intended to arouse their interest. Rather, his interest in ladies was very natural, very compelling, and his admiration of attractive ladies was completely sincere. And, the ladies realized that.

The first paragraph on page 8, about George being "included at many of the social gatherings". Not having been at every one of the social gatherings by any means, I nevertheless had the strong impression that the word "many" doesn't quite do it. My impression was that he was on the top of the list for all social gatherings.

One little minor matter: Peapack (New Jersey) is one word.

Lastly, and really the only specific change that I can suggest has to do with George Brice's automobile. It was a Ford, rather well worn at the time I knew him, and it was what at that time was known as an "open car". The technical term for a four door automobile of that era, having no wind up windows, and without a permanent top, but rather a folding up or folding down top of canvas or other material, is a "phaeton", or "touring car".

The term convertible was only then coming into the language, and it designated an automobile having a soft (and collapsible) top, but having wind up windows, which fit in a more or less weather type manner to the folding top. There were two door convertibles, and four door convertibles. There were of course two door "open" cars (no wind up windows), and two doors, and one seat across for the driver and a passenger. This was referred to as a Roadster.

The equivalent automobile with four doors (but again no windows and no permanent top) was a "touring car" or "phaeton". George had the latter.

And perhaps more significantly, it was not red. It was some more subdued color, of sort of a muddy hue as I recall it.

I realize that I have gone on with a great many words about matters that are quite inconsequential. Probably none of those who will read your account would be aware of the color of George's automobile; nor would they care.

George was a happy man, even though life dealt him some very difficult times, particularly in a financial way, as well as in his loss of wife and daughter. But, I cannot ever remember seeing George with a frown, or with anything unhappy or unpleasant to say.

He seemed unable to see anything but the bright side of life, and he enjoyed it to the full and relished all of those good things which came his way.

I hope that this may be of some little value to you.

Sincerely,
Jos. B Wiley, Jr. Joint Master of the Tewksbury Foot Bassets

ORVILLE ROBERTS—A SHORT BIOGRAPHY
by H. L. Todd Addis, MFH

From the inception of the Friends of the Penn-Marydel Newsletter, an old friend of my father's kept coming to mind. My only recollection of him was when he visited us on a Sunday morning to pick up offal for his private pack of hounds.

My urge to write a short biography of Orville Ellis Roberts finally came to fruition when a friend gave me a pamphlet on the History of Pickering Hunt 1911-1986. The Pamphlet was written by C. Barton Higham, who was a trustworthy insurance advisor, Master of Beagles and an enthusiastic foxhunter.

Barton mentioned in his pamphlet that huntsman Roberts kept a diary for the 1920-21 hunting season. His gracious widow Betty said all historical documents were placed in a box and turned over to the senior Master of Pickering Hunt, Dr. Theurkauf. Apparently, Dr. Theurkauf's attic is like ours, and the box to this date has not been located.

Another lead developed last spring when out of the blue the only grandson of Orville stopped by, he chatted about old family ties. He also expounded on a long chronic Lyme disease illness that was only cured by the use of wrap around magnets.

The grandson, also named Orville, said that his Aunt Ada was still living in Phoenixville, Pennsylvania.

I finally located Ada, the youngest of Orville's children. Even though her storytelling was sparse, the 90 year old petite lady was a chip off the old block. Her frame was straight like her father's and she has the same striking blue eyes and facial contours. She gave me four pictures of her father a newspaper clipping of the history of the Pickering Hunt.

William Clothier started hunting with the Radnor Hounds in 1904 where he came in contact with the Roberts' boys, who had a small pack of hounds in the southern section of Radnors' Country.

Orville Roberts, Huntsman for Pickering Hunt Club, and Master W. J. Clothier with hounds, 1935.

The Roberts' family farm was near Garrettford, in southern Delaware County. They were a big part of the farmer pack scene in Radnor's Hunt country.

Clothier, with Radnor's permission, financed their pack, hunting with them and finally invited the Roberts, with hounds, to integrate with the fledgling Pickering pack in 1910.

Mr. Clothier coaxed Orville to give up the dairy farm and bring his hounds and younger brothers, Pearce and Harold with him as whipper-ins.

Orville, with wife Katherine and children May, Bertha, Ellis (Bud) and Ada, bravely moved North and became a great hound and horse fixture for Pickering Hunt for 29 years. Ada was 2 years old. Brothers Pearce and Harold never married, their lives were shortened by illness.

My father and Orville would frequently swap hounds. No doubt, Orville would pick quality youngsters, while Dad would take in return the slowing down group. In an old vaccination book, of my father's, the following entry appears. Goofer, Girt, Gainer and Glory born November 1930- traded to Pickering, May 1933.

Another entry shows hounds Kay, Music, Maggie, Note, Lane, Leader, Luke, Montpelier, Master and Fury loaned to Pickering for one year, March 1933 - March 1934.

This is a 1923 photograph of Pickering Hunt Club Huntsman Orville Roberts with one of his legendary Penn-Marydel foxhounds on a lead. The identity of the other people in the photograph is unknown. The event at which they are attending is also unknown. Many thanks to Ada Roberts for providing all the photographs of her father Orville Roberts.

A few memorable days of hunting were recorded and appeared in the September 1996, vol. 20 no. 1 issue of the, The Historical Society of the Phoenixville Area, written by Miriam Clegg.

The Master of Pickering Hunt Club, William Clothier, describes a January 12, 1912, wintry Saturday Hunt.

The field on that January day included Redmond C. Stewart, MFH of Green Spring Valley Hounds, W. Plunket Stewart; later to found his Cheshire Hounds, Delaney K. Jay of New York, J. Hunter Lucas and Charles R. Snowden, both of Radnor Hunt.

They rode to a location seven miles north of the kennels and jumped a fox at 12 noon. The fox was put to ground after a 12 mile point in the Welsh Hills, just east of the Lancaster County line. They returned at a leisurely pace hacking 20 miles back to the club, well after dark.

Another account taken from Robert's diary December 12, 1921. Large field left kennel at 2 PM. Drew Phoenix Hill. Jumped fox in little woods near Benner's hill. Fast run over Geigers, Johns, O'Connells, Hallmans, Bibles, McCurdies, up to Calverts, crossed Conestoga Pike. Out upper end of Valley Hill, overlooking the Church Farm School, on up to Upper Forge Hill, turned to right- past Lionville- down ridge to Pikeland Churches, over to Phoenix Hill, pulled out after 5 hours. Hounds ran all night. Comment from the writer of this article "I have followed hounds in some of these hills and let me tell you- this is one hell of a hunt!"

A comment from myself- Let me tell you that many of these hounds had a weak back, were back at the knees, chicken footed, had too much leather in the throat and hocks too close to the ground. Probably every one of the hounds came home with their tails flopping off their hocks. Still, with all these faults, they were unbeatable.

Roberts recounted the following: four days after the previously described hunt, on Wednesday December 14th, a small field left kennel at 7 am. Drew Rhoads field, Phoenix Hill, jumped fox in Geigers and viewed fast run over Johns, O'Connells, viewing again. Past Pikeland Churches, over Bibles, Dunmores, Shuperts to McCurdies, up and out upper end of Valley Hill. Up to Forge Hill and viewed. On up past Hopewell Church. Hounds got away after 5 hours. Clear and Cold.

Remember, rural eastern Pennsylvania had few deer, few paved roads, very few cars. With a good pack of hounds, Orville Roberts had nothing between himself and heaven.

It is not clear whether my father helped Orville establish his own private pack after his retirement in 1939, after 29 years of service.

I do remember visiting his farm, just west of Phoenixville, PA. His stables and kennel were in a modest old red bank barn, they always looked immaculate. His dedicated helper and whipper-in was his second daughter Bertha.

Dad would send him our three year old horses. Although they were just halter broken the week before their training, Orville never called and said we'll need another month to work on them. They were always well broken after one month's training.

Both Orville and Bertha took immense pride in their work. This explains why he was such a success in training several Maryland Hunt cup winners. You can see by the pictures that he also took home some trophies from the Devon Horse Show.

Yes, hounds today and for centuries ate animal carcasses and the innards of the butchered stocks. I was young and strong, so I got the honor of forking these morsels to feed his hounds.

Before I was born, my brother Clarkson can remember Orville sending over a skinned out horse with their whip Ed Mooney for a $2 charge. In those days the financial reward was the sale of the hide.

I know, if this man was born in the 12th century he would have easily fitted into a suit of Armor, and most likely been Knighted by King Charles.

Speaking of Kings, our friend Billy King, MFH and huntsman for the Bedford Hunt in VA, said his mother and father thought so much of Orville, that they named his

Orville Roberts jumping, when and on what horse, is unknown.

brother Orville after Roberts. They named him Orville Ellis Roberts King. The senior Kings recognized something special in this man to give their son the full title.

The best I could do was being named after a dog hound, Todd, bought in February 1925. Todd, Brush, Stag, Reynard, Vixen- The best five hounds I have ever seen run together; One was as true as the other- My Dad's book entry in 1927.

Daughter Ada says "We were very private and reserved, none of us girls married. We all rode as kids, but when we moved to the club none of us were allowed to hunt, because this was an adult "gentleman's sport". Only Bertha stayed on line with horses and hounds and continued hunting her father's pack of hounds after his death in 1959.

Orville was a gifted storyteller. In his quiet manner he would assume the posture of the horse or hound he was describing. He made the exact move it took, sending me into spasms of laughter.

Character, honesty, faithfulness, and dedication to his job, coupled with the polished art of hunting hounds for 50 plus years, puts him, Orville Ellis Roberts, in my Hunting Hall of Fame.

ORVILLE ROBERTS TO BE INDUCTED IN THE HUNTSMAN ROOM

On the front page of our November 1999, Friends of the Penn-Marydel Newsletter, the subscribers enjoyed pictures and a biography of huntsman Orville Roberts. In the picture, William Clothier, Master of Pickering Hunt, stood by his side.

We Penn-Marydel hound enthusiasts had also read the story of Albert Crosson, huntsman for Rose Tree, Huntingdon Valley, Whitelands and ended his career with Pickering Hunt.

His daughter Marion and son-in-law MFH, Roger Scullion picked up the reins and presented Albert in nomination to be inducted into the Huntsman's Room.

For a decade and one half I was privileged to ride with Albert and spent many a Sunday hunting with him on foot.

Knowing Albert should not stand alone in representing the Penn-Marydels hound community. I submitted the articles of both Orville Roberts of Pickering Hunt 1911-1939 and Walter Hill of Eagle Farms Hunt 1929-1960 to the chairman of the Huntsman's Room Committee.

To quote a few sentences from my letter to chairman Sherman Haight- Both of these men were the George Washingtons of these prestigious Hunts- I wish to emphasize that both of these men were products of foxhunting families and were hunting their own private packs before being engaged by Pickering's William Clothier and Eagle Farms Hunt Joseph N. Ewing Esq." They took their home grown hounds with them.

To quote further- "As the Vatican sends a team out to investigate the beautification of a nun that performed miracles, may I respectfully suggest that your committee consider the possibility of placing these gentleman in nomination for the Huntsman's Room."

The first letter to stir excitement from chairman Haight stated in part. "Your research of the hunting experiences of Orville Roberts and Walter Hill is impressive. Both nominations will be brought before the committee for the Huntsman's Room at Morven Park well before the biennial selections of inductees in 2003."

The inductees of either one could not be realized on my say so- so a campaign was started by friends and family of these huntsman to give testimony of their character, dedication, trustworthiness and ability.

Only ex-MFH, Mrs. Harry I. Nicholas had hunted with Orville as a young lady. The rest of us knew him in our early years. I warned the family and friends that gave testimony not to be discouraged, if their Man was not inducted to the Huntsman's Room on the first try.

At the end of the day on last July 4th, I was watching C-span. The interviewer was interviewing William Martin, the author of historical novel titled Citizen Washington. The one statement that impressed me the most was, "After conducting so much research and getting so deeply involved in his life and thoughts, I became obsessed with his historical contribution." I must confess, working on Hill and Roberts lives has had the same effect on me.

So, when the letter from committee chairman Sherman Haight came declaring the induction of Orville Ellis Roberts to the 'Room' we were all thrilled.

REDMOND C. STEWART
by H. L. Todd Addis, MFH

Looking back over one's life there are certain events, associations, or activities that brought great joy. Some of these 'joys' were of short duration and some lasted for nearly a lifetime.

One of those joys has been meeting talented houndsman and reminiscing with them about great days with hounds. To go one better, I had the good fortune to join packs and see what sport these hounds could produce.

It's funny, but I can never remember being disappointed. Either standing on my feet or seated in the saddle, my association with some of these individuals come to mind. Albert Crosson, Orville Roberts, both huntsman room inductees, Jim Atkins, Billy Dodson, Ralph Ford, Guy Mercer, Billy King, Arthur Brown, Jake Carle, Bill Evans, and Bob Jeffries.

Recently, I was re-reading some of Stanley Reeves' and Charles Mather's diaries that qualify as antiques. Many of their sport entries mentioned joining a farmer pack. Sadly, the stories behind these packs lacking social standing, no doubt, would provide a story of great houndsman and great hunting. We know by the record that some of these farmer packs were recognized for sport and the wholesome families and individuals that were the heart and sweat that made them go.

Just to name two, first being Orville Roberts, of Delaware County, Pennsylvania. Orville and his two brothers, who William Clothier convinced to leave the farm, bring

Redmond, Landslide, and the hounds at Cliffeholme.

their hounds and start the engines for Pickering Hunt. Second being George Brice of Maryland's Eastern Short fame was coaxed to bring family, blue ticks, chickens and ducks to New Jersey and kick off a most successful 20 years for Essex Fox Hounds.

Another unfamiliar name in the hunting circles was John Bowen. The only entry anywhere in this world about this foxhunter was in Gordon Grand's biography of Redmond C. Stewart, Fox Hunter and Gentleman of Maryland (1938).

Mr. Grand quotes a story told by Redmond Stewart, "I often went night-hunting when a small boy (with John Bowen), and well remember when I was eight or nine years old getting back home between three and four o'clock in the morning on my little pony. I had to pass a graveyard and had just become calm when opposite the blacksmith's home, a Mr. Buckmans, a big dog jumped over the wall. The pony "Cliffton" and Redmond flew down the road.

We don't know very much about John Bowen. We are told, however, that he had white hair and whiskers and exceedingly blue eyes; that he rode out day after day foxhunting on his sorrel mare "Sally", and knew the whereabouts of every fox within hunting range; that he enjoyed dancing a reel known as "Down the Middle and up Again".

"My Master, John Bowen." It is the very truth that this old foxhunter exercised a deep influence on Redmond Stewart. Redmond refers to him through life:

For the C. Morton Stewarts to allow their 8 year old son to ride over to Mr. Bowen's for an evening hunt, one must know that Bowen reserved a big place in his heart for young Redmond and was want to say that he had taught him all he knew about foxhunting.

Bowen, lacking wealth, social standing and probably education, was never referred to by author Gordon Grand as being a 'gentleman' – It is clear that child Redmond loved to attend the foxhunters "Head Start" program that the white haired 'professor' Bowen provided.

"Redmond Stewart, the oldest of 14 children, was 'born to position and opportunity', and all his life he was surrounded by far more material security than is given the multitudes of men."

"Redmond was hardly past 10 when he began to assemble a hound or two. By the time he was fifteen he had been hunting a small pack of five couple for some years. No doubt Mr. Bowen's American hounds were the foundation pack for Redmond. When his hounds became so numerous that they tried the patience of the family domestic staff, an indulgent and ever sympathetic father supplied a kennel boy, George Holloway, in order that some semblance of peace and order be preserved at Cliffholme, the family home."

"When Ellinor, Plunket, and Redmond were about to set out on a hunting trip to Ireland, Redmond and his sister rode up to say goodbye to Mr. Bowen. They found him

My Master John Bowen

Redmond C. Stewart

sitting quietly on his porch. He expressed the hope that they would have good hunting in Ireland, then told Redmond, in a simple, matter of fact way that he would not be there when Redmond returned. True to his prophecy, he passed on that autumn."

I must confess that I started this article by writing about John Bowen and the good old boys that hunted with him. Before I finished with Bowen, I was engrossed by tales of the little boy who rode out to witness the great hound work of the John Bowen pack.

Henry Higginson and Julian Chamberlain Hunting in U.S. & Canada, report that a group of men met in the autumn of 1892 and founded the Green Spring Valley Hounds. Among the fourteen Baltimoreans, were of course, Redmond and brother Plunkett. Author Gordon Grand says Redmond was selected, (voted, coaxed, summoned, or appointed) as Green Spring Hound's first Master and amateur huntsman at the age of 18.

Redmond bought hounds from divergent sources. The famous Tom Firr of the Quorn pack in England writes:

I have sent the hounds off this morning by the first train. I feel certain they will give satisfaction. I shall be glad to hear the hounds go on.

Yours obediently,

Tom Firr

A letter from Hugh Davidson of Shelbyville, Tennessee:

I am glad to send you the July puppies. Trust they will keep up their reputation. I do know that the July Birdsong and Walker dogs are the best of all, everything considered.

Some years later Redmond wrote Harry Nicholas, Sr. (MFH of Meadowbrooke):

When I started keeping a few hounds and hunting, along about 1886, the hounds that I had were from a strain that John Bowen, an ancient foxhunter, had owned for many years, and which were said to be from the Old Maryland strain of hounds, dating back to Revolutionary times, however, I formed a close association with the Howard County foxhunters, John Hardy, living near Clarkesville, Napolean Bonaparte Welsh, a very old foxhunter, Dorsey Rogers, John Bentley of Poplar Springs. These men talked about the Brooke hound, a number of which strain were red hounds. They had beautiful notes, and had a reputation of being fox killers. It was said that along about 1850 a gentleman from Georgia procured one of these hounds and took it to Georgia where it became famous and was the progenitor of the July strain of American hounds. These hunters also said that these hounds were descendants by the male tail line from the original hounds that were brought over from Ireland by Bolton Jackson in the year I think, 1830.

The very first meet of our club," recorded in Redmond's diary, "was at Pikesville Station, Maryland (1892). In the little wooded hill on the Wilson Sanatorium a fox was found. At dark, hounds were called off."

Only after omitting the first year of the 25 years of Mastership, did Redmond keep a diary.

It was most gratifying to have a Stewart family member, Redmond C.S. Finney, to enthusiastically contribute to his grandfather's story. Without hesitation he went to his game room wall and dismantled several family pictures and sent me the three copies of Redmond and his Green Spring Valley American hounds. A number of hounds appear to be coupled and the stately Stewart home 'Cliffeholme' is in the background. Reddy Finney also introduced me to his great Aunts', Ellinor Stewart Heiser, 1940 book, 'Days Gone By', a wonderful historical account of growing up with her 13 siblings at 'Cliffeholme'.

Many diary entries show that Saturdays started early according to the season, but through the week most meets were scheduled in the afternoon at 2 PM to accommodate the businessmen working in Baltimore. Many entries read like this:

December 8th Pikesville, 2 PM George almost rides over a fox under a dead cedar and calls to me. Hounds are after him in a minute, making the woods roar. From this time, about 3 PM until quarter of six, we have a glorious run, seeing him several times. A quarter of six it is so dark we have hounds running and we go home. I hear afterwards that hounds put the fox in at about 7 o'clock in the middle of the valley.

Redmond Stewart and 'Philosopher'.

If there was going to be a Hunt diary, it was going to record the truth, so says Redmond.

October 14th Painter's Lane: The hounds are very wild and do not hunt well. They first run a black dog all the way to Chattolanee and run rabbits through the day with amazing readiness. The hounds work miserably and do not find.

Gordon writes, "Redmond Stewart loved the hills and vales of Maryland, and life's cards as they were dealt to him, took him continually into those green valleys and up over their pleasant, temperate slopes. For eight months of each year, during fair

On November 30th 2007, The Baltimore Sun reporter Gina Davis, featured an article on the historic Hampton Mansion. Redmond Stewart mounted on his favorite half bred hunter Tim Burr, and surrounded by his popular Green Spring Valley American Hounds, is pictured on the front lawn. Designated a national historic site in 1948, the $3 million renovation of the 217 year old mansion, at one time occupied 25,000 acres and was served by hundreds of slaves until they were freed in 1829. Seven generations of the Ridgely family, including a governor, occupied this majestic estate.

weather and foul, extremes of heat and cold, good footing or treacherous, often from rising of the sun to its going down, he hunted with country keenly, thoroughly and with high spirit.

And yet, during all these years he was constantly practicing before the bar, accepting his share of the care, incidental to rearing two sons and two daughters, Lattimer Small Stewart, Josephine Stewart Finney, Redmond C. Stewart, Jr. and Cassandra Steven Cassat. He gave unstintly of his time to civic and philanthropic causes, representing his district in the legislature, and playing a prominent part in the social life of Baltimore.

When on page 38 of Gordon Grand's book, I read the diary entry:

On February 17th, 1895 from Painter's Lane, the entire field consists of members of the C. Morton Stewart clan, Ellinor, Fanny, Lurman, Plunket and Redmond, a sporting family. It is snowing hard. We leave the hounds running on the snow at sunset. I am pleased with the pack, considering everything.

Redmond's father, a merchant importer and exporter, was apparently not shy at family matters. On page 39 author Grand states:

"The Stewart children were something to cope with. There were fourteen brothers and sisters, and it was a family custom for all of the children to make their appearance before retiring and bid parents and guests goodnight."

Redmond was a gifted horseman and brought out the most from his mounts. He rode 15 times in the Maryland Hunt Cup and placed first place once, second place five times, and third place four times.

To better prepare his book about Redmond, the author Gordon Grand lunches with Jervis Spencer, renowned Maryland Hunt Cup jockey, member of Green Spring Valley Hounds and cherished friend of Redmond.

Gordon writes, "I carried Jervis Spencer off to lunch – a lunch of lettuce salad and clear tea. When a man has ridden the Maryland Hunt Cup 20 times, won it 5 times and made himself one of the master horseman of his time, he can have a loss of words." Jervis Spencer never saw quite eye to eye with Redmond on all hunting matters. Spencer's emphasis was much the same as the majority of hunting people. He liked to ride and gallop on and believed, and with cause, that no amount of either patience or brilliant hound work would ever hold quite the same appeal for the average member of a field as a fast forty minutes.

Redmond's emphasis was on finding a fox, hunting it and accounting for it, irrespective of whether it took all day and part of the night or whether you stood still for half the day. People knew that his interest was in his hounds and loved him for it and did not complain.

No one in the world ever loved a long, hard, fast gallop more than Redmond, or was more pleased when his hounds flew on, but he didn't want this at the expense of not hunting his hounds as he thought they should be hunted. He was too well versed in the American hound to adapt British methods with them.

Redmond talked of the cry of hounds.

"If our coverts become smaller and the need of voice less important, we would not, through neglect or indifference, breed the voices out of our American hounds."

"He told me," Gordon writes, "That as long as 1860, a knowledgeable English observer had stated that 2/3 of all the hounds in England ran mute." Redmond attached great importance of voice and to remind me of how ancient this interest was, he quoted Zenophon as having vowed a part of the spoils of the chase to Apollo and put to Diana provided he should not lose his hound with the best note."

The Find

By Charles Kingsley

They're running – they're running. Go hark!
Let them run on and run till it's dark!
Well with them we are, and well with them we'll be,
While there's wind in our horses and daylight to see:
Then shog along homeward, chat over the fight.
And hear in our dreams he sweet music all night.
Off – they're running – they're running, Go hark!

American Past Masters

A. Henry Higginson, MFH; Feb. 28, 1941

Mention of the Green Spring Valley Hunt brings to me the memory of Bonsal's brother-in-law, Redmond C. Stewart, perhaps the greatest and best-loved master in the south. For twenty-two years Stewart ruled over the country, hunting hounds himself during that time, and though he was a busy lawyer, he always seemed to be able to find time to devote to the welfare of his country and his pack. Stewart was, I think, the best amateur huntsman that we ever had in America. That may seem to be saying a great deal but I have hunted with most of the amateurs in America and I am sure that none of them had the same control of hounds, the same knowledge of a fox's way that he had. He was a very keen student of hound breeding, and the hounds under his mastership were bred with the greatest care. Starting with typical Maryland hounds, bred in the country for many generations, he found that a certain infusion of English blood, obtained by using some of the Brandywine stallions, improved them in many ways. When the Patapsco Hunt was given up, in 1913, their hounds were acquired, and this brought another strong line of Maryland foxhound blood back into the pack. A very severe fall in 1914 made it impossible for him to continue the mastership, though he often hunted with the home pack, and also with the Harford, where his brother-in-law, Bonsal, ruled in after years. When I first hunted with the Green Spring Valley (in 1904), Stewart had his two amateur whippers-in, his younger brother W.P. Stewart, who is today president of the Masters of Hounds Association of America, and Frank Bonsal, of whom I have already spoken; so that it will be seen that Redmond Stewart shone, not only as a great master of hounds, but also as the teacher of two others whose names will always rank very high among the foxhunting men of America.

REDMOND STEWART

The critics of this book will no doubt question my placing Redmond Stewart as huntsman of a Penn-Marydel pack and not giving him full recognition of hunting a cross breed hound pack.

His beginnings as a boy and early hounds were unquestionably of the old Maryland hound—his great love and dedication to hunting was molded around this hound.

The second reason for entering him is that he made a great story.

GUY MERCER, 1911-2006
by H. L. Todd Addis, MFH

When you reach the age of 95, one would think most of your friends would have died before you. Not so with Guy Mercer, a Chester County Pennsylvania hound man and professional huntsman.

Guy was not known for his hard riding, but fox and hound sense kept him in the hunt.

His life began in 1911. He was raised as a farm boy and was surrounded with running hounds.

Besides his farming activities, he helped feed a young family by working the trowel at plastering, custom combining grains and feeding some livestock. In helping Devereaux Schools butcher house, Guy was able to cart home enough offal to feed his hounds.

The man who had a great influence and rapport with Guy and his friend Clarence Rice was Mr. Ewing's Eagle Farms Hunt's huntsman, Walter Hill.

The readers of 'Friends of the Penn-Marydel' may remember that Walter was featured several years ago. In fact, he was so well thought of that he was introduced to the Huntsman Room Committee, to be considered for induction at Morven Park, Leesburg, Virginia. He was turned down because he was not well known by his peers.

Guy had no trouble sounding his hunting horn since he played the saxophone, violin, banjo / mandolin every other Saturday night at the local Fire Hall square dances. His wife, Mary, was also a talented pianist, and often transposed popular songs to suit the instrument her husband wanted to play.

My experience in hunting with Guy was limited, but got its start when my father, sister and I were invited to hunt with Pickering Hunt. Guy was their professional huntsman between 1952 and 1959. Looking back, I believe Dad had some nice big New York reds in our chicken house and Guy needed to invite the one person who could provide a nice hunt. The big dog Fox gave us a 'big' hunt. MFH, Mrs. Josephine Betner, later became Mrs. Harry Nicolas was most gracious Master.

When Guy was engaged by Pickering Hunt as huntsman, he followed in the footsteps of long-time whipper-in and huntsman Ed Mooney, 1939-1952.

With the reintroduction of deer and its rapid population growth, huntsman Mooney lost control of his American hounds. When Guy took over, he hired George 'Reds' Albright as his whipper-in. Reds Albright, a paratrooper in the skies of Normandy in World War II, had his own five couple of Penn-Marydels in Northern Chester County. Reds had deer broken his own hounds by himself. The spread of bird-shot in the air was his 1st, 2nd, and 3rd whipper-in.

Guy took his own small deer broken hounds with him to help referee the Pickering pack.

It was not too many outings when the Pickering hounds made their break on the cloven hoofed whitetails, and slowly returned to the kennel by midnight. Huntsman Guy loaded them up in the hound truck and dumped them out. He returned home. The next day they were all back and were soon loaded up again and these exhausted, foot sore, deer running hounds went to their first lesson. Not one Pickering hound strayed off the path. There was a long line of tri-colors in back of the huntsman's horse. Guy's tried and true fresh hounds went on and started their fox. Any hound worth its weight in gold will hunt no matter how badly he hurts. These two men hunted those hounds from then on every day it was fit. Pickering hounds for over a half century have never bothered deer again.

Guy left Pickering Hunt in 1959 and was coaxed to hunt the Whitelands – Perkiomen pack from 1963-1966. Larry Miley, under Guy's tutelage whipped-in to him. Larry took over the huntsman duties until they disbanded in the early 1970's.

During Guy's budding days with his Eastern Shore bred hounds, he would team up with fellow farm boy Clarence Rice and motor south to hunt in Queen Anne County of the Eastern Shore of Maryland.

After a good day of hunting, they crammed their hounds in the extended rumble seat of his Old Chevy. They no sooner started back on their 2 ¼-hour trip when the lights went out. With a slight glimpse of a setting sun they limped over to the famous Joe Quimby's Centerville farm for help. Would you believe a substitute fuse was improvised by inserting a safety pin. They set out for home with Guy driving and Clarence Rice watching the red, hot pin glow in the dark.

Any old friend of Guy, whether on or off his horse will have a vision of his suspenders and his pipe.

When Guy was Pickering huntsman, he joined Albert Crosson's Whiteland's pack for an April 1st weekend fox chase at Mount Victoria, which is located in Charles County, Maryland. The place was the 900 acre Swan Point and its infamous ducking shack. The duck hunters left their bait-corn in the center of the floor, which became the attention getter of every bulging eye field mouse east of the Potomac. But somehow the hatching wasps drew more attention during the sleeping hours. Mornings were also attention getting. On one such morning when it came time to put his coat on and check his pipe pocket, Guy's hand emerged a hell of a lot faster than it entered the pocket; the hand was joined by one big, corn fed mouse.

Would you believe that the two hard running packs of Penn-Marydels during that April 1958-1959, seemed even to raise the tide in the Potomac River?

At Guy Mercer's funeral, I met a retired English School teacher who was kind enough to mail me a copy of the October 6, 2001 *Chester County Day Newspaper*. She had written a lengthy biography on Guy and I would like to quote a few sentences.

Guy Mercer in 1953, as huntsman for Pickering Hunt Club

Guy Mercer in the 1930's after a successful day rabbit hunting. This photo was Guy's favorite picture and was one of the few possessions that he took with him when he entered the nursing home.

"Using his resourcefulness and ingenuity, Guy also devised ways to make money by creating jobs for himself where none existed."

"Guy's natural talents were numerous and varied. In a literary way, we've all enjoyed his humor and adventures expressed via his story-telling ability. Few know that he was also an actor and participated in a group that performed in several local venues."

February 2007: "It was most appropriate that, as was always done at the end of a foxhunt, Master of the hunt, Dr. Todd Addis blew 'The Coming Home' bugle call as the finale of Guy Mercer's funeral. Guy was finally coming home."

LONGREEN FOXHOUNDS
BART MUELLER 1915-
by Susan Walker, MFH and H. L. Todd Addis, MFH
with excerpts from Longreen, 25 Years of Horse Sports in Tennessee

Why Bart? My newfound friend, Susan Walker, recently flew in from Germantown, Tennessee to witness the soggy 2004 Bryn Mawr Hound Show. She brought along a modest paperback book published in 1982 entitled: *Longreen, 25 Years of Horse Sports in West Tennessee.* It is not on loan, I hope! Just like Wilbur Hubbard's infamous Penn-Marydel huntsman was known as Hound Dog Brown, so too Western Tennessee has its 'Hound Dog' Mueller.

About a half dozen years ago, I got a call or letter (memory deficiency) from Bart Mueller wanting a Penn-Marydell bitch to breed to one of his dogs in order to freshen the lines in his pack. Reluctantly, I agreed and made arrangements to ship her out of Reading, Pennsylvania Airport. I called Mr. Mueller to alert him of her arrival time. No man kisses his hound goodbye, but I saw her carted off and whispered in her ear to do her job. Just by luck, I said to myself that I should wait around the terminal until she leaves the runway or until her parachute opens. In about 20 minutes, she is wheeled back and attendant said, "airline regulations will not let animals be shipped under 30 degrees". So home she came! Of course, Bart was disappointed with my call. The project was abandoned.

Bart Mueller and Whipper-In Pete Peters 1958.

The Longreen Master writes in the book, "My Maryland adventure and experience had by far the most influence on my knowledge and abilities as a horseman and huntsman."

Young Bart Mueller was exposed to farm horses, saddle horses, and polo ponies around the Minneapolis and Wayzata, Minnesota area growing up. He loved swimming, and won trophies for his style and speed in his youth. In the summer, along with swimming, he spent hours sailing. Wintertime found him mostly ice-skating and ice boating. His father, a landscape architect, moved to the Memphis, Tennessee area in the 30's. Due to this, one may read into Bart's early biography that he seemed to be a drifter; but his mind-set soon directed his attention to hounds.

He came to Germantown, Tennessee and writes "I got my first hounds in 1935. For the next four summers, I returned to Wayzata, taking some hounds with me, rode hunters and jumpers and had a dog pack until, when the Pine Tree Hunt was established at White Bear Lake, Minnesota. I was huntsman of this drag pack for two years."

During the winters, he built fences and barns at Wildwood Farms in Germantown, where his father was in charge of the landscaping and layout of the farm for W.L. Taylor and his wife Audrey. Wildwood was a world class American Saddlebred farm through the 60's. Needless to say, sometimes Bart and the workers broke off from the construction work early, so they could loose their hounds and enjoy the sport of foxhunting. Bart was hooked.

Mueller goes on to say that in 1939, he toured nearly all the hunts from Minnesota to the East coast looking for a hunting job. He lucked upon the Wythemore, just formed by some former Elkridge-Harford members after the Elkridge joined the Harford. "I had three wonderful years as their professional huntsman. We had only one blank in three years, and this in deep snow with it so cold we only drew one covert. There is no better hunting country in the whole United States. I had the best of it — I was in charge and could buy and raise hounds, had super horses, steeplechasers, and even a show ring champion."

What an area to learn about horses, hounds, and hunting. "The Billy Barton schooling course was in our hunt country. Billy Barton was Howard Bruce's horse — the first American horse to win the English Grand National. Ridgely Plantation, home of Mountain and Muse, the first foxhounds imported to America, was part of our country. I was learning the basics from an historic beginning!"

When not hunting, Mueller spend time working at the racetracks and schooling steeplechasers. He worked for Janon Fisher, trainer of Blockade, who was the first three-time winner of the Maryland Hunt Cup. "The Smithwick boys, Pat and Mike, were my first whips and became leading steeplechase riders. Hugh Wiley did his first foxhunting at the Wythemore as did Jean Bowman, the renowned artist."

One summer, Bart "worked for Charley White, who rode and trained steeplechasers. Substituting for Charley, I had a chance to saddle Stuart Janney's Winton, the all time greatest timber horse, for My Lady's Manor Timber Race, the Maryland Grand National, and finally, the Maryland Hunt Cup. He won all three."

In 1942, Bart served as a glider pilot in the Air Corp. Afterwards, he returned to the Memphis, TN area, took up a job as a crop duster and repaired planes. His love of flying gliders led him to the glider fields of Olive Branch, MS, just south of Germantown, TN, where is would spend hours soaring with the birds, always searching out the best thermal in which to gain altitude. He dated and married a young Germantown girl named Mary Ware, who's uncle was Nash Buckingham, a man known for his knowledge of fine hunting dogs, especially field trial bird dogs.

In 1945, Bart moved his family to Maryland for a graduate course in the sport of horses and hounds. Serving as a whipper-in for Elkridge-Harford under huntsman, Dallas Leath, with Ed Voss as the Master, Bart fine-tuned his skills in the traditions of Maryland style hunting.

After the '45-'46 season, Mr. Sidney Waters hired him to put together a pack of American Foxhounds for the Rolling Rock Club, to replace the English pack they had disbanded during the war. He toured southeastern Pennsylvania, Maryland, and northern Virginia, acquiring 15 couple, mostly Penn-Marydels.

"The best came from Arthur Webster, who sold us most of his famous pack at the then unheard of price of $100 each. They were great hounds, and many of their names are in the pedigrees of the present Longreen hounds, along with those of Ralph Ford's and Wilbur Hubbard's Eastern Shore pack."

Huntsman Mueller soon left Rolling Rock when they decided to hunt only drag. He returned to Germantown, TN, and with the help of W.N. (Sonny) Foster, Wib Magli, and Winston Cheairs, they founded the Oak Grove Hunt Club. Mueller says the pack was developed from both Tennessee and Maryland sources. The local Oak Grove Saddle Club of western and saddle horse riders, transformed into a traditional hunt and followed the hounds for about 10 years, at which time the members opted to get out from under the financial cost of a pack of hounds. Under the heading: "The Making of a Hunt", the author, describing a disbanding of the Oak Grove Hunt Club states: "This unusual situation was brought about by a power struggle within the membership of the existing Hunt Club which had resulted in a vote to give up hunting and to dispose of the pack."

Mr. Mueller took over the responsibilities and in 1957 established the Longreen Foxhounds with the help of youngsters who boarded their horses and ponies at his farm in Germantown, and who were part of the Longreen Pony Club. Bart and his wife Mary had established the Pony Club in 1954. M.F.H. Mueller goes on to say that while hunting the Maryland Wythemore pack, the hounds were kenneled at Longreen Farm, located in Hyde, Maryland, in the Long Green Valley. Hence the name of his farm and hunt.

Some recollections from the Master's Journal:

Nov. 23, 1957: A cold day following the first snow. The Cotton Plant fox was started in a cotton patch by the gum tree coop for the second time by Albus. A fast, loud chase for the first hour; they then cold trailed until they lost.

Dec. 7, 1957: Quick find in Cotton Plant bottom. Hounds crossed polo field, continuing to Wildwood Farm, on to McGammon's and back to Cotton Plant. Hounds made a second circle and then crossing creek at Kirby Bridge with water at flood stage. There was rain for the last 30 minutes, but we had about 3 hours and 15 minutes run.

Dec. 30, 1957: Holiday Hunt: Another super run, the kind we always hope for. Hounds found in Meadow Farms' bottom. Perfect hound work – wonderful cry. No over running, fast harking, close pack work by a tricky, twisting line, a run of one hour and forty-five minutes.

Nov. 19, 1959: Had a call from Mr. Collins, MFH of Radnor. He has arranged to buy and ship a stud dog from Rose Tree; also promises a bred bitch from Radnor in the spring.

The chronicle of the great runs continued in the book. Johann Bruhwiler writes: "While both red and grey foxes were plentiful as recently as 1975, the red foxes have not all but disappeared, and even the greys have become rare. One reason for this seems to be increased trapping activity; another is the appearance of coyotes.

Those of us who are huntsman or MFH-huntsman soon realize out lives are made immeasurably easier with a spouse that shares the work, joys, and frustrations of guiding a pack of hounds to produce top notch sport for a group of wonderful subscribers. Some subscribers, however, are always ready to create havoc. In addition, in her spare time, momma raises a family and leads the kids to the barn, pony club, the kennel, and finally to the hunt field.

My thoughts of the contributions my wife, Happy, has made to our family's involvement in hunting seem to parallel those of Mary Mueller, "The Mistress of the Hunt and Perennial Hostess".

Mary Mueller writes in the book: "The two older children were thirteen (Pinky) and ten (Allen), the third (Miles) only four and not yet riding. Both Pinky and Allen were avid Pony Clubbers and hunting was their sport. I hunted fairly regularly, too; but for me it grew to be almost too much. The Buckingham's Lodge meet was four miles away, and as we had no trailer, we hacked to the meet. Fine! Then we hunted for about four hours, then hacked home. At this point, all I wanted was a hot bath and a nap. What I got was: 'When do we eat?'"

Susan Walker, MFH Longgreen, Tennessee.

Longreen Master Bart Mueller hunting hounds, with Carlos Wilson Whipping-in, 1970.

"When you're dog tired, rubber kneed, and everyone else in the whole family gets to kick off their boots and sit by the fire while you stagger into the kitchen, the fun goes out. When I complained of the unfairness, they thought of a solution, they bought me a pressure cooker to speed up the meal. What a difference a microwave would have made back then."

Apparently, Mary Mueller's hunting days slackened and she frequently opened their home for hunt breakfasts with menus of spaghetti, a noodle and meat casserole which was dubbed "Longreen Pizza", huge cauldrons of stew or soup, and lots of hot chocolate.

One has a vision of Master and Huntsman Mueller finishing his stable and kennel chores, and then finding a rocking chair. Not so, he also provided his family with income from a landscaping business. As mentioned above, Bart recognized the value of the pony clubs while hunting in the east and imported it to West Tennessee in 1954. "He could not have dreamed how soon it could prove to be of vital importance, for just when foxhunting was at its lowest ebb, with the regular hunt members in disarray, a whole set of Pony Clubbers were passing their tests and becoming eligible to hunt."

Longreen Hunt, member of Nobel Prize fame, wrote a letter dated 3 May, '61 to Hunt Secretary, Mrs. Winslow Chapman. Two paragraphs were especially interesting:

"Thank you for the chance to subscribe and do my best to support foxhunting in our county: I would want to subscribe even if I didn't hunt.

I don't know what my status is, so I enclose the check in blank. Would be happy to subscribe the $75 even though I am not a member, if this is acceptable.

Yours Sincerely,
William Faulkner"

The huntsman's log had many entries in the 60's. Here are a couple:
Feb. 19, 1966: It is really the ultimate to gallop with this pack of tri-color, horn-

voiced Penn-Marydels driving a red fox on solid sod, well grazed pastures, and open ride-able woods.

March 23, 1966: During the Hunter Trial, I received word that 'Madam' was at the station waiting to be picked up. She is the brood bitch from Wilbur Hubbard, shipped in whelp to his Elmwood. She whelped in May and the six pups look mighty good.

In 1964 a pony clubber, Diane Taylor, invited the Master to survey the family's 3000 acre ranch for hunting. The Keith Taylor family and the Muellers had been friends a long time. It was a "foxhunter's dream". Mueller said, "The Twin Hill Ranch was our salvation." The original hunt country in Germantown was rapidly developing as people discovered the countryside and built suburbia. The ranch stayed a part of heaven from the 60's through the 90's. Diane became the 7th Joint Master in the 80's.

The romance of being a huntsman over took Mrs. Diane Taylor Newton, and she began to import hounds into a kennel of her own within the territory in the mid 90's. When some Longreen members made a fuss, she closed the ranch to the Hunt and pursued recognition for herself.

The last entry in the book is on May 30, 1982. "At the Preview Picnic of the Germantown Charity Horse Show, the Hunt gave me a lovely brass box engraved with:

Thank you Bart for twenty-five years of service and love of the hunt.'" It seemed the right place to honor Bart Mueller, since he was the landscaper who had seen this "bowl" in the center of Germantown and with tractor and grader and the help of others of vision, created today's setting for the Germantown Charity Horse Show arena back in the 50's.'

The book encompasses 25 years of Longreen history. 1957 through 1982. It did not end there. The half century huntsman, Master and horseman did not retire from the saddle until 1997. Today, Bart at age 89, is still West Tennessee's finest and helps to oversee the hounds in the kennel and continues to walk the puppies daily from age eight weeks to six months, a time that he firmly believes holds the key to their devotion to their huntsman, skill and bravery in the field, and firm bonding with the pack. His 90th birthday is January 13, 2005. In honor and respect for Bart Mueller and the Longreen hounds which he brought to West Tennessee in the 40's as the first organized traditional pack of foxhounds in the area, the Longreen membership, under the guidance of Mr. Mueller's son, Allen, will pursue new territories as civilization continues to creep eastward, in order that future foxhunters will be able to say: "I had a great day of sport behind those long-eared, long-legged, bugle-voiced hounds of Longreen!"

WHO WAS ARTHUR WEBSTER?

Phone conversation between Andy Ford and Todd Addis

Practically all editors are most pleased when they receive a 'Letter to the Editor' praising the story or publication. Being the father of the Editor, Beth Addis Opitz, will have to suffice in receiving praise for our article on Bart Mueller of Tennessee's Longreen Fox Hounds.

I could not record the phone call, so the best I can do is recall the phone conversation from Andy Ford and place it in the Longreen- Bart Mueller biography. Andy mentioned that Bart said in his biography that he purchased a pack of Penn-Marydels from an Arthur Webster for Rolling Rock Hunt in Western PA ('46-'47 season). Who was Arthur Webster? Well, back in the 20's, Andy Ford's father Ralph was leasing a farm in New Castle County, Delaware, near Jallyville. Jallyville's location is 4 miles north of present day Wilmington City limits and 4 miles due east of du Pont's Winterthur. Andy was in his beginning years in school with his father and mother building a dairy herd, developing a family and began entertaining themselves with 3 couple of fox hounds.

The story goes that the Arthur Webster pack drives a fox through the Ford farm and the next day sadly one hound goes mad with rabies, probably attacking unknown numbers in the kennel.

All the Webster hounds were destroyed and the fear spilled over to the Ford pack and they were destroyed also. For reasons not made clear one bitch was spared and farmed out to a relative, Herman Ford. After several years, she was returned to Ralph and soon was bred.

The Fords were on their way to a foundation pack.

Andy said he remembers Huntsman Bart contacting his father to get some hounds. "I was in school so did not meet him" Andy said. Some ten years later, Bart called for more hounds so "Daddy" built a wooden crate large enough to hold 4 dogs and took them to the rail station. The station master gave them a hard time in not having them in individual crates. "He finally gave in," Andy said.

The landlord or owner of the farm that Daddy was renting wanted to sell it to him, but he wanted too much money. He wanted $14,000. I said to Andy that it was overpriced back them; it should have been $5,000. Andy said, "Well, it had 240 acres." So Ralph and family bought the home farm at Kimbleville, PA.

Even though they rubbed elbows with Billy du Pont's 'caged' hunting territory, the Fords, Taylors, and Dougherty's actually managed to enjoy Pennsylvania's finest.

Ford's hounds produced great sport and attracted on a regular basis such notables as Ex MFH Jill Fanny of Essec Hounds and her mother Mrs. Miles Valentine. On one occasion in the middle 70's, the President of the MFHA Harry Nicholas, President elect

MFH Sherman Haight and MFH Wilbur Hubbard were treated to a "pretty good run", Andy said.

With the passing of his father, Ralph, and disposal of the dairy herd Andy changed addresses by buying a single farm on the Eastern Shore of MD.

When Andy moved to his new location in Maryland, he wisely added the ladies' touch to housekeeping – Nelda, the new Mrs. Andrew Ford has courageously taken on the task of listening to all those "huntin'" stories.

I said to Andy jokingly, "I guess you have a capital games problem."

"Yeah, I owe the government about $200,000."

"I think the rest of us owe the Fords a debt of gratitude for lowering President Bush's deficits and keeping the Penn-Marydel hound "true to the line". – T.A.

ONE HOUND CAN MAKE A DIFFERENCE
by H. L. Todd Addis

Those of us who have had the privilege of reading Charles E. Mather's diaries are well aware of his dedication to the English Hound. Mather, MFH 1890-1901, no doubt the godfather of Radnor Hunt and its American Hounds, secured a draft of 31 couple of Belvoir Hounds from England, and maintained them at his own expense at the Radnor kennels.

Even though Charles Mather's grandfather hunted an American pack some 75 years earlier near Coatesville, PA, he, Charles, turned to English Hounds to restock the Radnor pack lost to an outbreak of Rabies in 1884. The English Hounds were hunted alternately with the newly acquired local American hounds.

Because of discontent by Radnor's members with English hounds, Mr. Mather moved them to his Brandywine Meadow Farm along the Brandywine and resigned from Radnor in 1901. He died in 1928 and his son Gilbert inherited the pack and retained the huntsman Jack Smith.

The master of the adjoining Rose Tree Hunt, William Bell Watkins, told a story about Gilbert's experience soon after taking over the pack. "Gilbert, with his English hounds, bounced a red fox out of a covert but could do nothing with it on this cold day. Along came a farmer's lone fox hound, (no doubt of the Penn-Marydel characteristics), and gave reliable tongue on this fox for nearly two miles. Not a single English hound could speak to it. For Gilbert, this was the clincher."

I am told by long time supporter of the Brandywine Hounds Josie Cornwell Parman, that young Gilbert would accompany his father when following the hounds of Ross Taylor at his New London farm. When Taylor opened the kennel gate, 80 hounds, sometimes three and four deep, would exit. Of course, 80 (40 couple), driving a southern Chester County fox had to leave an impression on young Gilbert. It is frequently told, since New London is near the Pennsylvania, Maryland, and Delaware borders, that the Taylor hounds soon "fetched" a red fox in all three states in one good chase.

Following the "clincher" experience, Gilbert acquired seven couple of American Virginia hounds from Joseph B. Thomas, plus 2 couple of Walker hounds from J.L. Ridley of Thompson Station, TN.

Huntsman Jack Smith ended his Brandywine service after the 1937 season. Gilbert was occupied four days a week with the Mather Insurance business. He also hired huntsmen James McNair 1938-42, followed by Frank Turner 1942-48.

On a Brandywine 1948 hound list card, submitted yearly to the MFHA Stud Book, John White is listed as first whipper-in, accompanied by Miss Jane Mather, Mrs. Ann Mather Sullivan, and Mary Mather Bourdon. On the 1949 card John White was listed as co-huntsman. Whenever Gilbert would have to rush to the office he would hand his horn to young John.

On a Sunday afternoon in April or May, many a Chester County foxhunter and their families would gather in the YMCA building in Coatesville, PA and enjoy the silent films of Avie Hoffman. These films of the sixties and seventies showed the packs of Brandywine, Mr. Stewart's Cheshire Hounds, West Bradford Hounds, West Chester Hunt, Whiteland's Hunt, and Mr. Ross Taylor's Hounds. The crowd were nearly brought to their feet when Hoffman's projector and screen showed the fox breaking cover and hurried on by these wonderful American hounds. Hoffman gave Brandywine and John White top billing. For many of us the music of running hounds was still ringing in our ears from a season of hunting; so little was missed with only the sounds of a movie projector.

Alexander MacKay-Smith in his research of the hound Stud Books, reveals that Mr. Hubbard's Kent County Hounds, Huntington Valley, Rose Tree, and Whitelands all either bred to, or acquired, Brandywine hounds. This is the short list, the long list goes on with Blue Ridge, Bridlespur, Camden, Deep Run, Elkridge-Harford, Essex, Green Spring Valley, Keswick, Litchfield, Montreal, Myopia, Oak Grove, Quansett, Shakerag, Vicmead, Westmoreland, Wissahickon, and Woodside.

Whether you rode behind the Brandywine "old style" American hound, or watched them on film, you were a witness and could testify that huntsman John White knew his hounds and knew how to hunt them.

John White was raised on a 112 acre dairy farm and shared the chores with his 2 brothers and 5 sisters. I can only guess that the White Dairy changed from hand milking to machine milking sometime in the 30s. After the evening milking in the spring, and John being a good athlete, he joined the Jacob's Mushroom Canary Baseball Team. Hands that are conditioned to milking cows naturally placed him in the position of the ace left-hand pitcher.

An attractive young lady named Edith Landers also liked baseball. More than likely she enjoyed watching the young men playing the game. Edie, being one of 13 children, knew not only the game of baseball but also knew the game of double dating. Miss Landers, running the bases quickly, touched home plate and married John.

With John still working on the family farm he wasted no time in starting a family. Now at 23 years old, he was drafted into the U.S. Army on Dec. 7, 1941. His unit was called the Wolverines. After basic training he was shipped to the west coast and waited for assignment to the Pacific Theater. Military orders specified that fathers of three children were exempt from overseas duty. His wartime contribution was as an instructor. His discharge papers came on March 2nd, 1946.

John and Edie waited 9 years until they added a daughter, Brenda, to the family. Brenda now had 3 older brothers to play with—John Jr. born 1940, Richard 1943, and Gerald 1944.

Soon after settling back home, veteran John answered an ad in the local paper for a stable hand at the Mather farm. John, being somewhat familiar with horses at his Dad's farm, soon joined the Mather family in the hunting field. No doubt exposure to

Huntsman John White hospital visit by wife Edith.

the kennels went along with stable duties. Believe it or not, whether herding cattle or hounds, there are a lot of similarities! With John listed on the Mather's Brandywine Hound List Card in 1948 as whipper-in, and having been discharged from the army in 1946, it all calculates out to a very short whipper-in apprenticeship.

According to "Widow White," John was very dedicated to his hounds and seldom went to bed with a hound still out and not in the kennel. If a call came in as to a hound's whereabouts, John was out the door and in pursuit. One of these occasions prompted John to saddle a hunter and go looking. Horses do dumb things when not pursuing hounds. This horse shied at some standing water near the "act" of taking a fence. It placed John well out of the saddle, and when he landed, his symphysis (midline) of his pelvis had split two inches. I believe by John's account that he stayed mounted and made it back to the stable but could not dismount. The hospital photo shows John, with the exterior stabilizing pins anchored in his pelvis, and Edie, toasting Gene Gagliardi's huge lobster, with the exterior stabilizing pins anchored in his pelvis, or as it might appear as if they are anchored in the lobster carcass.

When it came to vacation time, John never asked for one nor took one, with one exception- in his later years he had a great desire to visit Cooperstown Baseball Hall of Fame, and Canton, Ohio and it Football Hall of Fame.

In 1970 the legendary Alexander MacKay-Smith published his American Foxhunting-an Anthology. Gilbert Mather contributed his story "A Great Day with Brandywine Hounds," joining some 78 other stories, essays, and poems, that Mackay-Smith thought worthy for his book. Mr. Mather's four page account starts with his early departure from New York's January 28, 1950 MFHA Annual Meeting and then catching the late train to Philadelphia. It only took until the fifth paragraph to mention whipper-in John White and his "welcome sound of a View Halloo." Defined in Webster's

The Brandywine hounds and their huntsman John White and whipper-in Frank Oas.

John White and his Brandywine Hounds.

Dictionary: 1) to shout to attract the attention of a person 2) to urge on (hounds) by shouting or calling out "halloo." That day John rode a game thoroughbred "Boston Buck" and returned to the kennels with hounds at 5:30 p.m.

John White's dedication and service to the Brandywine Hounds and the Mather family spanned nearly 50 years; he was huntsman from 1949 to 1996.

From far and near, masters, huntsmen, and foxhunters from every category you can think of thought well of his grace and character.

The third section of this book was supposed to be limited to the American hound of the Penn-Marydel Eastern Shore Strain.

However, the Brandywine hounds and their hunting like our PMDs popular huntsmen could not fade away from our fox hunting literature without a place in my book. Furthermore, his story may help propel him into The Huntsman Room at the Musuem of Hounds and Hunting.

Sat Oct 1, 1960

CHESTER COUNTY DAY

Gilbert Mather, M.F.H.

FOXHUNTING or riding to hounds is one of America's oldest sports, dating back to Colonial days and today in Chester County it is almost a way of life for many people. One of the most enthusiastic foxhunters of this area was the late Gilbert Mather of "Brandywine Meadow Farm", M.F.H. of the Brandywine Hounds and president of the Masters of Fox Hounds Association of America. He was a much-sought-after speaker on his favorite topic and those who were privileged to hear him will never forget the infectious pleasure he shared at such times. He usually demonstrated the use of the horn for the benefit of the uninitiated when one felt that his piercingly blue eyes were seeing, not several hundred fascinated human faces, but rather the faraway, vanishing brush of some old, well-known adversary—a smart but friendly fox. When sufficiently urged, he would even sing some of the old hunting songs.

Until the final year of his life, Gilbert Mather was able to enjoy the sport that he so loved and a poem, published in Hugh McDevitt's "Daily Doings" in the Local News seems almost prophetic even though it was composed by Mr. Mather on Thanksgiving Day, 1938 for his fellow-hunter, Kenneth Caswell of Pocopson. Some of the sixty-four lines follow:

> The Foxhunter was growing old,
> Too old, he thought, to hunt;
> Stiffly he rose from off his bed
> With many a groan and grunt.
>
> "My day is past," lamented he,
> "My step has lost its spring!
> Oh, grave, where is thy victory,
> Oh, death, where is thy sting?"
>
> "And yet the hounds are going out,
> The meet's not far away,
> 'By God', he said, 'I'll ride again
> If it's my dying day."
>
> Forgotten then the aches and pains,
> Forgotten, too, the gout!
> Our sportsman gathers up his reins
> And lets his hunter out.....
>
> And foremost in that thrusting throng
> Rides now our sportsman old,
> His eye is keen, his seat is firm,
> His heart is strong and bold...
>
> One hour and forty minutes!
> At last they mark to earth;
> Our sportsman reins his labored mount
> And eases up the girth...
>
> His heart is young, his blood is warm,
> No thought of cough or cold;
> Which proves this truth: NO SPORTSMAN TRUE
> NEEDS FEAR THAT HE GROWS OLD.

Gilbert Mather will be greatly missed. One can but hope that there is a special heaven for foxhunters where this gay and dauntless spirit may still be leading the field.

Chester County Day *Newspaper article on Saturday Oct. 1, 1960.*

WALTER HILL

by H. L. Todd Addis, MFH

I was privileged to have met Walter Hill in the early fifties when accompanying my father (a veterinarian) on his annual rabies vaccinations, at one of the Eagle farms in Chester County Pennsylvania. All the local hound-men would bring their hounds in pickup trucks in the evening. There was a rabies epidemic during this period, consequently, Dad vaccinated their hounds at cost.

Little did I know at this time that I was meeting with a great student of the Penn-Marydel hound. In fact, his classification, as I have learned through this research, should be full professor. All the men in the pickup trucks were his students.

My first interviewees for the research of Walter Hill were his daughter and son-in-law, Margaret Ann and Joe Sharp of Glenmore, PA. Mary Ann has old photographs and also an article written by Jane McIlvaine in 1949 about Walter Hill. The article was published in The Archive, in Downingtown, PA. Jane's title of her column reads, "The Hard Riding Huntsman of Eagle Farms Hunt, Is As American as the lean, Blue Ticked Maryland Hounds He Hunts".

In the early part of this century, Mr. William Clothier, Esq., MFH of Pickering Hunt maintained two packs in his vast hunting country. It is unclear what the circumstances were that led to Mr. Joseph Neff Ewing, Esq. taking over the second pack and purchasing the Eagle Farms near the village of Eagle, Chester Co. in 1928. Little is known of the Pickering pack at the Eagle Farm, except the name Pat Reilly. He was believed to be the huntsman.

William Ashton Esq. joined his brother-in-law, Joe Ewing, as joint MFH. This team put the word out that they were looking for a new huntsman.

Well known PMD houndman Roy Jackson, MFH of Radnor and Judge Hannum Sr. near Calvert Md. had firm ties with the renowned houndmen of the Eastern shore. Through this association, Walter Hill was approached and asked if he would come to Yankee Land. Walter's life at this time one the Eastern shore was not an easy one.

Walter was born on a farm in 1887 and in his early childhood he was constantly indoctrinated with hound-talk and hound music. Without his mother's permission, he was given two puppies on his sixth birthday. He told his mother they were beagles, but their adult size soon revealed the true breed, Foxhound.

Walter used to sit by the window of the old farmhouse and listen to the hounds run into the night. His mother would often come in and chase him to bed. One night when he was about five years old, his father left Walter alone with the three old maids while he went out with the "dawgs", Walter said. "I never had anything hurt me so bad in my life."

Hill never had a pony; he would ride saddlebags or Standardbreds raised at a neighboring farm.

Walter, his brother and two sisters were raised on a farm outside of Kennedyville on the Eastern Shore of Maryland. After his father's death, he farmed the home form for 21 years, farming on the halves with his mother.

His neighbor and cousin, Ray Jarrel, maintained a pack of hounds also. Walter was constantly lured to the woods to challenge every fox.

Walter married Mae Hurlock in 1908 at the age of 21. Sons Vern and William were the first and second followed by Francis. Fourteen years later, when her father was 41, Margaret Ann was born. She and the interviewee (me) no doubt were unplanned.

In order to be a successful farmer, one must pay attention to every detail, especially during the great depression. Walter's energies for detail were directed to his hounds. Walter was even sidetracked while babysitting. During his evening duties he would hitch up the driving horse to the spring wagon, put the baby in the back, release the hounds and road them to his favorite evening cover. Of course, the hound music and jiggling carriage ride put the baby to sleep.

This misdirected energy led to him being "sheriffed" out. However, the family farm was not involved.

Word of Walter's predicament was passed along to Mr. Ewing and Mr. Ashton by friends Roy Jackson and John Hannum, Sr.

Walter no doubt struggled with the offer of huntsman way up north. So his wife and family remained in Kennedyville for the 1929 year, while Walter explored the 'Outback' of Chester County. Mae and family soon followed.

Masters Ewing and Ashton did not live in the hunting community and neither were good at communicating with the local farmers.

Walter Hill was not only a gifted communicator, but also a tremendous recruiter and leader of young local farm boys into the world of hounds and hunting.

Walter was not only skilled as a communicator in farm and fox talk, he also became very involved in the local baseball and church activities. During the Depression and World War II years, being involved in the community reached everyone.

Walter's wife Mae was a great person in supporting her husband, while quietly enjoying his hunting thrills and hunting gossip. I have been told hunting was rarely discussed at the dinner table in the Ewing household, but you can imagine nothing else was discussed at the Hill dinner table.

Walter's starting salary in 1929 was $115 per month plus his horses. To his daughter's best knowledge, he was receiving $125 per month plus horses upon his retirement in 1960.

Eagle Farm's huntsman Walter Hill, with his legendary pack of Penn-Marydels. Photo taken in the 1950's.

In Jane McIlvaine's 1949 article, she relates several true accounts in Walter's hunting life. One such incident was at a joint meet with the West Chester Hunt. Walter was so excited that he jammed his lighted pipe into his pocket. Later, the field noticed clouds of smoke billowing out behind him. They called this to his attention before he had burned his breeches behind him, but not in time to save his coat pocket.

Another story was that of a hunt considered the best by Walter. Jane quotes him directly in this account.

"It was the last day in March, Guy Mercer, Bayard Hoffman, and I left the kennels at 4:30 am. We jumped a fox at Parker Hill that doubled back across country toward Pughtown (6-9 miles). It was so dark when we jumped that fox we couldn't see the dawgs, but old Jack and Dorothy, they got right on him. By the time we got to Pughtown the sun was up and the dawgs ran back to Sheeter Hill, an awful place! Our horses had been runnin' like they was on the track. The dawgs came back to Parker Hill and there was a boy yellin' Tally-Ho so loud he scared that fox clean out of the country. Those dawgs crossed the road to Mr. Anderson's and didn't stop runnin' till they got near Downingtown (another 6-8 miles). Bayard says he can't ride anymore cause his horse has a shoe off. I said, 'You don't have to ride, just listen to those dawgs, prettiest noise I ever heard!' They made three circles from Cemetary Hill and then doubled back to where they'd jumped the fox. It was then about 1 o'clock and old White Foot couldn't go no farther. I rode my horse back to the stable and jumped in my car to go after 'em. I asked Sexton, did he hear any dawgs? And he says he hears them back by Parker Hill. I then met a farmer and he says, 'We got that fox in a box in a cellar. The Missus is mad, 'cause she says that fox has been eatin' her poultry'. I tells him that that fox done more runnin' that any fox I ever rode a horse after and persuades him to let me have him. I took him back to Parker Hill and put him into a hole. He never ran but once after that. I'd just like to know how many miles that fox did run that day. I had 43 dawgs out and they was all up at the end!"

Mr. Hill, by design or just being good-natured, encouraged a number of the surrounding farmers to hunt with the Eagle Farms Hunt and, also, to get some hounds of their own. This concept is totally opposite to most masters and huntsmen in ones hunting country. The normal attitude is to discourage every other pack that hunts in your country; to selfishly have it all to oneself.

Walter would meet at these farms and insist that they throw in their 6, 8, or 10 hounds with the Eagle Farms Pack. These boys would know every neighbor and knew how to find the best running fox in that country. This fellowship and cooperation led to the finest hunting in the world. Maybe the rides could get a little rough, especially in a hillier country, and maybe the rocks could be tiring when the going was soft, but this country provided foxes with a greater sense of security. A fox, feeling secure and measuring the distance of these great voiced hounds, would run all day and all night.

Walter did not come north by himself; he also brought his blacksmith and best friend Albert Hague and family of five. Albert whipped-in for Walter all of his career.

Walter's early days with the 'hand-me-down' Eagle Farms pack was not an easy one. One of his first students and farm boy favorites was Guy Mercer. Guy maintained a small pack and went on to be a distinguished huntsman for Pickering Hunt and Whiteland – Perkiomen Hunt.

Guy tells of the day he was out rabbit hunting with his favorite old beagle bitch when the Eagle pack came through. Some wide skirting Eagle dogs soon picked up the scent of his rabbit hound and promptly killed her. Mr. Ewing sent a letter of apology and a check for $25. Later on these same ornery hounds chased Mrs. Sloanmaker's house dog and ran it around the house three times. The caring widow opened the kitchen door for her pet to escape into the house. She was slow to close the door and seven of these hounds followed, breaking up the poor dog underneath the table.

Walter, needless to say, took care of the problem and headed back to the Eastern Shore to retrieve some of his Maryland 'dawgs'. He came north with 10 hounds with a different set of genes for the Eagle Farms pack.

In addition, he bought an all white hound called Bigboy from Webb Moore in 1951, and Punch from Claude Anthony in 1949. These two hounds influenced the makeup of the Eagle Farms Pack for years to come.

Albert Hague told the story about a cold day Walter was trying to get with hounds and his horse broke through the ice while crossing the Baptism pool at St. Vincent Baptist Church. Walter said, he always wanted to become a good Baptist, but Albert Hague said he could never become one with the language he used extracting himself from the baptism pool.

Another one of Walter's 'students' was a kid who lived on a gently rolling farm several miles southeast of the kennels. This kid, Paul Hannum, had the right spirit in Walter's eyes. When he got to a stiff box jump that stopped many a hunter, Paul managed to squeeze his small white pony under an adjacent wire fence and stayed with hounds. Walter knew the best way to discourage a kid from continually hunting was to keep him in the field. So he would tell Paul to 'Come ride up with me.' Paul paid attention!

Paul tells the story when Walter was hunting the Longwoods on his father's farm and the good fox was jumped on this good scenting Saturday afternoon. Walter beckoned Paul to come on and ride with him because he knew this fox would take off straight away and go for miles before he would turn at Parker Hill. As young Paul rode by the slow-paced field, the master beckoned to Paul, "Hold up! Hold up!" Paul ignored him and galloped on to catch Walter, as they were leaving the normal boundary of the local foxes. Unfortunately, the master and obeying field were dumped. The next day Mr. Ewing appeared at the dairy barn at milking time. He confronted Paul's father and said, "Paul was welcome to hunt anytime, but he must stay back in the field." Paul's daddy asked, "Where did this happen?" "On your farm," was the reply. The senior Paul told Mr. Ewing, "If you don't have enough horse to stay with hounds, you can't expect the boy to get out of the hunt, especially on his own farm." Later on, Paul's father remarked that Mr. Ewing had too much starch in his collar.

After Paul graduated from High School, Walter took him and Bob Wilson

Walter Hill, 1949

(ex-Huntsman from Radnor) to Sudlersville, Maryland and bought six hounds. Walter's pack and the farmer's pack had to mesh perfectly. We can see now that there was a tremendous gene pool with this community of hounds.

The territorial line between Eagle and Pickering Hunts was not far from Eagle's main hunting country. Walter would call the night before and tell Paul to go hunt that good fox in Parker Hill (Pickering's country). If we hear them, these hounds are going to 'break', so we'll join you, (legally, by MFH rules). He would often use Paul and other farmers with hounds as point men. You go ahead and get the fox jumped, I'll hunt your way, especially if it was in Whitelands or Pickerings' territory.

One morning soon after the pack moved off, Walter's horse refused a chicken coop. Mr. Ewing told whip Albert Hague to give Walter a lead. Albert said, no sir, he was staying out of Walter's way as the Eagle Huntsman was warming his horse up at a full gallop, in a 30 acre field, before turning the horse at the fence! It must have been quite a sight. Walter always rode with his coat unbuttoned even on the coldest days.

One evening Walter came to Paul's house and said his hounds got away from him and left the country, so Paul drove around with Walter into the night looking for them. After knocking on a few doors and being told by one lady to 'get the hell out of here', Walter finally had a premonition where they were. "They probably holed and were laying down." The night air was still and chilly, so Walter reached a lonely spot, stopped, stepped out and let one hell of a bloodcurdling yell that carried for miles. A few young hounds were near enough to hear and returned his call. "We found them."

His faithful, supporting wife rarely heard her name called out as Mae. She only can recall hearing 'O-Mae. Walter seemed to always be hunting and would come in from stable work to get dressed for the day, and would constantly be trying to locate his stock, stock pin, clean breeches and gloves, etc. His daughter Margret Ann recalls hearing Daddy hollering downstairs "O-Mae, where's my---".

Walter never joined the church because he said he swore too much around the barn. Mae always had dinner ready when the day's hunting was over, no matter how late it was. He said his hounds ran all day and all night and when he rose in the morning, he saw the fox silhouetted in the sun, he said "They must have set the whole world on fire."

There is a quote that comes to mind when thinking of Walter. "Try to be, what your dog (hounds) thinks you are." Walter definitely was everything his hounds thought he should be.

"Too many hounds are bred to run too fast – to beat one another." In Hills opinion, "That's not foxhunting!"

I have been privileged, to have hunted the gentler southern part of the county on occasion, but have fulfilled any man's dream, of hunting my own pack, in the more rugged northern part of the county.

Thanks to all of Walter's "students": Paul Hannum, Guy Mercer, Clarence Rice, Bud Able, Earl Mercer, Charlie Barns, Dave Finger, and Chester Ortlip. They shared their sport, puppies, and, of course, friendship that helped me to introduce Walter to you.

There are many more tales in my notes about Walter Hill, but I have been told by the editors of the Friends of the Penn-Marydel, that I must end this story. Remember behind every good man there is a good woman, - O' Mae.

Walter's huntsman duties started in 1929 and ended in 1962. He died in 1963 at the age of 75.

The Hard Riding Huntsman of Eagle

Walter Hill, Huntsman For Eagle Farms Hunt, Is As American As the Lean, Blue Ticked Maryland Hounds He Hunts

Jane Louise Davis Rhoades

Richard Walter Rhoades
(410) 479-3175

27042 Burrsville Rd.
Denton Maryland 21629

August 16, 2002
Mr. Sherman Haight
Chairman of Huntsman's Room Committee

This letter is directed to your committees consideration of Walter Hill Huntsman at Eagle Farms Hunt, Chester County PA. as an inductee into the Huntsman Room at Morven Park VA.

May I say that as a young girl growing up following hounds I was enraptured with Walter Hill. He was the first huntsman for Eagle Farms Hunt (1926) mastered by Joseph Neff Ewing Esq. and the Honorable William H. Ashton. Mr. Ewing met Walter during both of their stints as league baseball players. Walter lived on the Eastern Shore of Maryland near Chestertown. He farmed, foxchased and played baseball. Mr. Ewing hired him to come to Chester County and help build a pack of hounds at Eagle Farms. That they did and quite successfully. Anyone who was fortunate enough to have The experience of riding to hounds with Eagle Farms was elated with

2.

From Louis Davis Rhoades

Richard Walter Rhoades
(410) 479-3175

27042 Bursville Rd.
Denton Maryland 21629

Their voice, drive and good sport.

Walter was extremely influential in the breeding of the Penn-Marydel hound with Mr Ewing and Mr Ashtons support. Their pack soon became the envy of many. In 1934 when The Penn-Marydel Foxhound Inc was formed Mr Ashton was one of the original members. Mr Ewing served as a director in later years.

Walter encouraged local folks and others on the attributes of the P.M.D's. He took excursions to the Eastern Shore (MD.) to select stud hounds and brood gyps that would enhance the qualities of the P.M.D.s. My Dad, a dairy farmur had a pack of hounds and soon became one of Walter's boys. He whipped hounds and chased with him for many years. In later years C. Rupert Davis (my Dad) became the Huntsman for Eagle Farms Hunt until its disbandment upon the death of Mr. Ewing.

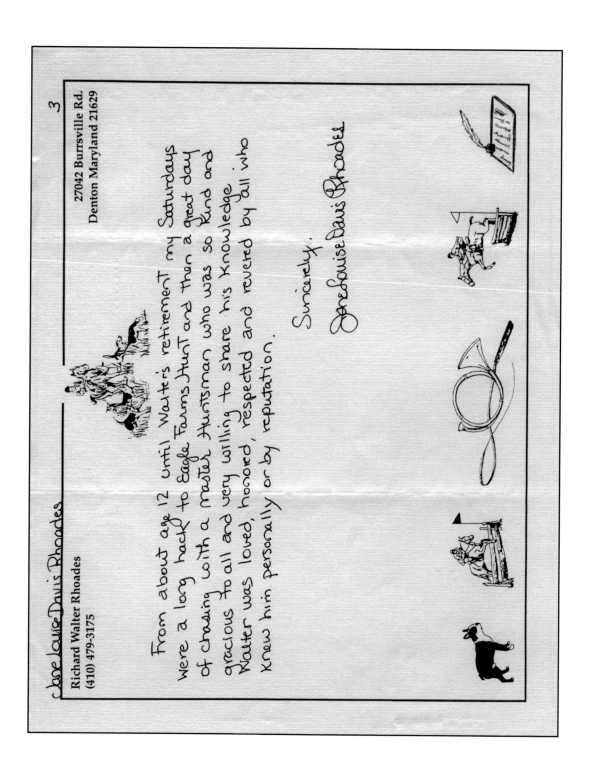

Jane Louise Davis Rhoades

Richard Walter Rhoades
(410) 479-3175

27042 Burrsville Rd.
Denton Maryland 21629

3

From about age 12 until Walter's retirement my Saturdays were a long hack to Eagle Farms Hunt and then a great day of chasing with a master Huntsman who was so kind and gracious to all and very willing to share his knowledge. Walter was loved, honored, respected and revered by all who knew him personally or by reputation.

Sincerely,
Jane Louise Davis Rhoades

Walter Hill (Huntsman); Albert Hague (Whip)

Walter Hill — Making a final decision in regard as to who would be going to the hound show (I think it was the first hound show after World War II).

Mr. Hubbard's Kent County Hounds. Pictured from left to right is Whipper-in Joan Hill, MFH Mr. Hubbard, Arthur Brown, (friends called him Brownie), and known to everyone else as Hound Dog Brown. Person on far right is not known.

HOUND DOG BROWN
by H. L. Todd Addis

Everyone has a vision of priming an old pump to draw some water. Finally, there is lift, the pail is full and we have water. This same scenario occurred in my long sought after interview with Hound Dog Brown (Arthur Brown), the legendary huntsman for Mr. Hubbard's Kent County Hounds.

My friend James Yerkes of Calvert MD, passed the word along to an old Wallace Township foxhunter, Sally Maenak, who moved to the Eastern shore about a decade ago and teamed up with Brownie, chauffeuring him in pursuit of the Penn-Marydel.

I finally called Sally to alert Mr. Brown that I was coming to Chestertown on May 9th. Our agreed meeting spot was at the local McDonald's parking lot. Sally suggested to meet at the adjacent mall, "Everybody meets there" she said. I hemmed and hauled and said I believed McDonald's was better.

Ten o'clock sharp we circled McDonald's looking for a little white convertible. No Sally, so we parked out front. Finally, we went in for a cup of coffee and sat next to four old timers chewing the fat. It was now nearing 10:30 AM, so Happy went over to ask if any one was a foxhunter. One spoke up and said "yes". This was the break we needed. We tried to introduce ourselves, but they did not listen – they were off and running with their own hunting stories.

One old boy named Bill Taylor, said he used to have hounds and his pack had joined with Brownie many times. Sometime during the story telling he volunteered to take us out to Brownie's.

We were off – A few miles outside of town we pulled into Brownie's yard. Arthur came to the door and seemed most surprised and pleased to see his old stable mate Bill Taylor. We all piled into the modest cottage and Brownie's housekeeper, Carol, put a call into Sally on her cell phone. Sally soon arrived and politely explained that we parked on the wrong side of the McDonald's.

It only took 10 minutes of idle conversation before we got into "The Story". To my surprise the 88 year-old huntsman was not of Eastern Shore stock, but rather born and raised in Westminster, central Maryland.

His first position as a young man was caring and training horses for William Martin. Bill Martin was he father of Duck Martin, the current President of the MFH Association. He started this job in 1936 and with the help of his pretty wife Peg, they raised two boys, Buster and Dick and a daughter Ruth Ann. One of his most memorable mounts that he galloped for Mr. Martin was Insure, winner of the Maryland Hunt Cup.

One of these trainees broke Brownie's leg; he was consequently laid him up for nearly 9 months. Apparently, Mr. Martin reduced his wage by one-third while injured and wanted to keep him at this salary after recovery. Arthur's temper flared up and he quit on the spot and moved in with his sister.

On the second day at his new perch, the phone rang and it was Harry Straus asking for Arthur. Mr. Straus was a charismatic man of wealth, who either invented or developed the racing tote board. He had an extensive hunting and racing stable, and was Master of the Carrolton Hounds, near Westminster, Maryland.

He asked if Arthur would come and be first whipper-in and kennel-man. Without hesitation, Brownie took the position. Henry Moltand was the old Hunstman. Before Henry Moltand they had Otis Hays, former huntsman for green Spring Valley Hunt. Otis drank too much for Green Spring subscribers.

Mr. Straus was killed in 1949 when his private plane crashed near Port Deposit, Maryland. Within two weeks of his death, his widow released all the help and I assume the hunt and racing stable was emptied also.

Mr. Hubbard, MFH of Mr. Hubbard's Kent County Hounds, was soon on the phone and asked if he would like to come to the Eastern shore and hunt his hounds. This date, 1951, was the beginning of "Hound Dog Brown".

Brownie said, when he arrived at the kennels, "They were a mess". Hounds were riddled with fleas, ticks and mange. He had a bunch of Crossbreds and English hounds. "None of them were worth a damn," he said. I asked, "What did you do with them?"

His answer – "I hit them over the head". I don't know if this was a figure of speech or the actual method of euthanasia. I did not pressure him.

He said he scoured the local packs for hounds and brood bitches. He took a number of bitches up to Essex Hunt and bred to a great hound named Farnam.

He turned partially in his chair and pointed to a painting in the living room and said, "That hound Layman was the best hound I ever hunted". "Layman was by a Pickering dog, Albert Crosson gave him to me as a pup".

Hound Dog's voice was strong, loud, and clear. It reminded me of Radnor's distinguished Hunstman Bill Evans. It was hard to get him to describe any one hunt, but rather he would describe some funny incident with his hunting visitors and friends.

Years back, Oscar Crosson, brother to Huntsman Room Inductee, Albert Crosson, brought his Vicmead Crossbreds down for a meet. Arthur said to Oscar that he would have to go over to Delaware for a bunch of cowbells. Oscar said, "What for"? Brownie answered, "If we are going to hear these hounds, we will need bells on their collars".

On another occasion the Kent County pack was invited to bring their hounds to Old Dominion, Virginia for two days following Thanksgiving. At the last minute Brownie came down with pneumonia and was hospitalized. Mr. Hubbard called him at the hospital and told him he was going to cancel the trip, since Brownie was sick. Brownie told his Boss to do no such thing. He will have his two whipper-ins, son Buster and Eddie Houghton, pick out 15 couple of our best hounds and you hunt the hounds. Well, the old man could not resist and followed the directives of his huntsman.

Arthur Brown, better known as Hound Dog Brown, hunting Mr. Hubbard's Kent County Hounds.

Following the first hunt in Virginia, Mr. Hubbard was on the phone calling his servant. He was thrilled. "The best hunt they have seen in Virginia in two years. Two hours and 45 minutes," he said.

Mr. Hubbard would often visit other hunts, particularly when goose season was going strong. He had a keen eye for the work of the staff and their hounds. From these visits he only invited those to hunt Kent County that he thought were worthy of it.

One such hunt was the Essex Hunt from New Jersey. Essex huntsman Buster Chadwell on arrival laid out a bet – that he could drive any red fox out of a cover in full view of the field and earth him for 20 minutes. The Master, Jill Slater (Jill Fanning) soon doubled the $20 bet.

Brownie knew he had a good running fox across the road that no body could hole, so he took them straight to him. "They got their view, but they could not earth him".

Early on Howard County's Gus Riggs sent over three Crossbreds to help build the pack. My question – "How did they work out"? His answer, "All they did was fight like hell, I hit them in the head too."

Another gift hound was a good-looking Eastern Shore, white hound from Joe. Quimby. "Joe, what's wrong with him?" Brownie asked him. The former Sheriff, of Centerville Maryland, said, "nothing, except we can't break him from running deer". Brownie took him and laid the lead into him when he came roaring out of the first cover on deer. We got him deer broke, but he soon took off to the neighbor's barking dog. The barking farm dog was a call to challenge. About this time, "Mr. Ramsey, from one of those fancy hunts in California, called for Penn-Mardel. We had the perfect hound. Within a month, Mr. Ramsey, Harold C. Ramsey of Pine Valley Hounds (Pacific), send $110 to Brownie with a note enclosed, "This is the best running hound that we have ever seen". Dog or coyote, not much difference.

Much to my surprise, I thought the Eastern Shore was strictly red fox country from near Colonial times. But, Brownie said, when he came in the 1950's, there was nothing but gray foxes. So, he told Mr. Hubbard that he would like to stock some reds. "How many do you need?" the boss asked. Communication was off this day, because Brownie said 50 and the old man thought he said 15.

"We had them shipped in from Ohio by train to Fallston. We picked them up and took them back and put them in the corncrib. Mr. Hubbard came out of the farm to see the 15 foxes. When he looked in the crib and saw 100 eyes staring back at him, he nearly croaked."

"How did you get rid of the grays?" I asked. He said, "We went out with a couple of old beagles and shot gun. We just kept getting their numbers down."

"You know that Master up there from Connecticut, Sherman Haight?" I said yes. "He called and wanted a bunch for stocking. He came down and met with a bunch of those Virginia Masters and we went over to Charles Town. Somewhere in the back streets we met a truck." "How many were in the truck?" I asked. Brownie answered "800". It's a wonder the game officials did not smell them 10 miles away.

The interview was pressing past 2 hours, so I knew it was time to rein it in. So, I took a look at the numerous hunting pictures on the living room wall. The large picture of hounds, huntsman, Master and whipper-in Joan Hill, I could not touch that one, but several other small ones I took off the wall and asked if we could use them in the newsletter.

Brownie rose and used his walker to enter the living room and said take them.

Whether this distinguished huntsman is ever proposed for a place in the Huntsman's Room, I do not wish to speculate, but I do know from all my friends, who had the privilege of riding behind his pack, were not cheated from the very best.

He said several times during our visit that, "The most thrilling part of a days' hunting is having the pack start the fox on a cold trail and build on this track for a half hour then go to running for the rest of the day."

On the front page of the Kent County News, dated January 20, 1993, there is an article titled, Hubbard Retires His Hounds. The author is not identified, but from all indications he interviewed Huntsman Brown, whipper-in Joan Hill, and kennelman Sam Pickrell.

One quote of interest came from Pickrell. "We could have got rich on dog turds, at a penny a piece." Brownie said, "I remember times when we'd be out before the kids were going to school and get back when people were coming home from work."

Whipper-in Hill was a horse person before she came to work for Hubbard. "All my lift I wanted to foxhunt," she said. When she first was offered a job as a receptionist, "I felt I had to take a more secure job with pension and security a large corporation would give," she said. That was Friday. When she arrived at work on Monday, she found she already had been laid off. She immediately took the secretarial job with Hubbard.

Brown lamented the change in times. "Up until the middle 1980's the old farmers all had a couple of hounds, and would foxhunt. I've left here with 35 or 40 hounds and when we got back there'd be 65 or 70," Brown said. "When the farmers heard the sounds they would turn their dogs loose for the exercise, and pick them up later at the kennel."

Whether or not Mr. Hubbard had his two hunt servants on a 401k pension plan, I do not know. However, the two hunt servants were well recognized in his will.

At the 2001 Virginia hound show evening dinner, we ran into Ex-MFH, Sherman Haight, from Litchfield Connecticut. Our conversation finally touched on Mr. Hubbard and huntsman Brown. Mr. Haight told how Wilbur invited him down one winter for a few days. "Because of soft footing we took our combined packs to Kent Island. The ground level at Kent Island is only 2 feet above sea level, so foxes don't hole too easily," he said. "We hunted it on foot. We entered this big cover and perched on a big fallen log. The pack settled on a common running fox. After several hours of circling in the same direction, Brownie got tired of this and beckoned me to come along. When they arrived at the predetermined path of this circling fox, Brownie cut loose with a war hoop." The boredom was broken.

Mr. Haight's position as MFH and huntsman was of no deterrent to the host Master. Both caught a verbal dressing down for turning the fox.

It would be most rewarding if the above conversation was just Part 1, in a series of stories about Hound Dog Brown. How about you readers send in a letter with your tale, so the rest of us can enjoy a little more about Hound Dog Brown and Mr. Hubbard's Kent County Hounds.

STRIKING GOLD
by H. L. Todd Addis

When researching material for the 75th anniversary of the Penn Marydel Association Inc. back in the early part of 2009, I frequently would see the name of Benjamin Funk of Chester County, Embreeville, PA. Just a few paragraphs copied from Alexander Mackay-Smith's book of the American Hounds 1749-1967.

"Except for the years 1937-1940 when he was with Howard County (MD), Ben Funk who came to Goldens Bridge at age 33 in 1924 and continued to hunt hounds through the 1956-1957 season retiring at the age of 66. For more than 30 years he showed remarkable sport in this cramped, heavily wooded and deer ridden county, being one of the first huntsman in North America to develop a deer proof pack. He was undoubtedly the most literate professional huntsman of this century, his accounts of runs with Goldens Bridge, written for The Chronicle, being outstanding in their field. Ben Funk was also unusual in his interest in pedigrees." (page 281)

I was curious under what circumstances Ben Funk 'excused himself' from Goldens Bridge and hunted Maryland's Howard County Hounds. I asked Master of Hounds Roger Scullin of Howard County-Iron Bridge Hounds if their archives would have any records of Funk's employment. He could not recollect any written documents that would answer this question. Still building my enthusiasm and curiosity of Benjamin Funk, I must digress to another hunt in the east named Vicmead Hunt, Delaware.

"The Vicmead Hunt was organized in May 1920 by a group consisting of Mrs. Victor DuPont, Mrs. Holliday Meads, Messers Henry B. Thompson,

Benjamin Franklin Funk's brother Joseph settled in Detroit, Michigan after his baseball career in Chester County. While walking and viewing some shop windows he was startled to see a hunting picture in the display window of a camera store. On closer examination, "by golly it's my brother." He entered and found the picture to be a promotional picture for Eastman Kodak's colored film. He asked for a copy and had it sent back East.

Norman F. Rude, A. Felix DuPont, E.C. McCune, John B. Bird and others. As a compliment to the ladies, the name of the hunt was compounded from their names. A pack of tri-colored Penn-Marydel type American Hounds was secured from Benjamin Funk, then of Embreeville, Chester County, PA, who later became famous as huntsman for the Goldens Bridge Hounds."

Of course after reading a few of Mackay-Smith's remarks, I turned to the index of American Fox Hound book and found no less than fourteen page numbers listed behind Benjamin Funk. When I questioned MFH Russell Jones of Mr. Stewarts Cheshire Fox Hounds whether he ever heard of Benjamin Funk and his farm, he replied immediately, "Yes, we meet at Funk's Gate." From what I can learn, the buildings of the farm are no more. It was later purchased by a Strawbridge and eventually by billionaire Jerry Linfest and finally, just before he could sell his properties including the Funk farm for development, Nancy Hannum of Unionville tackled Mr. Linfest and persuaded him to place these historical fox hunting properties in Natural Land Trust.

Without troubling myself to research the Funk farm history, one can assume Benjamin Funk inherited his hounds and huntsman knowledge from a father, uncle, or grandfather. Whether a spell of crop failures, economic depression or tired of milking enticed young Benjamin to leave his farm, I do not know. From his farmer pack, hounds were drafted to Delaware's Vicmead Hunt, West York, Fairfield/West Chester and Goldens Bridge.

The next question that comes to mind is, how did Ben Funk become huntsman for Goldens Bridge? The most important call that I made in my research of huntsman Ben was to the Chester County Historical Society.

The Historical Society's receptionist transferred me to the librarian. She, the librarian, after listening to my story said she would "work

Benjamin F. Funk

Benjamin F. Funk, ardent sportsman and former independent baseball player, died late Saturday night at his home in Chatham after an extended illness. He was in his 69th year.

Born at Embreeville he was the son of the late John W., and Mary Barry Funk. As a young man he lived at Embreeville, and, in that small community, organized and managed a baseball team which was among the best independent teams in the county. He was a playing - manager, appearing mostly as a catcher but also at times as an infielder and outfielder. His brothers Norman and Jacob were among stars of the team. Norman later played Minor League baseball.

After World War I and through the 20s, the deceased played occassionally with West Chester and other independent teams.

He was also interested in the sport of fox hunting and rode to the hounds with area hunts. Before establishing his residence at Chatham he was associated with Goldens Bridge Hounds, at Brewster, West Chester county, N. Y.

Surviving are his wife, Virginia Brown Funk and two daughters, Margaret F., wife of Harvey G. Shortlidge Jr., West Grove and Mrs. Marie Baily, Oxford. Three grondchildren, three brothers, Joseph W., Detroit; Jacob M., Philadelphia and Norman T., Garrett, Ind., also survive. A sister, Mrs. Anna E. Musiel, is deceased.

Benjamin Funk Obituary

on it." 'Pay dirt' was realized on my second call. The librarian found a 1969 obituary column on Benjamin Funk in the Chester County Daily Local. She read the names of his three brothers, Joseph W., Jacob M., and Norman T. and one sister Anne Funk Musiel. Next came his deceased wife's name, Elsie, and present wife Virginia Brown F. Two daughters, Margaret (Peggy) wife of Harvey G. Shortledge Jr. and Marie Bailey of Oxford, PA.

My next plan of attack was to go to the phone book and look up the name Shortledge. Luckily there were only five listings under Shortledge. When I called Howard G., he gave me a number to call of Harvey G. Shortledge III. Of course, I got an answering machine and left a message. The heavens opened up two days later when I got a call from this great sounding lady. The 87 year-old Marie Coulter, Ben's youngest daughter.

So, now what you read and the pictures, including the first page, are all produced by the excited youngest daughter Marie and referred to as Baby Funk by Langhorne Gibson's account published in his 1930 diary.

The spry 87 year-old Marie insisted in driving to our farm with pictures and documents on November 22, 2010 to help rewrite and clear up her father's biographical events.

"Just finding the information was a major challenge; it was a treasure hunt, and it was addictive. And the more I got into it, the more the pieces began to fall together." – A clipping from someone's paper

Back Row: Funk, Murphy. Front Row: Young, Jackson, Marshall

My conclusion that the Funk family had hounds for generations was unfounded. Ben developed his own pack of hounds. The farm with kennels was a family farm and he inherited it in 1937 with his siblings. He proceeded to buy out their share so he would realize sole ownership. This was, no doubt, the reason he resigned the huntsman position from Goldens Bridge and pursued the occupation as farmer.

Facing the absence of a monthly check, he was approached by August Riggs, MFH of Howard County and accepted the position of huntsman. He not only took on this new Maryland huntsman job but also met and married Maryland's Virginia Brown after losing his beautiful wife Elsie at her prime age of 47. A ruptured blood vessel in her brain was the cause of death.

In pursuing the M. (Mack) Roy Jackson story as huntsman and MFH, we need to realize he developed his own private pack of Eastern Shore hounds in Delaware and moved on as Master and huntsman of Rose Tree in Media, PA, 1914-1918. No doubt a relationship and a mutual admiration developed between Ben Funk and Roy Jackson while in PA.

Mr. Jackson then moved north to Connecticut's Fairfield and West Chester Hunt in 1918. Usually a move like this is the result of business or a lady friend. His influence with Fairfield and West Chester was strong and changed the complexion of their pack to the Eastern Shore hound type. He was elected JT MFH in 1921, joining MFH John McE Bowman. Mr. Jackson, overjoyed with his type of hounds, hunted them for three years.

Roy Jackson's (now 55 years-old) great love of hunting was greatly supplemented with

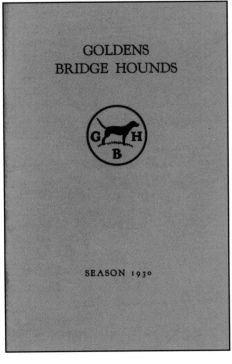

1930 Goldens Bridge Hounds Diary

the marriage to 21 year-old Almira Rockefeller in 1929. Mr. Jackson soon returned to PA establishing his plush Kirkwood Kennels and eventually assuming the Mastership and huntsmanship of the Radnor Pack on July 31, 1929.

Both of Ben Funk's daughters were accomplished equestrians and re-established themselves back in Chester County, PA. Neither one returned to NY Goldens Bridge on their father's return in 1940.

While on our second visit with Marie in Oxford, PA, she confided that a bad fall, fracturing her skull and rendering her unconscious for three days, ended her fox hunting

continued on page 195.

SPRING

THE 1930 season opened several months earlier than usual, and what is more strange yet, the Goldens Bridge Hounds had their first run of the year over the lands from whence came their forebears.

As a result of a very kind invitation from the Blue Ridge Hunt Club (Captain Ewart Johnston, M.F.H.) to come down and hunt their country with our own Pack for the period of one week, a goodly crowd of women, men, hounds, horses and automobiles left Goldens Bridge in the early morning of March 20th; while Marion and I left the following night by train. Among those who went down by motor were Ben, Mrs. Funk, Peggy, Percy and one or two grooms; about twenty couple of hounds in the hound van; a horse van with six horses; and last but not least, the Funk baby. Everyone seemed to be driving a car, except the latter infant, and the whole procession looked more like a circus than an invading Hunt contingent.

This "troupe" passed the first night in Westchester, Pennsylvania, and then proceeded on towards the Blue Ridge Country, which can best be described as lying in the Shenandoah Valley, in the vicinity of Winchester, Virginia. It is a country rich in apples, Civil War history, horses, limestone and beauty. Insofar as native foxes are concerned, it is rather poverty stricken, as we were soon to find out. Horses, humans and hounds were received amid ovations and everything possible was done to provide them with comforts. It was a large order having so many descended upon them, but with true Southern hospitality those good people did not allow themselves to be fazed.

I shall not bother to describe all the hunts we had, there being five in all;—four of them being hunts in which our hounds were the sole and main feature; while the fifth hunt was a joint-Meet with the Blue Ridge Hounds. On the sixth day we hunted with the Cobbler, across the mountain in the Piedmont Valley. Beside the many other pleasures afforded us, you can see that we all had plenty of exercise. Of course we had not brought enough horses to hunt all those days, nor did we have to beg mounts, as they were offered to us by each and everyone.

I cannot say that the sport we had was of the very best. In the first place it was hot and dry, and in the second place, as I have said above, foxes are not too numerous in that particular locality. However, we had short and frequent bursts every day but one, which was a total blank. Our hounds did not know what to make of that day, nor did

[15]

Page from the 1930 Goldens Bridge Hounds Diary. Written by Langhorne Gibson.

we, so strange a coincidence was it! All of the local Packs had the same trouble at that time, as did we—weather and fox-trappers.

The country is a very nice one indeed. Like all others, it has its woodland and open sections. The going is excellent with the exception of frequent limestone outcroppings, which have to be watched out for. Because of the great amount of wire, it will require considerable more paneling. As it now stands, the panels are placed in the corners of very large wire enclosures, which make it hard to follow in a direct line. Our hounds were not long in catching on to the trick of wiggling through this pig-wire, although they are a distinctly heavier type than the Virginia hound.

I must say that our hounds created a very favorable impression, as they naturally would. As to the impression created by the Goldens Bridge riders, I had rather leave that up to the Virginians to say!

In short, we had a most successful trip and it was well worth while from every point of view. We did not lose a single hound, which I think, is quite remarkable. In addition, we acquired two Virginia hounds; one of them being the black and tan "King" that is now doing so well at Goldens Bridge. The other one died. We bought one horse while down there, as did Ben.

It was not in the spirit of any criticism of the Blue Ridge Country that we decided that after all, there was no place like home, and by "home" we meant our own native hunt-lands. One has to go far before one can see a country nicer than ours—a country with more native beauty and a country without monotony of any kind. I, for one, would not swap it for any other. No, not even for Leicestershire! A country must possess qualities which offer riding and real hunting in the truest sense of the word. Nature has given us both and we may well be thankful.

[16]

Above: Page from the 1930 Goldens Bridge Hounds Diary. Right: Donald Philhower, presently huntsman for Millbrook Hunt, NY.

Map of Goldens Bridge Hounds Territory

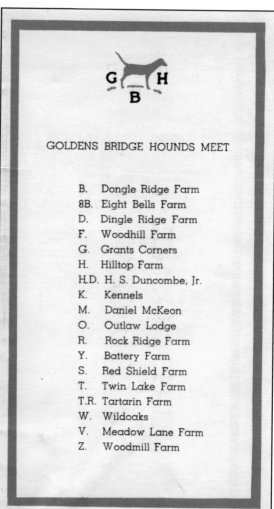

GOLDENS BRIDGE HOUNDS MEET

B.	Dongle Ridge Farm
8B.	Eight Bells Farm
D.	Dingle Ridge Farm
F.	Woodhill Farm
G.	Grants Corners
H.	Hilltop Farm
H.D.	H. S. Duncombe, Jr.
K.	Kennels
M.	Daniel McKeon
O.	Outlaw Lodge
R.	Rock Ridge Farm
Y.	Battery Farm
S.	Red Shield Farm
T.	Twin Lake Farm
T.R.	Tartarin Farm
W.	Wildoaks
V.	Meadow Lane Farm
Z.	Woodmill Farm

activities. So sister Peggy, being 10 years older, really was into hunting with her dad until his first departure from Goldens Bridge in 1936.

In the neighboring NY Counties the Fairfield-West Chester Hunt (Recognized 1915), Mr. John McEntee Bowman, a man of wealth, and proprietor of the Miami-Biltmore Hotel, was voted in as Master of Hounds in 1921. On one occasion during his mastership, he persuaded huntsman Funk to bring the pack to the Biltmore Hotel and paraded the hounds before some important guests on the ballroom floor. The hounds handed the elevator with class!

In 1924 Mr. Bowman resigned from the Fairfield and West Chester Hunt and started his own private pack. He purchased his hounds from Fairfield-West Chester Hunt and named them Mr. Bowman's Hounds. Bowman, with the help of Roy Jackson, engaged Benjamin Funk in 1925 as Huntsman and Tom Wallace as his whipper-in. Bowman also established the Coral Gables Hunt near Miami, FL in 1925. During Mr. Bowman's mastership of his private pack, he would bring Ben Funk south after the winter closed in on the north to his Coral Gables Hunt (1925-1929, page 258).

Mr. Bowman's Hounds were recognized by the National Steeplechase and Hunt Association in 1927. Due to major conflicts (territorial dispute) with the Fairfield-West Chester group, he moved his kennels and changed the name to Goldens Bridge Hunt in 1928. Mackay-Smith goes on to say, "The pack in 1928 consists of about 40 couple; some of the original purchase and some of the homebred are of excellent type, great size, and first class hunting ability." According to many diary entries, deer chasing became a problem, however, Mackay-Smith again is quoted, "By the early 50's when the writer first started hunting with The Essex, he saw deer actually running in the middle of the hounds, who paid no attention to them whatsoever. During the same period, Ben Funk, huntsman from Golden's Bride, made that pack similarly deer-proof." Bowman continued as master until his death in 1931.

The readers of this presentation of Ben Funk's Huntsmanship must recognize former Golden's Bridge huntsman, Donald Philhower, for his preservation of Golden's Bridge Hounds 1936 booklet and well-written 1930 diary written and published by joint master Langhorne Gibson. Mr. Gibson was a very popular Master, according to Marie Funk Coulter and authored numerous works including The Riddle of Jutland, which I entered 'for the record'.

A few lines take from the October 7, 1930 diary entry of MFH Gibson stirs one's imagination as to huntsman Funk's abilities.

"We could hear hounds giving tongue in the thick of this immense wood. By stopping at frequent intervals and 'harking', Ben was able to mark the line, and after one hour of riding through the most impassable woodland, we came out onto a dirty road below which flowed a gently meandering river. This very spot we met up with the main body of the pack, it was the finest piece of work on the path of huntsman that I have ever seen. It is not so much the galloping and the jumping, nor even the viewing of the fox that makes good for hunting; it is rather the viewing of the perfect coordination and understanding between a man and his hounds – that's hunting!"

October 25, 1930 the master was at his best when writing this account of the hunt. Some lines in the two-page account follow:

"Away we went, across the cement road, over lovely open fields and all that country heretofore mentioned as the 'cream of vale' at every point we were at least two fields behind Ben and only by pushing our horses to their utmost, we were able to catch a fleeting glimpse of his scarlet clad figure silhouetted against the bleak skylines. Had the Prince of Wales been out with us, we might have laid a drag in order to show him our best country, our cleanest jumps or somebody equally important was out, saved us the trouble and must have said to himself, 'I am just going to treat these people to the best they ever had.' I do wish my pen could express my enthusiasm over today's sport in such a way that would not only gratify me personally, but that would make it really live for all time in the annals of the Golden's Bridge Hounds."

Golden's Bridge Stallion hounds had been used by Battle Creek, Fairfield Co. Middleburg, Tryon, Midland, Smithtown, Kirkwood, East Aurora, and Fox Chapel up to 1961.

Clark (dog hound #44) was out of W.G. Merion's Judy, the daughter (Lucifer-Tutler) secured from Philip Bowen, huntsman of the Howard Co. Maryland Hunt.

Many Fox-hunting establishments curtailed these hunting activities during World War II and Golden's Bridge was no exception according to Ben Funk's daughter. Member and Master R.L. Parish during the early 40's employed huntsman Funk part time.

My July 9, 2009 letter addressed to the Chronicle's Editor asking for assistance was conveniently ignored, so my wife and I detoured from our trip home from Berryville, VA log house one September day in 2010 and began our search for Ben Funk's articles.

The big question was where to start? Did he start to submit articles early on in his professional huntsman career (1924) or near the end (1957) or anytime in between? Why I chose the 3-inch thick 1956 bound Chronicle magazines I do not know, but it was the right decision. My untrained thumb somehow managed to stop on the Hunting section of the 52nd bound magazines and then I looked for the GBH emblem and titled Golden's Bridge Hounds. None of the many articles were signed or initialed. So, who really wrote and submitted the articles? While scanning page 20 of the hunting section of April 20, 1956, these three sentences sealed the identification of the real author.

Our second fox was found in a swamp between the two pinewoods on 8-Bells Farm. This proved to be one of the old-fashioned fox hunts that we farmer packs used to have in Pennsylvania and Maryland. This good red ran for two hours and five minutes and was marked in on Pinewood Hillside on 8-Bells without a single check.

At this point in time only God knows how many 'write-ups' Ben Funk submitted with the contents of so many great hunts.

Daughter Marie (Baily) Coulter told this little story on Happy's and my second visit.

"Golden's Bridge Penn-Marydels were in hot pursuit of a good running gray fox when all of a sudden it decided to climb a weak limbed tree. Suddenly, the fox fell, only to be half-swallowed by a hound. Huntsman Funk leaped from his horse and grabbed the fox to save his life. The loose horse, in the excitement, let go with both hind feet, hitting Ben and knocked him cold.

Recovery is not during a helicopter or ambulance ride, but laying still while life returns. The staff and field crossed their fingers and waited. Many minutes passed before the caring huntsman was able to breathe and stand; he found a helpful stone, and mounted – the hunt resumed."

GOLDENS BRIDGE HOUNDS
North Salem,
New York.
Established 1924.
Recognized 1925.

It was only a couple of weeks ago, Reynard, as we call him, began to invade our hen house and kill chickens for the fun of it, leaving them on the floor.
"What will we do about it?" I asked Tom Christopher, the farmer.
"I don't know," he answered frankly without too much thought. "Maybe we could shoot him," he added.
But he was too wily and recognized the shotgun which we carelessly stood in the corner of the chicken house. The next morning there were five casualties. So I got to thinking, and an idea struck me.
"What the hell is a fox hunt for if not to hunt foxes?" I asked myself.
So I called up Ben Funk, Huntsman of the Golden's Bridge Hounds, and an obliging fellow, and explained my predicament.
"I'll be over in the morning with the hounds," he promised.
Sure enough, not only did he and about 50 dogs show up, but about 50 riders of both sexes besides. Zanuck could have made a movie of it. They turned the hounds lose in the swamp, and pretty soon they began to holler and bay and along comes Mr. Fox up across a field toward the hen house with the hounds and the horsemen after him. He went through the chicken yard with the canines yelping and scaring the hens so they didn't do any laying for three or four days. But they caught t h e marauder and killed him. It was the most stylish hunt in a chicken house in the annals of sport.—John Wheeler
(From the New Haven Evening Register of December 17 by permission of the North American Newspaper Alliance.)
σ *1956*

1956 Goldens Bridge Hounds Article.

GOLDENS BRIDGE HOUNDS

North Salem,
New York.
Established 1924.
Recognized 1925.

Thursday, Sept. 1 — Opening of cubbing season. About forty met at Galway Stable, a new stable on Baxter Road, and cast in back of the house of our former M. F. H., R. L. Parish, after hacking down Baxter Road. Hounds opened up at once on a red cub. He quickly went to ground; almost at the same time an old red bounced out of the pine woods on Battery Farm. Hounds ran with great cry over Charles Wallaces' and Billy Meldrum's, crossing De Lancey Road, on over Salem acres via Harry Caesar's and marked under a ledge overlooking Liticus Reservoir. The day was very warm, with a heavy dew, scent excellent.

Thursday, Sept. 8th — Met at Galway, drew north to Starr Ridge and two cubs broke out of swamp east of the Miller home and one quickly went in. The second fox truned back to starting point and ran through David Vail's swamp to Peach Lake outlet, then swung right through Pach Lake Manor and went to ground in a very convenient earth. We crossed over towards Red Shield Farm where hounds opened up and they were off on the heel line which was quickly discovered. Hounds quickly harked back to voice and were off. Hounds never ran faster or gave more cry and marked in near starting point. At one time, while the hounds drew near Hardscrabble, one of the largest deer, about a 12 point buck, hopped out in the road, listened back over his shoulder and cantered off to the south. In about twenty seconds another buck, equally as large, followed the first deer. So it looks like another good season, with fox hounds to follow instead of the deer hounds which so many gallop after.

Saturday, Sept. 10th — Met at Galway and found at once, and quickly marked in. We drew north to Hardscrabble where two fox had been viewed crossing the road. There were two woven wire fences which held up the hounds, especially the puppies; once straightened out they ran over the section near Star Lea. I viewed this good cub running near Peach Lake. He looked like a drowned rat due to the heavy dew. There were so many commuters going to catch the early morning trains.

causing volume of gas fumes. that hounds had to be helped for the first time this season. Once off the road they ran fast and marked in on the former Red Shield Farm. A third fox found near the Shack on the Rock. ran around the Von Gal swamp and was marked in near Kennels. A few wanted to take off for the Fairhill Races by plane so we called it an early day.

Thursday, Sept. 15th — We foolishly started out in the teeth of a heavy electrical storm and just as hounds opened on a line near a good earth. lightening and thunder and rains were upon us and as we galloped the pack toward the Kennels a bolt of lightening struck a hickory tree within 30 yards of Dick Lundy and myself. It split the tree to the ground. Dick and I both felt that the Lord must be on our side and that people are certainly foolish to go out in such weather.

Saturday, Sept. 17th — A large field met at Galway stable; the day was warm and the footing, mucky. A small cub was found within five minutes after moving off. This run lasted one hour and twenty minutes without a check and hounds marked within twenty yards of where the field was checked in Dan Raymond's field and woods. The run was over some of our best country, such as Auson Lobdell's, Rock Ridge and that section. It was more like an October or November meet, scent breast high.

Saturday, Sept. 24th — Met at Galway stable again and found near Windswept; Hounds marked in near starting point. A second fox, found in rocky field on the Lobdell Farm, crossed Hardscrabble and ran over via Red Shield where he made many big circles, crossing back by Bill Meldrum's house, then on south to Salem Center and marked to ground in a wooded knoll near starting point. A wonderful run of over one hour. It rained during the entire run and we were all soaked and really were surprised to find a fox out as it had rained very hard all night.

Saturday, Oct. 1st—Opening meet at Meadow Lane Farm, the home of M.F.H. and Mrs. Carlo M. Paterno. We drew down over the Lake and Race Course and after crossing 124 a young deer bolted right through the pack and following this one came two more. Hounds paid no attention to them. About two minutes later hounds opened up with a roar, Moonshine spoke first. He is an all tan, the old fashioned type of Pennsylvania hound (no show hound, but my kind of hound, always on the move, a long high bawling voice and nothing on his mind but fox). Hounds ran this fox for an hour and a half with only one check, that being when the

Continued On Page 17

Goldens Bridge Hounds Article
Friday, February 24, 1956

HUNTING

fox found a hole in the fence around Ex-M. F. H., R. Laurence Parish's lawn and we prevented the pack from going in the front drive to give the fox a chance to get out, which he did. Hounds were put on the line and away over Raymond's where they marked in. This is where the joke was on us, unless there were two foxes. While hounds marked in under a fallen tree—it was leaning on top of another tree—Lightfoot and a couple of other hounds climbed this tree, but gave no tongue and were called off. After we left the tree , we found that the fox was perched in the crotch of this tree, at least sixty feet up, a nice young Red. We have enjoyed some great runs on this fox.

Tuesday, Oct. 4th—Met at Hilltop Farm, the home of Mr. and Mrs. Fred Tompkins. A very good field turned out. We cast in Hunting House Hill, a section which is a haven for deer, fox and partridge. Within five minutes after moving off, old Striver spoke on a fox, which had just left the rocky ledge and we were off for about thirty-five minutes of as nice a volume of music as only American Hounds can give, and marked in on a hillside overlooking Field Lane. As we were running this fox, a second fox jumped up, crossed Fields Lane and stopped back of Gene O'Riordan's house. Three hounds, Boulder Monday and Moonshine chased this nice lanky Red by sight down Fields Lane (a dirt road). We quickly harked the pack to them and, while the Hunt to Ride members might not have enjoyed this Hunt too well, the real Fox Hunter who rides to Hunt enjoyed this as one of the best. After two hours of a continuous chase and a great volume of cry, our fox was marked in on the south side of Hunting House Hill. One of the real great days.

Saturday, Oct. 15th—The big flood, meet called off.

Sunday, Oct. 16—The Hunter Trials called off due to the weather.

Joseph Johnston Farm. This was the same fox we treed on opening meet day. A great shame; I would call him one of the best running young foxes.

Tuesday, Oct 25th—Met at The Foxes, the home of Mr. and Mrs. Frank Fox. We failed to find near the place of the meet. We crossed Wallace Road and found and ran fast and straight to the Murdock Farm where fox was marked in. A second fox found on the Ross Farm, ran over Dongle Ridge and as they ran through the swamp on the Stuart Farm two foxes broke out of covert. We stopped a few couple on one nice, big Red and harked to the running pack and finally marked in on Hillside adjoining a pond along Spring Valley. The Foxes entertained the wield at Breakfast.

Thursday, Nov. 3rd—Met at Galway Stable, hacked through the village of north Salem, cast in over Miss Bessie Smith's property, over Dingle Ridge and Merrys W o o d section, blanked, found on 8-Bells, ran fast for thirty-five minutes and marked in within 100 yards where we found. A second fox found on Joseph Delhi's. Hounds were bothered by his Jersey Herd chasing the hounds off the line. We lost this fox near Ridgebury Church. This was the first fox we did not account for this season. A third fox, a grey, found in Stuart Bates' swamp, gave a short run and was marked in under a stone wall near his dairy barn. Very heavy going, but a nice morning for hound work.

———————— O ————————

GOLDENS BRIDGE HOUNDS

North Salem,
New York.
Established 1924.
Recognized 1925.

Tues., Nov. 8th — Election Day. Met at Rock Ridge Farm, drew north over the Misses Lobdell property, on by Peach Lake, found at lower end of Starr Ridge Continued On Page 20

swamp and over Ted Miller's farm. At first all hounds struck back line along wall except Bugle Anne and Songstress, two real fox hounds. Pack was harkened to the right line and after about fifty minutes of real American Hound Music, around the big Peach Lake swamp, fox was driven out into open. About this time we heard two shots and as we came to the place where we figured the shots came from hounds came to a dead halt at a barway along a stone wall and could not carry the line beyond. We could see a city gunner hurrying toward his car. I galloped after him but he said he had not fired his gun all morning. We knew he was guilty, but a dead fox would not provide further sport. After all tempers have to be controlled, for the fox has few friends, and so we had to call an end to a beautiful chase.

Thurs., Nov. 10th. Met at Waterfall Farm. Mr. John Wheeler, a very popular neighbor who lives in Spring Valley, Ridgefield, had told me about this crumby looking fox killing his chickens and the geese on the Dunning Farm. I told John I would try to kill him on Thursday. I cast the hounds down between his cattle barn and chicken house and even though we had had a heavy frost and it had evaporated hounds picked up our mangey Red. After twenty five minutes of as deafiningly heavy voiced music as I have ever heard, they killed within 100 yards of where we jumped him. Our second fox was found in a swamp between the two pine woods on 8-Bells Farm. This proved to be one of the old fashioned foxhunts that we farmer packs used to have in Pennsylvania and Maryland. This good red ran for two hours and five minutes and was marked in on Pinewood Hillside on 8-Bells without a single check. All the men members had fallen by the wayside except my good whip, Dick Lundy, and four of the fair sex, Mrs. Westa, Mrs. Franken, Mrs. Marsh and Mrs. Lord. So we agreed to bring names in of people who will stick and stay—a great day.

Tues., Nov. 15th. Met at the Foxes on Hunt Lane. The day was very windy and blustery. Cast west toward Keeler's and from the first covert eight deer bounded out in front of field. All the two year and older hounds paid no attention; a few of this year's puppies opened up on the deer. Dick Lucy, my very good whip, stopped this right away. In the meantime I cast off to the north over towards Ridgebury and found in an open rocky field on the former David Vail Farm, ran fast for a quarter of an hour and marked in the old den on the hillside near the Murdock Farm. A second fox found in a swamp on 9-Bells Farm gave a good run of over an hour and was marked in near the starting point. As everyone was heading toward home, we cast in the small swamp on Stuart Bates' swamp. After waiting on the edge of the swamp and sounding the horn to call hounds home, deep in the lower end of the swamp I heard the high long note of Mandy. Immediately the hounds all joined this great young bitch and for over an hour we all enjoyed one of those old fashioned foxhunts—sometimes fast at other times they had to get down and hunt it like an old cold trail. Finally, when the fox ran the dirt road back of Ernest Russell's stable, we lifted hounds and hacked back through North Salem to the kennels. A great day.

Sat., Nov. 19th. Met at Dongle Ridge. It was our first snow also the first snow hunt for our young entry. When we left kennels the ground was bare out by the time we cast hounds we had about an inch of snow. We cast in the small swamp on the Bates' property. Hounds spoke a few times and I noticed a partly filled print where a fix had leoped on a large flat stone. The old hounds, who knew how to bury their noses in the footprint and get a whiff of reynard, spoke a few times. By this time it was snowing hard and I could not get this old red afoot. We drew on north to the reliable pine woods on 8-Bells when we heard those three great voices, Monday, his litter mate, Mandy and Bugle Anne —open up. For over two hours we enjoyed a great chase. Horses balled up quite a bit and we finally called off near Mr. Murdock's when hounds were still going strong.

Sat., Nov. 26th. Met at Arigideen, the home of our Joint Master, Mr. Daniel M. McKeon. About ten minutes after moving off, we found a grey, our first run on a grey in a long time. We ran this grey for about half an hour and marked in on a rocky ledge in Merrys Wood. We drew all the usually good coverts blank due to the deer hunters and bow and arrow hunters. As a last resort we were drawing the big Von Gal swamp. Most of the hounds were giving up when all at once I noticed that great white and tan bitch, Bugle Anne, throw her head in the air. Evidently she had winded a fox stirring deep in the swamp. At least six hundred yards from this point she opened up hot, but the wind was high so she was joined only by four of the older hounds who knew how to stop and listen and then hark to a reliable voice. About this time, the rest of the pack jumper a red and ran within thirty yards of the kennel yard over Carlo Paterno's race track, via Salem Center, finally marking in near the Misses Barry and Ficher Studio. A nice windup for a windy day, which I dislike.

Thurs., Dec. 8th. Met at Springbrook Farm, the home of Mr. and Mrs. Joseph Johnston. After circling the swamp north of Peach Lake, hounds opened up near the road and a red loped down the road in front of the field. Hounds were running with great cry. About this time, we could hear them split on two foxes. In this big swamp we could do nothing to get them together, so we followed the pack rurnning the fox we had viewed. They carried this line well until we came to Dingle Ridge Road and lost. As we could hear the other hounds running strong we picked the hounds up, galloped back and harked them in. Shortly thereafter we viewed a nice big dog fox crossing Peach Lake Road. He looked tired and they pulled him down along a wall on Eugene Mendel's Farm. The fox had been running for over an hour and was all in. This was one of our very good days even if it was slippery going and a sharp north wind biting our faces.

Sat., Dec. 10th. Met at Dongle Ridge, another very cold day. Drew north through 8-Bells Farm. Blank. As we entered a rocky field on the former Converse Farm, I noticed a rabbit hunter standing on a large rock. Just to pass the time of day I asked him if he had any luck. He said he had just shot at a fox about three hundred yards below from where he was. Hounds picked up the line and ran fast for about two fields and marked in on the late Lyman Keeler's Farm. We were anxious to see if he was hurt, so we blocked him in. I went back that night to make a little test and found out he was not hurt at all. A second fox gave a good slow type of hunt that brings out the trailing ability of the old type American Fox Hound.

Wed., Jan. 25th. We drew up through the Von Gal swamp where Mandy and Monday opened up on a grey. They circled the swamp for about thirty-five minutes and treed; as we have a lot of fun with this grey we let him live to enjoy another day. As we were drawing over the upper end of Lobdell's woods, crows began to mark a fox under a pine tree on the Bloomer property. Hounds opened up where he had run along the top of a stone wall and then swung right towards the pine tree where the crows had spotted their hated enemy. Evidently there were two foxes afoot as one went in on the hillside of Dr. Nichols near the chicken coop jump. While hounds were marking, Larry Mallon viewed a nice big red crossing the upper end of Rock Ridge. We ran this fox for over an hour and marked to ground on Rock Ridge Farm.

Sat., Jan. 28th. We drew north of the kennels and around Peach Lake blank. As we were drawing near Windswept, Monday, an all-white hound (except for a black four leaf clover on her side) opened way off to our right on Charles Wallace's and they fairly flew to honor this old reliable. Though the ground was as hard as a concrete road, we enjoyed an excellent run of two and a half hours before the fox dropped in an earth on Lobdell's just north of the big shelf on Rock Ridge. This fellow is a very large dark red and old enough to know all the tricks to puzzle a pack. He would run the ice on all the brooks he could find and they had to work it out at a walking pace.

Wed., Feb. 8th. Ground hard, softening a little just enough to make scenting conditions about the best you could find. Immediately after casting hounds in the swamp that adjoins the kennels, two reds ran north by the Shack on the Rock. You could hear hounds split, one half swinging by the old fallen down barn and marked in on Rock Ridge. We quickly put these hounds in with the others who had crossed the concrete road and were running south over that nice open country towards Windswept. From that time on it was just ride and cut around to view this big red either running the top of a stone wall or just in front of the pack across the open country. Hounds only had to be helped once where he ran the concrete road. Finally after three hours, they marked in the same earth they marked the vixen in earlier in the day. Just before they marked in they formed a most wonderful silhouette, as all the hounds were running on top of a stone wall. I cannot recall a better hunt in a long time.

Sat., Feb. 11. Hounds found in north section of 8-Bells Farm and fairly flew north over Dr. Ratchford's, swung right into Connecticut and then back over Lee woods and came to their noses on a heavily manured muddy corn field. Then on south to Dingle Ridge over the Ross farm and had to work foot by foot over a new grass field where the fox was picking up mud. Crossed Dingle Ridge Road where they hit it off hot; then over an old sod field and marked in on Frank Fox's Farm near Vail's golf course. The run was about an hour and a half. A very good day.

GOLDENS BRIDGE HOUNDS

SEASON 1936

Here's one for you old-timers. Remember Ben Funk? Well, in case you don't, here's a little reminder. Ben—along with his brothers Jake and Norman—was one of the stars of that great Embreeville baseball team that thrilled Chester county fans for many years back in the 1920's. Ben was manager and second baseman for the nine, which was one of the best ever put together here in the county. Some of the big events of the year were the games between the local nine and major league teams brought in by Herb Pennock.

Those of you who remember Ben will be sorry to hear that he's been in West Grove Hospital for the last month or so. However, hospital authorities t e l l us he's improving rapidly, and we think he might like to hear from some of his old pals in the area. So, if you get a chance, drop him a line, care of the hospital. Maybe you can give him back a few of the thrills he used to give you.

Left: Morris 'Mox' Fell, Center: Benjamin Funk, Right: Unknown

Attacking the deer problem.

THE MASTER KNOWS BEST

An entry into Langhorne Gibson's September 27, 1930 diary entry should not be passed over without quoting a few sentences.

"Thanks be to the weather, the caterer, the guests, the Hunt members and Ben Funk that the Farmers' Party was a huge success.

The Goldens Bridge Hounds members proved themselves as good waiters and waitresses serving at least 650 persons.

The whole tone of the party was in keeping with the spirit of foxhunting and that is why it was so successful. We were reminded once again of the respect which Ben Funk commands in our countryside. This, after all, has had more to do than anything else, with the success of our organization."

Left: Morris 'Mox' Fell, Center: Benjamin Funk, Right: Unknown

HISTORY OF THE PERKIOMEN VALLEY HUNT
by H. L. Todd Addis, MFH

Some readers of this issue may be thinking, "Is this guy (meaning myself) monopolizing this newsletter?"

This answer in this issue is yes.

For several years I have considered writing a story on the Perkiomen Valley Hunt. The founder and the only Master for 21 years was my father, Clarkson Addis.

The main reason I finally finished the story can best be explained from an excerpt from a letter I wrote to Mr. James Young, MFH.

"A little over a year ago I developed the same feeling, that an archaeologist must feel when he discovers the 'missing link' dinosaur that explains all. The euphoria developed when my older brother, Bud, showed up at the door with a metal box. He said it was stored in his attic for nearly 35 years.

The enclosed note written by the last hunt secretary shows how close this 3-inch box, with a stack of club records dating back to 1926 was almost destroyed.

I have searched my mind and conscience as to why I never asked my parents why, when, and how they organized the Montgomery and Perkiomen Valley Hunts. The Box had the answers.

Having Van Urk's volumes of *The Story of Foxhunting* in my library, plus your article Digging at an Historic Earth, in December 2000 of Covertside, renewed my urge to brag about my father and mother in story form.

The Friends of the Penn-Marydel newsletter has featured some legendary houndsmen and I plan to add my father to this list.

I am curious as to what you have in your treasure chest of historical hunting records pertaining to Montgomery Hunt, 1926, and Perkiomen Valley Hunt 1934.

Dr. Clarkson Addis, Sr., as Master and huntsman of the Montgomery Hunt and one of his favorite mounts, Bob. The Montgomery Hunt, which later changed its name to Perkiomen Valley Hunt, was co-founded by Clarkson Addis in 1922. This photo was taken in 1931.

Dr. Clarkson Addis as Master and huntsman of the Recognized Montgomery Hunt. His pack was made up of American hounds, later known as Penn-Marydels. Photo taken in 1926.

If I can help in my amateurish attempts to gather material, I am "biddable to the horn."

What prompted this letter to Mr. Young was the December 2000 issue of the Covertside, MFH James Young wrote an article describing Herculean assignment to complete Volume III and Volume IV of J. Blan van Urk's, The Story of American Foxhunting. To quote from Young's article: "To advance van Urk's efforts to complete *The Story*, I plan to pick up the scent with those hunts, still extant, which he first described in Volume II and bring their line forward through the twentieth century. In addition, I anticipate featuring all of the major hunt histories which have endured through the twentieth century and mentioning those smaller or transient packs."

In the beginning of Volume II, of The Story of American Foxhunting, page XV – Publisher Notes three lines read as follows – "In Volume III and IV will be found *THE STORY* of all packs and organizations

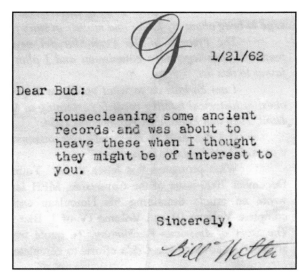

established between 1907 and 1940, among which will be the following present day recognized Hunts."

I am aware of a number of packs, some of which are thriving today, that have stood the test of time for a century.

A number of reasons account for these not being recognized, nonetheless, the intentions of van Urk's telling The Story of American Foxhunting would be incomplete, if these accomplished private or subscription non-recognized packs were excluded from *The Story*.

World War II slowed hunting activities for Perkiomen Valley Hunt Club. Pack size was reduced to 10 couple. I was 7 years old at the Wars' start up. My most vivid memories during the War years were not of hunting or riding, but the several 'real lickings' that I received for being bad. Whipper-in Jason Regar was assigned to heavy artillery and served in the European theater and my sister Betty Jane's husband Bill Batchelor was thrown into the Guadalcanal and Okinawa campaigns. My brother Bud came of draft age near the end of the war and joined the Merchant Marines.

Perkiomen Valley Hunt in 1947. Master and huntsman Dr. Clarkson Addis, Sr. surrounded by his family. Left to right, sons Todd and Clarkson Addis, Jr., Ann H. Addis (Clarkson Sr.'s wife), his daughter (riding side-saddle) Betty Jane Addis Batchelor, Betty Jane's husband William Batchelor and Hunter Addis.

Hunting activities and membership took off in the mid to late forties. Unfortunately, the misguided Game Commission declared all out war on the fox in order to assure plentiful game for the returning soldiers. With this depletion of native fox, Dad was forced to provide sport by laying drags and then have Mom drop a fox near the end of the drag. Of course, buying foxes particularly from New York was illegal and releasing them was also a no-no. These weekly activities continued into the early fifties when we were hit in 1952 by a rabies epidemic in Montgomery and Chester County.

The Game Commission continued their intensified demise of the fox. Besides intense trapping and encouraging the shooting of the fox by gunners, they began a wide poison bate program. Some local wardens would ride the caboose of the rural trains and throw poison out at an appropriate spots.

I really became proficient in handling these big wild New York foxes. It is too lengthy to describe snaring a wild red in a chicken house and placing him in a burlap bag by oneself.

Unfortunately, Dad got bitten on the finger by a gray fox that turned out to be rabid. I remember the Pasteur treatment. It was a series of 16 shots in the abdomen.

I am convinced that the houndsmen were responsible for the rabies epidemic, by releasing foxes, in the incubation stage, in order to replenish their countries.

Dating from the late 30's, Dad had vanned to adjacent Chester County and hunted with Whitelands hunt.

1949, Huntsman Albert Crosson called in desperation for Dad and sons to come and represent Whitelands field at a joint meet with Rose Tree Hunt, since not even one Whitelands member, nor its Masters would be there. We were the only ones.

Following this hunt, Dad and Albert's friendship and respect for one another grew.

His long time fondness for Chester County hunting eventually led to his recruitment as Master of Whitelands Hunt in 1955.

Dad's Mastership and magnetic personality brought astonishing growth to Whitelands membership. Perkiomen hounds were absorbed into the Whitelands' pack, as Albert Crosson continued hunting Whitelands' hounds.

Not until post puberty and the development of manhood did I realize why so many families with flowering daughter joined the hunt to grovel for Dr. Addis' three sons.

It worked – all three of us married girls that hunted. Temperament of the first bride led to a divorce from brother Clarkson.

But my brother Hunter's marriage to Judy Harrison, of a distinguished foxhunting family from Radnor, and my marriage to Hampton Crain, from a sporting and hunting family from Southern Maryland, stood the test of time.

Perkiomen Valley Hunt

Written by Charles Belz in 1940 as a response to a solicitous letter from J. Blan van Urk. Grammatical and spelling mistakes were intentionally left in, as is explained in one of the letters on the previous page.

In 1923, Dr. Clarkson Addis called together several of the leading sportsmen of the community, and proposed the idea of organizing a club for foxhunting. Whitemarsh was then hunting Montgomery County, but did not cover the country north of Norristown. Pickering confined its activities to the west bank of the Schuylkill in the vicinity of Phoenixville and the territory west of it. Nevertheless in his work carrying him through the back country of the Perkiomen Valley, Dr. Addis ascertained that there was enough native fox, both red and grey, to justify the existence of a Hunt Club. He was familiar with Hunt Club organization having grown up in Huntingdon Valley's country, and having followed their hounds as a boy, and knowing personally many of their members. The men he called together to consider his plan were J. Hansell French, who was State Secretary of Agriculture during the Earle administration, and a resident of Collegeville, Ralph Beiber Strassburger, the Norristown publisher, John Keyser, and Harvey Plummer who were active sportsmen in the Valley.

Needless to say, the plan was enthusiastically received. It was decided to contact others to form a membership, and after the groundwork had been laid, hounds were finally purchased from William J. Fotterall who maintained the pack then known as the Chester Valley Hunt. Thirteen couple of hounds were purchased, and they were represented as containing the blood lines of the famous Gloucester Hunt.

Dr. Addis acted as Master, and maintained kennels at his farm. Hunting proved most successful, in fact so successful that a number of Norristown sportsmen finally prevailed on their moving the kennels to Norristown, making Norristown, the County seat headquarters of the Club. Recognition was applied for in 1926, and granted in the name of the Montgomery Hunt. Its territory included all the townships east of the Schuylkill River northwest or Norristown to Pottstown. Some friction later developed between the Collegeville group, who wanted to hunt fox, and the Norristown groups who wanted a Hunt Club. As a result, the Collegeville group, including Dr. Addis, withdrew and re-established their kennel at Dr. Addis's Tally-Ho Farm, taking with him those of the hounds that were his personal property. This Club was reorganized as the Perkiomen Valley Hunt, and it confined its sport to the Perkiomen and Skippack Valleys. By 1932, hunting did not continue very well with the Montgomery Hunt, and many of their members came to hunt with the PVH, and finally bringing their Charter with them, they rejoined the PVH Club as a body. Steps were taken to change the State Charter, and to change recognition with the Masters of Foxhounds Association to the name of Perkiomen Valley Hunt. It has continued successfully as such since that time. In 1933 additional territory was granted, extending our country into Berks County and including three townships on the west side of the Schuylkill River opposite Reading.

The original hounds were quite a mixed pack, and while all American bred, including tri-colors, black and tans, red-bones, and what have you. Dr. Addis, by systematic breeding for nose, voice and color, has since 1934 achieved a pack uniform tri-color, all looking so much alike that he alone can on sight name every hound in the pack. We now have in kennel about 25 couples, and for an obscure, and unimportant hunt we feel that we have a magnificent pack. Dr. Addis gives his personal attention to every detail of kennel management and breeding.

Dr. Clarkson Addis hunting hounds followed by his family. From left to right behind Dr. Addis, son Clarkson Jr., daughter Betty Jane and his wife Ann, hunting on a cold winter day in 1931. (Picture taken before Todd was born.

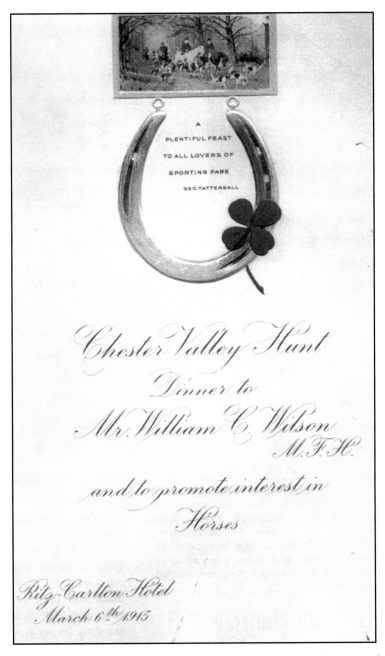

A
PLENTIFUL FEAST
TO ALL LOVERS OF
SPORTING FARE
GEO. TATTERSALL

Chester Valley Hunt

Dinner to

Mr. William C. Wilson

M.F.H.

and to promote interest in

Horses

Ritz-Carlton Hotel
March 6th 1915

The above invitation to a 1915 dinner party hosted by William C. Wilson, MFH of Chester Valley Hunt, is of interest because Dr. Addis purchased his hounds from Chester Valley hunt in 1922. Also of interest, the founder of Chester Valley Hunt, which was founded in 1898, was R. Penn Smith, who is the grandfather of Mrs. John B. Hannum, MFH of Mr. Stewart's Cheshire Foxhounds. The contents of the invitation appear on the next page.

Menu

OYSTERS

―――

CONSOMME MADRILÈNE

―――

NUTS   SALTED ALMONDS   OLIVES

―――

LOBSTER NEWBURG

―――

FILET MIGNON BEARNAISE

PETITS POIS FRAIS AU BEURRE

POMMES PARISIENNE

―――

CRÈME DE MENTHE PUNCH

              PALL MALL
              CIGARETTES

POULET ROTI

SALADE

―――

FROMAGE

CRACKERS

―――

MERINGUES GLACÉS VANILLE

―――

COFFEE

Hunting Echos

BETTER TO HUNT THE FIELDS FOR HEALTH UNBOUGHT,
THAN FEE THE DOCTOR FOR A NAUSEOUS DRAUGHT.
OLD PROVERB

. . . . NOW MY BRAVE YOUTHS
STRIPP'D FOR THE CHASE, GIVE ALL YOUR SOULS THE JOY.
SOMERVILLE

. . . . AND NOW IN OPEN VIEW
SEE, SEE, SHE FLIES! EACH EAGER HOUND EXERTS
HIS UTMOST SPEED, AND STRETCHES EV'RY NERVE.
SOMERVILLE

WHEN DEW HANGS ON THE THORN
THE HUNTSMAN MAY PUT UP HIS HORN.
OLD PROVERB

. . . . WE GENTLY BOAST
AT LEAST SUPERIOR JOCKEYSHIP, AND CLAIM
THE HONOURS OF THE TURF AS ALL OUR OWN!
COWPER

PURSUE THESE FEARFUL CREATURES O'ER THE DOWNS
AND ON THY WELL BREATH'D HORSE KEEP WITH THE HOUNDS
SHAKESPEARE

ONE TOPS IT, ONE BAULKS IT, AND, CRANING, TURNS AROUND,
WHILE A THIRD QUITS HIS SEAT FOR A SEAT ON THE GROUND.
WILLY

A RIDER UNEQUALLED—A SPORTSMAN COMPLETE.
A RUM ONE TO FOLLOW, A BAD ONE TO BEAT.
WHYTE-MELVILLE

FILL UP YOUR GLASS, EVERY MAN;
HE IS AN ASS WHO WON'T HUNT WHEN HE CAN.
DELME RADCLIFFE

Committee

FRANCIS R. STRAWBRIDGE

CHARLES W. WALKER

HARRY C. YARROW, JR.

NATHANIEL EWING, JR.

CHARLES W. BRAY

FRANCIS B. REEVES, JR.

WALTER G. SIBLEY

WILLIAM F. FOTTERALL

CHARLES R. HAMILTON
CHAIRMAN

Items appearing clockwise on this page were pages, in the invitation to a dinner party, hosted by William C. Wilson, MFH of Chester Valley Hunt. The picture is of popular Master and huntsman William C. Wilson, also on this page, an interesting menu, Hunting Echoes, and committee members.

VACCINATION RECORD

VIRUS		Total Charge	REMARKS	History and Condition—Autopsy Record / No. Sick—No. High Temps.—Other Treatment
Serial	Amt.			

Old Chester Valley Hunt Club Pack.
Hounds bought from Mr. Wm Fotterall Valley Forge, Pa. 1922

Red Fox — Black whit Tan
Sister — " " "
Dad — " " "
Mommy — " " "
Brust — " "
Todd — " "
Woody — Red Bone
Scotty — " "
Searcy — Black White Tan
Bill — " "
Mike — " " " — Killed
Lady — " "
Teddy — " "
Leader — " "
Queen — " " "
Jack — " " "
Pete — " "
Mary — " "

Red Fox to Mary. Ten in litter.
Gift to Montgomery Hunt Club.
This pack was put in kennel at Jeffersonville at time of union of two clubs. This was foundation of the pack that became recognized
Other hounds was purchased from White Marsh V.H. from J Maldis Valley Forge from F. Clark Schwenksville

VACCINATION RECORD

VIRUS		Total Charge	REMARKS	History and Condition—Autopsy Record / No. Sick—No. High Temps.—Other Treatment
Serial	Amt.			

VIXEN — *Best five hounds I have every seen run together. One was as true as the other.*
TODD
VIXEN
CHIMES F
CHASE F
MUSIC F

REYNARD
BAY
JIM M — Whiteland Hunt 1933 died
JAKE M — killed
JOE M
JUDY F
JANE F
JOAN — FURY
JEAN — JUDY

MASTER M R — killed all
MAX M R — but 1 pup
MUSH M R
MONTPELIER M R
MONMOUTH M R
MASK M R
MAGGIE F R
MICKEY F R
MINNIE F R
MUSIC F R
MINERVA F R

Notes written by Dr. Addis about the purchase of and breeding records of the Montgomery Hunt hounds. Above Left: of most interest on this page is the note at the top listing the original hounds, by name and description, purchased from "Old Chester Valley Hunt Club Pack." "Hounds bought from Mr. Wm Fotterall Valley Forge, PA 1922." Above Right: of interest on this page are the five hounds listed at the top. "Best five hounds I have ever seen run together. One was as true as the other." The hound listed at the top of the list, Todd, is the hound Todd Addis is named after.

Above: Hound name plates, note the phone number. Right: Dr. Addis, with his medicine kit, arriving home from his Veterinary calls, surrounded by foxhound puppies.

END SECTION III

Sometimes an author may find it more difficult how the ending of the book should be rather than how to start it. Well, I have gathered 98% of the material for *Our Penn-Marydel Hound* before my brain awoke to use the correspondence to my father from J. Van Urk and publisher Eugene V. Connett, founder of the Derrydale Press. Taken from The Publisher Notes in Volume I of the story of American foxhunting Connett writes:

"When Mr. Van Urk and I first discussed his undertaking to write "The Story of American Foxhunting", we both visualized the work as comprising a single volume. However, research into early records of the sport in this country uncovered an unsuspected abundance of material, and we soon realized that we had underestimated our subject — we might have to utilize two volumes. As time went on, it became evident that in order to cover properly the amazing extent of American Foxhunting since its inception, four large volumes would be required."

"Never in the history of sporting literature on this continent has such a painstaking and accurate search been made for facts about a sport, and in my position as founder and head of The Derrydale Press, I state unequivocally that Mr. Van Urk's story is the most important and fascinating sporting book ever written in America."

Volume I 1650-1861 entertains the reader with stories covering some 130 packs both privately owned and placed in a 'Club' status.

Volume II 1865-1906, no less entertaining than Volume I, records some 250 packs. To quote from an article written for the March 2001 Friends of Penn-Marydel Newsletter:

"In the beginning of Volume II of the "Story of American Foxhunting" under Publisher Notes, these lines read as follows — In Volumes III and IV will be found the story of all packs and organizations established between 1907 and 1940, among which will be the following present day recognized Hunts."

To the best of my knowledge, James Young's assignment stalled and this assignment was awarded to a few who only chose to include hunts that would only have been included on The Queen's List.

The colorful MFHA Centennial Book, which may have been an attempt to complete Van Urk's Volume III and IV omitted many successful packs born and died in the 20th century.

In my review of the Centennial Book, I failed to see one chapter or one picture of a Penn-Marydel Pack or one PMD hound. To continue with one sentence of my response to Mr. Young concerning his Covertside article, I quote myself:

"Remember the baseball's Negro League, they too contributed greatly to baseball and had their Hall of Fame-er's Too."

I have chosen to reproduce letters from publisher Eugene Connett and author J. (Jack) Blan Van Urk to help contribute foxhunting history to Volume III and Volume IV of "The Story."

Van Urk, who still hunts and rides on weekends, is happily at home in horse country on his Sugar Hill Farm in Unionville, PA. There he keeps and trains his timber horses, has several indoor and outdoor dogs – no foxhounds – and, he says, "every time I see a fox in the field, Little Charlie keeps cropping up."

J. Blan "Jack" van Urk, creator of "Little Charles, the Fox." From the Wilmington Delaware Evening Journal, *December 12, 1977.*

The Princeton Club of New York
Park Avenue and 39th Street

March 7, 1940.

Dear Dr. Addis:

The Derrydale Press has commissioned me to do a comprehensive, serious and up-to-date book on Hunting in America, and I am at present working on it. In order to do the task properly and thereby make a sound contribution to the Sport, I should like to solicit your assistance and cooperation.

Would it be possible within the next few weeks to have sent to me data on your Hunt, especially that which might be difficult to find in the normal course of research?

This work is to be thorough and detailed and I am interested in the past as well as the present: Masters, hounds, country hunted, interesting and important characters, horses, anecdotes, legends, etc. Also, perhaps you have a record of a particularly famous run of the past and one of recent date.

Because of the book's size, it will be profusely illustrated -- the more photographs and snapshots you can send me the better. (This also applies to any interesting scenes or pictures of the past). I hope to have not only Masters, Hunt servants, Fields and individual followers, but also hounds (single, when outstanding, and packs), horses, maps of hunt countries, etc. Please have explanations and names marked very clearly.

I am a little embarrassed at asking so much and I know these requests are a strain on cordiality, but perhaps someone is sufficiently interested in the ultimate results so that he would be willing to assemble the material upon delegation from you. Obviously, in starting a book of this sort I was not attracted by any commercial inducements, for such an effort cannot make money for an author. I mention this as my excuse for presuming upon you to such extent.

I am sure, with your help, a book can be turned out that will serve as an accurate and interesting record of the development and present status of hunting in this country.

I should be pleased if you would favor me with any suggestions, ideas or advice pertaining to make-up or contents of this book.

Sincerely,

J. B. van Urk

vU:N

Dear Mr. van Urk,

Dr. Addis forwarded to me your request for material on the Perkiomen Valley Hunt. Since receiving this we have had considerable sickness in our family, and I have given little thought to correspondence. I am sorry I neglected your letter for such a long time.

Your request is for information within the next few weeks. If it is not too late, I will attempt to get something on our little Club together for you. We are only a modest little group, and I warn you beforehand that I can give you nothing of extraordinary interest to the fox-hunting world. However, if for the sake of thoroughness you still desire a report on our history and activities, I shall endeavor to dig up this information for you.

Please let me know if I can still be of any help to you.

Very truly yours,
Charles A. Belz, Secretary
R.D. #2 Landsdale, PA

The Princeton Club of N.Y.
Park Ave. & 39th Street
N.Y.C.

The Princeton Club of New York
Park Avenue and 39th Street

April 3, 1940

Dear Mr. Belz,

Thank you for your letter of March 31st. I am sorry to hear of the illness in your family. Hope you are all completely recovered by now.

The size of a Hunt his no bearing on its importance. It is the attitude towards the sport that counts; and while some Hunts might have more things to write about than yours, I certainly want to record in my book what-ever information you care to send me about the Perkiomen Valley Hunt Club. It is not too late for you to send me this data. Any time before the middle of May will be all right, in fact.

Again thinking you for your attention, I am

Sincerely,
J.B. van Urk

Dear Mr. van Urk,

I am enclosing herewith half a dozen pages of random notes on our Club and its activities. I wanted originally to do a great deal of research, but time flew by so quickly, and I have been so very busy that my good intentions turned out to be just another one of those paving stones.

Perhaps even this is too late. I don't dare edit these sheets, -then you'll never get them. I must confess that I have never been able to think coherently through a typewriter, and since you couldn't decipher my penmanship at its best, there was nothing to do but hammer out ideas as they arrived, phraseology, form, syntax, spelling etc. be damned. It had to be this or nothing. I will leave you to judge whether "nothing" might not have been better at that.

I am enclosing a picture of Dr. Addis. The Club is his child, and he is its Master in every sense of the work. Mrs. Addis might almost be called a Joint-Master, and in reserve we have their oldest son, Clarkson Jr., who, as far as a fox-hunting is concerned, is a carbon copy of Clarkson Sr.

I do not send other photographs, -fox hunting snap-shots are like news-reels, you've seen a dozen and you've seen them all.

Very truly yours,
Charles A. Belz

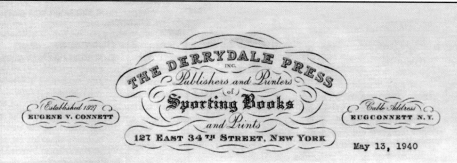

May 13, 1940

Dr. Clarkson Addis
Perkiomen Valley Hunt Club
Collegeville, Pa.

Dear Dr. Addis:

You have already been apprised by Mr. J. B. van Urk of the fact that he is writing a complete story of American foxhunting (from its beginning to the present) for the Derrydale Press. Since commencing this work Mr. van Urk has uncovered so much of interest that is vital and which has hitherto never been published, that we have decided to publish his treatise of some 200,000 words in two volumes. The first will take in everything from the very start of the sport in this country to 1906, inclusive; and the second, from 1907 to 1940.

The recognized packs established prior to 1907 and still in existence will be given full accounting, through to the present day, in Volume One. If your Hunt falls within this group, we hope you have sent the data Mr. van Urk requested so that he may not miss any informative detail. If this has not gone out, may we urge you to direct its course as quickly as possible.

We will start printing Volume One upon its completion in time for fall distribution. While this is being done Mr. van Urk will continue the writing of Volume Two. In order that he will not be delayed in the writing, we repeat our request regarding information being sent to him promptly about Hunts established since 1906.

Because no work has ever been attempted or published which so completely tells the story of American foxhunting (it will not be a glorified Hunting Directory), we are of the firm opinion that these volumes will remain the most important contribution to American foxhunting literature ever published.

As you undoubtedly know, we publish only limited editions; and because this work is of such importance, we are endeavoring to determine how many sets should be printed. Already many inquiries have come in regarding this work. Consequently, should you care to authorize your Honorary Secretary to send us a list of your members or subscribers, so that we might solicit an expression, we would be most grateful. This manner of determining what the demand is likely to be will in no way interfere with purchase through favorite booksellers. We are simply anxious to find out about how many copies will be wanted before going to press.

Sincerely yours,

Eugene V. Connett

EVENING JOURNAL

WILMINGTON, DELAWARE / MONDAY, DECEMBER 12, 1977 · · · 25

FROM: EVENING JOURNAL NEWSPAPER, MONDAY DECEMBER 12, 1977

Author Van Urk Captures The Fantasy of Foxhunting
by Betty Burroughs

Every foxhunter knows Charlie. He's been around about 200 years.

It's a name English devotees of the hunt gave their quarry, whose oldest and best-known alias is Reynard. Charlie is named for English statesman and orator Charles James Fox (1749-1806).

But "Little Charlie, the Fox," is the creation of author J. Blan "Jack" van Urk who, after living with this charming character for more than 30 years, finally has introduced him and his friends to young readers.

The book, just released by Van Urk's Serendipity Press ($10), is the author's first venture into fiction on a child's level.

For the distinguished 75-year-old publisher-writer-sportsman, the materialization of "Little Charlie" involved treading on strange territory. While he is an international authority on hunting, writing for the very young is a whole new world and called for a drastic departure in style...and role.

"I took my publisher's hat off for this one," says Van Urk, who moved to the Wilmington area from Mt. Kisco, N.Y., in 1959, to become president of National Publishers Service, Inc., then at Second and Market streets. It now is Serendipity Products, Inc., of which Serendipity Press is a subsidiary, with offices in Greenville Center.

In fact, it was that, plus a lot of hounding by his writer wife, Virginia, that forced him after all these years to resurrect the story he had woven in his mind while working for the N.W. Ayer advertising agency in New York City.

"It was about 1945," he recalls, "and I was into a lot of things – free-lancing, raising Great Danes and renting them out to models at $15 an hour for advertising copy."

In 1945, he also became Encyclopedia Brittanica's authority on "hunting" (fox, stag, hare and otter) in Europe and North America. He still is.

But busy as Van Urk was, Little Charlie was a persistent personality and, he says, "I discussed my dream of this fresh little character with one of the agency artists, Milt. R. Gutsche. He was in Ayer's Philadelphia office."

Immediately captivated, Gutsche "roughed out some drawings, then later did some more. I set them aside and then…well, I was involved and ambitious and did a lot of traveling."

Understandably, the years passed and in the movings from one place to another the drawings were misplaced. Then one day when Van Urk was going through some old papers, "I came upon the drawings."

Not to discount his wife's producing ("that's why the dedication to Virginia"), Van Urk said that finding the Gutsche artwork is what really got him going again on Little Charlie.

It also caused him great consternation because all efforts to trace Gutsche have failed. "I don't know if he's dead or alive and I'd give anything to find out. Ayer wasn't able to help at all."

Only the drawings in the delightfully illustrated book are by Gutsche. The other more detailed drawings are fashioned after the unsigned originals for which the author, in his opening remarks, credits Gutsche.

Van Urk says he'd feel much better if he could share Little Charlie's debut with his artist collaborator who caught the young hero's sly, mischievous and bright expressions.

Truly an ardent admirer of the red fox and lover of all animal life, Van Urk says his purpose in writing this book is to portray the exciting game of foxhunting through storytelling.

The cast of characters includes the superstar fox's family; friends Pookie, the bunny, and Red Jacket, also a fox; Whiskers, the hunter (horse); Windy, the foxhound, and Mr. Cheerful Thinthatch, master of foxhounds.

There also is an anonymous "baddie" billed only as "Man with guy."

In his "Remarks (to and for parents)," the author notes: "While essentially a fantasy, with slight overtones of satire, the background of this tale remains in some degree authoritative, and the occasional hunting terms used are accurate."

The book carries a glossary of hunting terms; also some factual, legendary, and historical information about foxhunting and a tribute to the red fox, nature's smartest animal," from Encyclopedia Brittanica.

Indeed, Van Urk maintains, the oft-maligned fox is cunning in an admirable, not evil, way and is an attractive creature in the bargain.

The Holland-born writer and sportsman was "blooded into foxhunting" as a boy visiting in England. Van Urk not only loves the sport but also has a higher regard for the animal participants than he does most people.

"I have much more respect for animals than for human beings," he explains. "In their 'ethic' background, animals respect each other. They kill only for food, which is more than we can say for ourselves."

In his new book as in other writings, Van Urk seeks to dispel the misconception that foxhunting is a cruel sport.

"It is very rare that they have a kill in a foxhunt," he explains, "and in those instances where foxes are killed it is to keep the balance of nature. In England they have earthstoppers — men who go around before a hunt stopping up all the holds the fox can run into to hide."

Even then, he adds, the fox may outfox hounds, horses, and riders because "he's just so smart."

All these characteristics of fox, hound, hunter (both hoofed and human) and other animals and people are brought out amusingly, appealingly, and, sometimes poignantly in "Little Charlie, the Fox."

Van Urk calls his first book for juveniles his literary "young entry." It is bound to charm adults as well — at least those of a whimsical turn of mind and those who know and enjoy foxhunting.

Because it is an entirely new adventure in a lifetime of writing, the author awaits the reception of "Little Charlie" with some diffidence.

When you consider the man's literary accomplishments, this may sound unreal. A 1924 graduate of Princeton, he started out as a reporter on the old New York Journal-American.

"I covered police and city hall, then began writing animal features, which is what I enjoyed doing most," he said. "I became an itinerant journalist, traveling and free-lancing. I went where there was horse interest."

Among his previously published books are, "The Story of American Foxhunting," published in two volumes, and "The Story of Rolling Rock," about hunting and published by Scribner's.

Yet, Van Urk says, "I was afraid to try writing a book for children. I wasn't sure of myself. The style is so different from anything I've ever written."

And so he concentrated on winning young readers with appealing characters and simple but lively dialogue while still maintaining the true structure, sentiments and sporting strategy of the hunt. He builds in excitement, action, plot, comedy, pathos, a villain, a lovable hero, and, ah, yes, just a touch of romance.

And Jack Van Urk, who at the outset wondered, "God, how do I write a juvenile book?" may have a winner in "Little Charlie, the Fox."

There will be many critiques of this book but the one who I live with, my wife Happy, says I must have the last word in this book.

Occasionally watching and listening to these Evangelical preacher on television who are in the KNOW leads me to believe that I will "Talk to my death" when that final judgment day comes.

My chief concern is that my two years of the French language in high school and one year in college has long departed from my brain. Can I find a fox hunter interpreter in the hereafter to communicate with all those thousands of French houndsmen?

With the help of a left ear hearing aid I will have little trouble communicating with the English and Irish houndsmen.

Until we meet again, Doc.